SAM   BRANNAN
Builder of San Francisco

D1615921

BY LOUIS J. STELLMAN

Port o' Gold
Mother Lode
Mate o' Dreams and Other Poems
That Was a Dream Worth Building
Sam Brannan, Builder of San Francisco

Sam Brannan

Sam Brannan

Builder of San Francisco

A Biography by

L O U I S   J .   S T E L L M A N

Preface by

Albert Shumate
President Emeritus
California Historical Society

With an introduction
by
Kevin Starr
State Librarian of California

1996
James Stevenson Publisher

1500 Oliver Road Suite K-109 ● Fairfield, California 94533
(707) 434-0210

1996 Edition:

This edition of Louis J. Stellman's book, *Sam Brannan, Builder of San Francisco*, has received a facelift, with a new cover design. Albert Shumate, President Emeritus of the California Historical Society, and Kevin Starr, State Librarian of California, have graciously prepared introductory remarks. Inside are illustrations, gleaned from the *Annals of San Francisco*. Other photographs are included courtesy of the Sharpsteen Museum.

ISBN 1-885852-05-3   James Stevenson Publisher

Original edition:

Published by the Expositon Press Inc. 386 Fourth Avenue, New York 16, New York. 1953-1954

TO MY WIFE

Preface

Sam Brannan, what awe that name conjures!

I first became intrigued with this remarkable pioneer in 1954, when I was Noble Grand Humbug in the Yerba Buena chapter of E Clampus Vitus, a fun-loving historical society. This chapter had been first established in San Francisco in 1852. One hundred two years later, I led chapter members to the site of Brannan's Calistoga spa, where a plaque in his honor was placed on a shaft of petrified wood. It read, in part, "Sam Brannan, dreamer, promoter, Prince of Californiacs. Here in 1859 he created the name of Calistoga."

Brannan has been called "Builder of San Francisco," "California's first millionaire," "California's first entrepreneur" - and rightly so. He established one of California's first four mills, San Francisco's first newspaper, built some of the first houses in San Francisco's Happy Valley, was a founder of the Society of California Pioneers, a leader of the first Committee of Vigilance in 1851, and a large landowner in Sutter and Sacramento counties - to list a few of his many accomplishments.

His exuberance was demonstrated in May 1848 on his return to San Francisco from the newly discovered gold fields. As described by Oscar Lewis, "He strode down Montgomery Street holding aloft a small bottle filled with nuggets, shouting - 'Gold! Gold! in the American River!' " This sent most of the male inhabitants of the town rushing to the hills.

Brannan's final years - enduring poverty, illness, and being largely forgotten - were tragic. Another native of Saco, Maine, I. C. Woods, met a somewhat similar fate. Woods was born in Saco a few years after Brannan; in California he became president of Adams & Co., the largest express company on the Pacific Coast. After its failure and Woods' flight from San Francisco, he became known as the "Notorious" I. C. Woods.

There are few place names bearing the name of Brannan- an island in the Sacramento River and a street name in San Francisco - but this remarkable man is not now forgotten. Jim Stevenson is to be congratulated for reprinting Stellman's biography of Brannan. While it is not a definitive work, it does give a good portrayal of this dynamic entrepreneur, a pioneer who deserves to be remembered.

Albert Shumate
President Emeritus
California Historical Society

"Sam Brannan
A Flawed Founder"

Introduction

by
Dr. Kevin Starr
State Librarian of California

The re-issuing of Louis J. Stellman's *Sam Brannan, Builder of San Francisco* (1953) by James Stevenson Publisher reintroduces to a new generation of readers the enigmatic, energetic, and frequently outrageous Founder of California, Samuel Brannan (1819-1889).

Note that I describe Sam Brannan as a Founder with a capital "F". Mormon missionary, land developer, founding politician of San Francisco, playing a crucial role in the promotion and provisioning of the Gold Rush, Sam Brannan deserves as much as any other figure - as much as Junipero Serra, Mariano Guadalupe Vallejo, John Sutter, Thomas Oliver Larkin, John Fremont, the Big Four, the Silver Kings, Thomas Starr King - the designation Founder. Yet this designation has not been accorded Sam Brannan. No statue of Brannan stands in San Francisco, a city he helped organize, or Sacramento, a city he once nearly half owned, or San Diego, the city of his sad and lonely last years.

Why is this? To put the matter simply: Sam Brannan had more than his share of faults. He was a boozer, a womanizer (even a bigamist), a ruthless businessman (capable of exploiting the misfortunes of his business partner Sutter), a Mormon unfaithful to the tenants and discipline of his church, a filibuster (in the original sense of the term, an American trying to seize control of a Latin-American nation, in Brannan's case Mexico): a confidence man, in short, George Washington

Harris' Sut Lovingood, Mark Twain's the Duke and Dauphin, or Herman Melville's Confidence Man from the novel of the same name. The American frontier was replete with such characters: shrewd, entrepreneurial, energetic, intensely flawed, walking a fine line between creative entrepreneurialism and crime. In their folkloric dimension, they stand at the center of enumerable frontier legends and tall tales. Harris, Melville, and Mark Twain transmuted such characters into fiction with gusto. And yet - with the clear exception of Sam Houston of Texas - such figures are rarely enshrined in the pantheon of founders of former frontier states. The very virtues which made them survive and thrive on the frontier - above all else, their capacity for self-invention and self-renewal, the constant con-man masquerade of their lives - render them, once a frontier state has become a respectable commonwealth, somewhat embarrassing to later generations, so strong is the genteel tradition in these United States.

At the conclusion of Mark Twain's *Huckleberry Finn*, Huck says that he is going to "light out to the territories." Had Mark Twain written the novel about Huck in his adulthood, the adult frontier Huck Finn would have very much resembled Sam Brannan. Like Huck Finn, Sam Brannan had a father from hell: a dipsomaniacal Irish farmer from Saco, Maine, given to beating his wife and five children when he was drunk, which was often. Thomas Brannan seems to have exercised a particularly sinister control over his oldest daughter Mary Ann, who protected her younger brother Sam like a second mother. Not until she was twenty-seven, a considerable age for that period, was Mary Ann able to escape the sinister hold of her father, marry, and take her fourteen year old brother Sam with her to her new home in Ohio so as to get him away from the abusive Brannan household.

Sam Brannan, then, like Huck Finn, began his life in a condition of violence and abuse, perpetrated by a drunken, avenging father. The psychological relationship between adolescent experience and the choice of the frontier in adulthood has not been sufficiently studied. One suspects, however, that there were many Huck Finns and many Sam Brannans in 19th century America: young men who could never bond to their locality in the settled states because that locality had been the *mise en scene* of a tangled experience of violence and abuse which they had to flee, indeed, which in one sense they were fleeing for the rest of their lives. From this perspective, the frontier offered not only land and entrepreneurial opportunities, as formulated by Frederick Jackson Turner in his famous 1893 essay "The Significance of the Frontier in American History," but a source of psychic release as well: a place into which one might flee the hated father and the dead-end life the drunken, abusive father embodied.

As if further to intensify the representative, even archetypal life he would lead on the frontier, Sam Brannan chose as a young man in Ohio, the one calling above all other frontier callings which could give a young man without prospects - Samuel Clemens, for example, or William Dean Howells, Henry George, or Harrison Gray Otis - sufficient tools for survival, self-improvement, and even dominance. Sam Brannan became a printer. A printer's workshop was the Harvard and the Yale of the frontier. Handling letters as physical entities, young men with little education learned to assemble words as material properties: first words, then sentences, then, in time, to make the transition towards an equal mastery of the language which was structuring and propelling the printed page. Benjamin Franklin had made this transition from printer's devil to savant in the 18th century. Thousands followed him, including America's greatest writers in literature. While Sam Brannan never became a writer (his was the call to a life of pure action), he nevertheless kept a lifetime association with printing and newspapering, which he brought to California in 1846 and through which he acquired his education.

Not even the frontier could protect Sam Brannan from tragedy; indeed his entire life seems an epic of defiant survival against misfortune after misfortune. In 1838 he joined his older brother Thomas in New Orleans, where the brothers Brannan opened a publishing firm. Then came the cholera, and Thomas Brannan, Jr., was dead. On to Indianapolis, where a second business failed.

At this point, Brannan came into contact with a movement, a force, Mormonism, which was even then, in 1842, sweeping the frontier. Converted to Mormonism after the death of his mother, Brannan married a Mormon girl by the name of Harriet Hatch. Sam was not a steady and faithful spouse. Nevertheless, he sought ordination as a Mormon missionary, most likely to get out of Indianapolis, missed the birth of his daughter, spent time in Connecticut, where he acquired a second spouse, Ann Eliza Corwin, whom he married after seeking permission from Mormon leader Joseph Smith.

As far as the history of California is concerned, at this point, Sam Brannan, despite his failings, edges into greatness. After the expulsion of the Mormons from Illinois in 1846, Brannan became convinced that the Mormons would have to sail half-way around the world, to Hawaii and California, to get far away from a persecuting American society, which was especially affronted by Mormon polygamy. With the backing of the church leadership, Brannan chartered a ship in New York, *The Brooklyn*, refitted it to carry 215 people, then in February 1846, took his Mormon colonizers, men, women, and children, around the Horn to Honolulu, which they reached in 136 days, then on to San Francisco.

When Brannan and his colony left New York, they thought they were removing themselves to a Mexican province.

Landing off Yerba Buena cove in late July 1846, they spotted the American flag flying over the sketchy Mexican village of Yerba Buena. "Damn that flag!" Brannan was later quoted as saying. Mormons were not destined to be persecuted in California, however; indeed, a battalion of Mormons serving under General Stephen Kearny assisted in the conquest of Southern California. Far from being a member of an alienated minority, Sam Brannan and his Mormon brethren found themselves at the center of the establishment.

Across the next twenty busy years, Sam Brannan achieved an epic of entrepreneurial action - land development, one of the first two newspapers in American California, industrial construction, railroad, banking, a bookstore, a biscuit factory, a lumber mill, a resort - that would make him, if only temporarily, a rich man. In an era of entrepreneurs, at a time when ordinary men and women made and lost fortunes in the service of the new American empire on the Pacific, Sam Brannan was the undisputed leader of the business community.

In his first year or two in the military territory of California, Brannan kept close to his Mormon brothers and sisters, for whom he served as de facto leader. At the confluence of the San Joaquin and Stanislaus rivers, he established the Mormon settlement of New Hope, which Brannan envisioned as a Mormon metropolis where his persecuted community might find sanctuary, prosperity and peace. Indeed, Brannan travelled across the Sierra Nevada to the Great Salt Lake in an effort to convince Brigham Young and his followers, then camping on the Green River, that California, not the Great Salt Lake region, offered Mormonism its land of milk and honey. When Young decided that the isolated region of the Great Salt Lake offered Mormons better protection from a persecuting American society, Sam Brannan saw his dream of California as Mormon utopia go up in smoke. Soon, however, he conceived of another idea, vaguely schismatic. Why should the Mormons of America confine themselves to one chosen place? Why shouldn't the Mormon community of California, even now being augmented by the young men discharged from the Mormon Battalion, stay put and create in California a new and equal Zion, with Sam Brannan, and not Brigham Young, as their chosen leader? To this end, Brannan continued to collect tithes from the Mormon community: funds which had a way of remaining under Brannan's control in San Francisco. An exasperated Brigham Young sent agents to collect the money. Brannan refused and was excommunicated. No matter, he was not a very good Mormon anyway.

By early January 1847, Sam Brannan was publishing the *California Star*, one of two newspapers in the state. In April 1848, Brannan shipped a special edition of 2,000 newspapers to the East, announcing the discovery of gold. Legend has it, in fact, that Captain Sutter, having learned of James Marshall's discovery of gold on the south fork of the American River on 24 January 1848, told Brannan about it but swore him to secrecy. Not on your life! Brannan understood instantly what the discovery of gold would mean to entrepreneurs such as himself who controlled the shipping and transportation infrastructure of what would soon be known as the Mother Lode, not to mention the hotels and taverns of San Francisco and the choice waterfront properties in Sacramento which Brannan began to acquire from his partner Sutter when Sutter got into financial difficulties.

The 1850s was for Sam Brannan a decade of exhausting involvement. He served on the City Council of San Francisco, helped organize the Committee of Vigilance of 1851, acquired properties in Hawaii, opened a bank, developed the resort of Calistoga at the northern end of the Napa Valley, constructed the Napa Valley Railroad running between Vallejo and Napa to serve it, while all the while straying from the path of righteousness in the matter of women and drink, much to the exasperation of his long-suffering wife, Ann Eliza, who dreamed every day of moving with Sam and her three surviving children to Europe.

At any number of times in the 1850s Brannan might have cashed out and lived a life of leisure, whether in Europe or in Calistoga. Was it the drink that was propelling him: the drink that had slurred his tongue when he wanted to name his resort "the Saratoga of California" and it came out "the Calistoga of Saraphonia"? Was it the exhilarating prospects of even more land, especially after Brannan and his political ally Senator William Gwin pushed through Congress a bill establishing a Land Commission in California which offered Americans a virtual right to steal Spanish and Mexican properties? Was it the womanizing? The affair with the internationally known Lola Montez, such a boon to his ego as well as his libido, a country boy from Maine carrying on with the quondam consort of millionaires and kings?

Whatever its psychological origins, this wild hunger for something better, something more, it propelled Sam Brannan through the 1850s like a remorseless force. He grew thinner and thinner from dissipation. He developed a chronic cough and spit blood. He was using himself up, but he couldn't stop. There, ever before him, always and everywhere, was the promise of the next big deal, the next big score, the next possibility of escaping the scars of childhood.

By 1856, Sam Brannan was perhaps the wealthiest man in California. Frustrated by his alcoholism, workaholicism and womanizing, Ann Eliza took the children off to Europe, settling in a chateau in Geneva, Switzerland. No matter, Sam had his brother Captain John Brannan for family, who also acted as Sam's business manager. And then there was Hattie, Sam's first wife, and their daughter Elmira, whom Sam brought out to San Francisco, where Hattie found another husband but

In the 1860s Sam Brannan got heavily involved in the effort to roust Maximillian from the throne of Mexico. Ann Eliza, by this time, was back in San Francisco, ensconced by Sam in a luxurious home at 930 Clay Street in San Francisco. Already, however, Sam's fortunes were on the wane. The Mexican venture - in which Sam had organized and trained a group of volunteers, then shipped them into Mexico to fight for Benito Juarez - had depleted his finances. The loss of his brother John to tuberculosis deprived Sam of an all-important calming influence. He continued to drink and to womanize, and his business affairs ran down hill. In 1868 he was shot and severely wounded while trying to repossess a saw mill. Ann Eliza divorced him in 1870, demanding a settlement of a half a million dollars in cash, an extraordinary sum for that era. Sam paid the settlement, but it finished him. In 1877 he returned to Mexico, hoping to pull off what he had accomplished in California in the 1850s, the development of a new empire. He lost money in land and silver. Old age and bad health debilitated him, yet he must have maintained something of his earlier charm, for a young Mexican woman by the name of Carmen, whom he eventually married, kept him steady company. Even Carmen, however, had had enough by the mid-1880s after having moved from Mexico to Arizona, where Sam was reduced to selling pencils for a living, before heading on to yet another venture, this time in Guaymas, Mexico. He was so serious of making a go of it once again that he even quit drinking.

The year 1888 found Sam Brannan old, tired, in ill health, living at a boarding house in San Diego, making an effort to establish himself as a fig-grower. A stroke had shrunken his once robust frame. One arm shattered by gunshots in the saw mill dispute, hung limply at his side.

And yet, despite all this, not for Sam Brannan would

this be the last act. Not for him would there be the expected end in a seedy boarding house in San Diego. An earlier investment in a cemetery, made in conjunction with his Odd Fellows Lodge in San Francisco, suddenly yielded a cash settlement of $49,000. Sam Brannan returned to San Francisco, now the tenth largest city in the United States, claimed his money, paid his debts, with his last days solaced by the kindly care of a Mexican woman.

Huck Finn had come home. The territory to which he had lighted out in 1846 was now the commonwealth of California. Before the end, which came on 5 May 1889, Sam Brannan, facing the shores of the sundown sea in Southern California, must have had the opportunity to think back across the years, remembering it all: the terrifying father, the print shop days, the Mormon missionary years, and the sudden, unexpected establishment of an American commonwealth on the Pacific. One hopes he realized that his life had, after all, yielded much. He was much more than the sum total of his faults. In and through California, Sam Brannan had achieved a certain kind of greatness.

Foreword

Far too little is remembered of Sam Brannan during these history-celebrating days in California. He, his children, and his children's children have succumbed to time. His vast fortunes are long dissipated. Only scattered monuments of his great endeavors stand, here and there, like the ghost towns of the West, and in San Francisco a street bears his name. The Mormon Church has written him off as an apostate or worse, and his grave is marked by a modest headstone provided by the charity of a man who never saw him.

Yet Sam Brannan's influence on western America's history was colossal; his deeds formed a pageant of spectacularly important events from the day he brought a shipload of Mormons to sleepy, Latin-Indian Yerba Buena Cove (later to become San Francisco), three years before the Gold Rush. Brannan's followers trebled its population and made it, almost overnight, a young city, for, among the *Brooklyn*'s debarkees were expert craftsmen, traders with stocks of goods, farmers with domestic animals and equipment, doctors and lawyers.

Brannan printed San Francisco's first newspaper and its first book that transcended the proportions of a pamphlet; he was a defendant in its first trial by jury; he performed its first marriage ceremony, preached its first Protestant sermon, promoted its first school and opened the first flour mill. He started the first store in the Sacramento Valley, which furnished materials for historic Sutter's Mill, where the first gold—which led to the stampede of '49—was found. He precipitated an exodus from San Francisco to the goldfields which left seven male adults to run the town. He almost succeeded in a plan to bring Brigham Young and his Mormon hegira to California. He was the state's first millionaire; he made it one of the world's great wine-growing regions.

Sam Brannan did more, perhaps, than any other man to

organize the historic vigilance committees of 1851 and 1856, which restored order and law to crime-terrorized San Francisco. He was a foremost figure in colonizing Sacramento and driving out its lawless squatter element. He built railroads, established a curative spa, opened a bank and issued his own currency. He helped to finance the Union against the Confederacy. He aided materially in overthrowing the French "protectorate" in Mexico by a lavish purchase of revolutionist bonds and by organizing an army among American unemployed, which he armed, equipped, and transported at his own expense to reinforce the patriot, Benito Juárez' untrained and tattered peon forces.

Drink and domestic troubles checked Sam Brannan's upward curve at last. Men and women whom he trusted fleeced him and betrayed him. He went down and almost out. But, even at the close, his dauntless spirit triumphed. Aged, poor, partially paralyzed, he nevertheless wangled a fortune out of a grateful Mexican government in satisfaction of his claims for vast lands south of the Rio Grande which he had tried to colonize. His "international lawyer" kept a lion's share; but with what was left he returned to San Francisco, wiped out all his debts, entertained his cronies with a splendor reminiscent of old days, and died in the arms of the boarding-house woman, deliriously happy in the belief that she was his third wife, Carmelita. With his last gesture, two hands filled with gold coin, he laughed at the prediction of a Mormon elder that he would die penniless and forsaken.

Such is a rough résumé of Samuel Brannan's life. The detail of it is astounding and—to me, at least—absorbing. I have tried to make it so for the reader. And, if I have resorted to the more fluid narrative style which smacks of fiction, the framework of truth is none the less solid. I essay to present a living man rather than a case history. . . . To accomplish this, I have linked known facts with established legend and coherent probability. Every fundamental statement in this book is based on dependable evidence. Much of it is shown within these covers. The rest is carefully deduced and checked conclusion.

I consider what follows a true picture of the man after all relevant records have been explored. Much enticing but unprovable report has been ignored.

L. J. S.

Contents

Illustrations

SAM BRANNAN
Builder of San Francisco

. *1* .

American Transplantation

Thomas Brannan was the son of Patrick Brannan, a farmer of Waterford, in the county of Waterford, now a part of Eire. On the twenty-fifth day of December—Christmas Day—1755, Thomas Brannan was born there. He was one of the younger sons—no great asset to the farm, though big and strong.

After he had got his growth, he went to work in the distillery where they made good Irish whisky. He liked that and the way of making it and the companions of his labor. The whisky went to England, for the most part, but a tidy bit of it was shipped down the Suir River and found its way to the taverns of Dublin, less than a hundred miles away.

In the distillery and the town, Tom Brannan heard about America, where there were vast, unsettled tracts of land to be had for the taking, red Indians and pretty colleens. He watched the big ships sail up the river from the Irish Sea and talked with the men in the shipyards. By first and second hand, he heard many tales of the colonies, where life was freer and fortune easier to win than in Ireland under English rule and landlord domination. They fired his imagination, and the swigs of young, hard liquor he got from the still did the rest. He was weary of the old country, of life that promised little for the future, of patronizing elder brothers and a father who had no great use for him. His mother—God rest her soul!—was dead this many a year. At twenty, Tom Brannan made up his mind. He took his savings and the small patrimony his father allowed him with dour prophecies, and sailed away to the new land. He debarked at Portland, Maine, and found work in the hamlet of Saco close by. He liked the look of things. He sang, often, at his work and drank heartily in the ale house when evening came. He began to look the women over. This was the place for his future.

The following year some brave fools at Philadelphia signed a paper which they called the Declaration of Independence. They were ready to fight England for their freedom, if need be. That was fine—and foolish—Thomas Brannan thought. Ireland had tried it and failed. He wished them luck, but he took no sides openly. He was more concerned with the thought of marriage.

Mary Goodrich, the daughter of a small farmer, worked in a shop. When Thomas went there, as he often did, they talked together: of the Revolution, which—if God were just and gave the English tyrant his deserts—would one day make an independent nation of the colonies. Mary was about Tom's age, big and strong like him. She would make a fit wife for him, a good mother for young ones; and she seemed to like him. So Tom asked her, Would she marry him?

"Yes," she said.

They took up a piece of land with her dowry. Their combined labor made it pay them a living during the early, unsettled years of the new Republic. Later, prosperity came; but it was ten years before a child was born. The baby was a son and they named him Rufus, for Mary's father. The second son, Thomas, was named for him; the third, a girl, they called Nancy.

Tom Brannan had bad luck with his sons. One died of yellow fever before he was twenty; another was drowned in the Saco River when he was half grown. On top of that, Mary, his wife, died in 1805. Nancy, aged nine, was too young to take over the household. So, after a decent interval, Tom married again.

By this time he was a well-to-do farmer. He married a lady:

Sarah Emery, the niece of General Knox, who had fought with George Washington and was a member of his cabinet. Sarah was eighteen years younger than Tom, who, by this time, was fifty. They had a child the following year, and four more afterward. The first was Mary Ann, born July 4, the natal day of the American Republic. The second was named Tom, the third Dan and the fourth John.

Six years later the last child came, a gay, smiling tyke who, always from the first, managed to have his way. Mary Ann was thirteen when Sammy was born and her mother was ailing, so Mary Ann took charge of the babe. She petted and coddled him. They all made much of little Sam. Even old Tom Brannan, now sixty-five, ailing with bone fever and given to blind, drunken rages, often smiled at his youngest son.

He had become a cruel father and a bad husband in his latest years. He beat his sons and, some said, his wife, on occasions. He drove the boys from home as soon as they were old enough to fend for themselves.

Nancy, youngest of his first wife's children, long ago had married and left home. Mary Ann was the mainstay of Tom Brannan's household now, for Sarah was delicate and often ailing. She had been reared a fine lady, and the heavy tasks of even a gentleman farmer's home were beyond her strength. But Mary Ann, the firstborn of her brood, was equal to them. She mothered the teen-age boys and pacified her father when the angers caused by drink and aching joints made him difficult. She was twenty-seven now and he hoped, selfishly, considering her plainness and years, that she would never marry. Thus, when Alexander Badlam, from a near-by farm, came courting, old Tom did his worst to thwart the match. But he was unsuccessful. Mary Ann and Alec were united in the spring of 1833.

Old Brannan, in his fury and frustration, sought the public house for solace. He returned at dusk, muttering and brandishing his cane. John, who had the evil luck to cross his path, was cruelly beaten and left home never to return. Sarah feared for Sam, who was her "baby." He was fourteen now and big enough to brook no more chastising by his father. If they clashed, thought

Sarah, something serious might happen. And so, reluctantly, because she loved the boy, she arranged, in secret, his departure with the Badlams, who were going to Ohio. Sam was eager for the change. He and his sister were congenial spirits and young Badlam readily agreed, for he, too, liked the boy.

Painesville, Ohio, was a border town between established civilization and a half-charted wilderness filled with hostile savages and predatory beasts. There Badlam took up land and built a home. He sold his surplus crops to travelers and traders. Finally he built a store and added stocks of merchandise. Sam was working for a printer who did job work. He had been apprenticed for five years and liked the trade. Some day he should have a shop of his own, he boasted.

Almost everyone was speculating in land values. Some made fortunes overnight and others lost their all in the mercuric, fluctuating values. It fascinated Sam. He had had enough of printing when his fourth year ended. With money borrowed from his sister, he returned to Saco to demand his patrimony, though he was not yet of age. And, between Sarah's urging and his father's irresponsible condition, he succeeded. Back in Painesville, he bought off the final year of his apprenticeship and became a speculator.

Badlam and his sister warned him, but Sam would not listen. One night he came home with a long face and turned his pockets inside out with an eloquent gesture. "Well, I'm broke," he said simply.

"Oh, Sammy!" Mary Ann cried in distress.

"Never mind," he told her. Suddenly he laughed. "I've lost the first round, but the fight's not over. Some day I'll be rich. . . . I've got it in me.

"Tomorrow I'll hit the road," he said, and he squared his shoulders. "I want to see the world. I'm eighteen now and have a trade. A printer can always get work."

"Where do you plan to go?" asked Alexander skeptically.

"To New Orleans," said Sam, "by easy stages. Brother Tom is there. He writes that it's a grand city full of fine houses and beautiful women. . . . I can work in towns along the highroad—

a month or so in each place—and save money. And I can get rides on the river boats as a deck hand."

He started next morning. First he went to Saco for a farewell visit to his mother. He was shocked to note how she had failed since his departure. She was overjoyed to see her youngest son and marveled at his growth. It seemed only yesterday that he had been her little boy. Now he was a great man, going out into the world.

Sarah gave him money—more than he had hoped for or expected. "Be a good boy, sober and industrious. Promise me," she pleaded.

Readily and quite sincerely, he said, "Yes." One look at that drooling, human wreck, his father, was the best of temperance lessons. And industry would be the natural outcome of his driving, sharp ambition to succeed.

He kissed his mother fondly, clasped his father's palsied, bony fingers in a gesture of farewell and, whistling gaily, went his way. Here and there, throughout the next few months, he found work in the printshops or at anything that offered. There were many large towns on his route and each one different. The farther he got from the coast, the livelier and freer men were in their habits and their views of life and law; and so were women in bestowing favors. Sometimes Sam was forced to move on hurriedly—for his was a nature that attracted feminine affection, and he was no lad to say them nay. He reached New Orleans in the spring of 1837 just before the carnival of Mardi Gras, in which he and his brother Thomas joined with glee. He was captivated by this romantic southern city. It was like fulfillment of his schoolboy dreams of Paris. Sam wanted to stay there forever with his brother, who worked on a river boat. They lived in a French *pension,* and there Sam met young men and women such as he had never known before: darkly handsome, full of fire; poets, artists and musicians. Encouraged and abetted by this gallant coterie, the Brannans pooled their monies in the publication of a little magazine, hand-set and printed on an old French press which Tom, a mechanical expert, reconstructed from a damaged antique. This fledgling of the graphic arts was well received in

Bohemian New Orleans and might have burgeoned into something really notable, had it not been for the fever epidemic which struck suddenly throughout Louisiana and claimed many lives. Sam saw the brother he adored sicken and die within twenty-four hours and many of his friends go to their graves overnight. Even though the plague subsided almost as swiftly as it had appeared, Sam was through with New Orleans. He sold his type and placed his press in storage when no ready purchaser appeared. Short of funds but horrified and fearful, he fled northward, pausing only long enough en route to earn fresh traveling expenses, till he came to Indianapolis. There he stayed for several years, and the news of his mother's death brought him new sadness.

Sam liked Indianapolis. Life was brisker there, if less romantic than in New Orleans. Yet poetry and art were not neglected by the volatile and brilliant hoosiers. The son of Sam's employer scribbled verses—not like the classic ballads of his southern friends, but full of homely vital humor that was novel and refreshing. Another friend made woodcuts for a weekly, the *Gazette*. Sam found himself the center of a group of eager and creative spirits. When the *Gazette*'s little press broke down and creditors removed the rest of its equipment, Sam and his friends sent for the Brannan press in New Orleans and revived the little paper. Once again before he had attained to his majority, Sam found himself a publisher.

But this, too, proved an ill-starred venture. The *Gazette* made many friends but ate up most of Brannan's salary. At last, reluctantly, almost tearfully, he sold out for enough to pay his debts, and he packed his bags once more. He had money to take him to Painesville. He longed to see Mary Ann and his kinfolk again.

The Badlams welcomed him into their home. He found work readily enough with his old employer and prepared to "settle down." He had had enough of "bumming," he informed his sister. Mary Ann laughed doubtfully and said she hoped so.

Sundays they drove to Kirtland to hear Joseph Smith expound his new religion: Mormonism. Badlam and his wife were converts. They had been baptized, were devout adherents and urged Sam continually to join the Church of Latter-Day Saints. But he was skeptical of Smith's claim for the new, "true gospels" revealed in a dream by the Angel Moroni and written on plates of gold. Sam liked the fiery evangelist and listened to his stirring sermons with respect. He answered Smith's persistent pleading for his personal conversion with a "Later on, perhaps." He wanted time to think it over. He enjoyed these Sunday outings with the Mormons and made friends among them. Like the Badlams, they were honest and well-meaning folk.

One of them, indeed, upset him strangely: the young daughter of a widow who attended Joseph Smith's meetings. Mary Ann introduced Harriet Hatch to her brother and watched, with satisfaction, their growing interest in each other. She wanted her beloved and mercuric Samuel to renounce his wandering habits, and marriage was the best approach she knew to such a change. Hattie was still in her teens, big-eyed, blonde and handsome in a rather bovine fashion. Sam fell head over heels in love with her and, after a tempestuous courtship, they were "sealed" by Joseph Smith.

Hattie proved a docile and compliant spouse. She met Sam's passionate advances with a yielding rather than responsive spirit. But it was not a happy marriage. Sam returned at night to a disordered home and tasteless meals. Hattie's coiffure, once a golden halo, had become a stringy aureole about her characterless features. Approaching motherhood to her was an excuse for dowdiness, neglected household tasks and sleepy inattention to Sam's talk of future plans. Desperately he turned at length for consolation elsewhere; met the jealous rages of his wife with silence that infuriated her the more. She progressed from name-calling to the violence of hurled dishes and hysterics. Finally, she threatened to divorce him.

Then Sam's Irish temper flared out suddenly. "Go ahead— and be damned to you," he thundered and flung out of the house. He never re-entered it. He did not even take the trouble to discover if she had carried out her threat. Thereby he made a mistake.

New York, in the early '40's, seemed a great, imposing city to Sam Brannan when he reached it after months of indirection spent in small-town printshops in a restless, gypsying effort to forget his marital fiasco. He had left Painesville without even a change of clothing and requested his sister to forward certain belongings to him at the first stop. After that he had not even written to her concerning his movements. He desired, savagely, a complete break with the past.

In the metropolis, he found his first surcease. He loved its busy streets, its smelly but enticing docks, where ships of all nations rode at anchor and people of all races jabbered in foreign tongues. He found modest lodgings in one of the city's quieter sections and for a time amused himself at theatres or public meetings. An election was in progress, and everywhere men, mounted on soap boxes or more elegant rostrums, abused their opponents with lavish gestures and sharp words. At night there were parades with bands and uniformed organizations, carrying torches, and lighted transparencies extolling the virtues of their candidates.

For a time Brannan was happy and bemused by all these unfamiliar activities. But presently an overwhelming loneliness beset him in this multitude of strangers. Almost against his will, he looked up William Smith, a brother of Joseph, the Mormon leader, hoping to find social contacts. Smith welcomed him eagerly. He had heard Joseph speak of Sam, he said, and he was about to tour the New England states, seeking new converts.

"Why not come along with me?" he said. "You have a limber Irish tongue. You can help me." Sam replied that he was a printer; he was not interested in religious proselytizing. "Well, I'll tell you what we'll do," urged Smith. "We'll campaign for funds to start a Mormon paper in New York. If we can get enough donations for a press and type, I'll have my brother authorize it. You can use the shop for private printing on the side. That's better than working for somebody else."

Sam thought it over and at last consented. He even allowed Smith to baptize him into the Church. They could work together better if he were a Mormon. And he didn't care. He could quit if he didn't like it.

They journeyed here and there together. Smith told him that his brother had a rival, Brigham Young, who wanted to be leader of the Saints. He was bitter against Young and warned his hearers everywhere against "this arrogant impostor." Sometimes Sam, who loved to talk and feed on public admiration, swung his arms and bellowed in his rich and carrying voice the Mormon credo. He had never met Brigham Young, but he knew and liked Smith, so he fought the latter's battle valiantly.

They returned to New York with ample funds to start a printing office. Sam bustled about looking for secondhand presses. Finally he found one suited to his needs and a complete equipment of type, etc., in a shop that was going out of business. At No. 7 Spruce Street, not far from newspaper row, he rented a storeroom and set up his machinery of trade.

Joseph Smith had authorized the publication of a church paper to be known as *The Prophet*. William Smith wrote the editorials and booked subscriptions. Brannan found a few advertisements among Mormons in New York. Others came in presently from members of the Church, who were in business throughout Illinois, Ohio and New England. Occasionally Joseph contributed an article from Nauvoo, where a great colony of Saints was being formed. Elders Orson and Parley Pratt sent poems and editorials. The paper prospered.

Sam found customers along the docks, where he loved to roam: orders for manifests, invoices and the like. He visited political meetings and solicited printing from campaign committees, cannily promising both sides Mormon support at the polls. He was in a new boarding house now, in a better street, kept by Fanny Corwin, a widow from the South who called her boarders "paying guests." All of them were people of refinement, schoolteachers, clerks, bookkeepers and the like.

Lisa Ann Corwin waited on the table. There was an air of genteel grace about her that attracted Sam, though he found her rather offish. She responded to his boisterous sallies of friendliness with a reserve that daunted him a trifle, but she smiled now and then at his jokes. She was like his mother's people, he decided, not his father's.

Sam did not write to Mary Ann about his new surroundings or his latest enterprise, and he asked William Smith not to mention his address in letters to Painesville. Nor had he written to his wife. Sometimes he wondered if the child were like him, but he was not deeply interested. He remembered Hattie's angry farewell message, "I hope I never see or hear from you again." Well, she should have her way.

. 2 .

Marriage and Migration

Nauvoo, the Mormon colony-city in Illinois, was growing fast. There were hundreds of houses and many outlying farms. A great tabernacle was in building for public assemblies, and a temple for religious services was planned. It would have a pipe organ and a boy's choir.

Everywhere throughout the larger cities groups of Mormons met and worshipped. From them, into the back country Mormon elders and apostles with persuasive voices and enticing arguments appealed to the people, seeking converts. They spoke of fertile soil, large crops and communal security, "the helping hand" which allowed no man to suffer unaided, the fellowship which made all men brothers, the new Word of God which avoided the evils of old and misunderstood gospels.

From the barren hill districts, from the worked-out farms of Connecticut and other regions, came men and women, eager to try the new religion, the new plan. They brought their farm machinery and stock; wagon trains began to move toward the Mormon center, which, some said, would soon outclass Chicago.

On the wharves where foreign vessels discharged many immigrants arriving from Norway, Sweden, Italy, England and

France, a proselyting band worked for the Mormon Church. They sought especially the large-framed, light-haired women from the Nordic lands. They would make good wives for farmers. They were docile and strong. It was Brigham Young's idea that many of them should be brought to Nauvoo. He wanted plenty of women, he told the apostles, in case polygamy became essential to the need of Mormon growth. It was provided for in Mormon gospels. But, at present, it would stir up enmity with other sects. It were better to bide one's time—until the Church had grown more powerful.

A schism grew and widened between Brigham Young and Joseph Smith. The latter was a prophet and dreamer, the former an executive, astute and clever. He played politics with organizations and officials, using as a trump hand the many votes he controlled. The Smith factions said that he overdid it, that he built up oppositions, hatreds which might one day be his ruin. Whether or not they were right, a growing animosity to Mormons and their practices began to manifest itself, and political enemies did not overlook the opportunity of using it to their advantage.

Young's ambitious schemes included foreign cells of Mormonism. Wilfred Woodruff was selected to invade the British Isles and spread the gospels. He arrived in New York to look over the field endowed with much authority. There he conferred with William Smith and Brannan. The former distrusted and disliked him, as he did all friends of Brigham Young. It is possible that he threatened Woodruff, a clever and resourceful man who had heard of the evil reports Smith and Brannan spread throughout New England concerning Young. He tried to patch up a peace between the factions, but Smith would have none of it. Woodruff wrote back bitterly to Nauvoo concerning these two men. Presently he departed for England, and Parley Pratt, a new worker, also appointed by Brigham Young, came to New York with his brother Orson. Both of them were elders of the Church.

Affairs went on more smoothly for a time. Sam liked the Pratts, especially Orson, who was a poet and a scholar. They convinced him that Brigham Young was not as black as Smith had painted him and that he had much to contend with in the ever-spreading antagonism toward the Church. There had been acts of violence against the Mormons by masked night riders who set fire to their homes and even assaulted their women. Smith had appealed to the governor of Illinois, with little success. They might have to leave Nauvoo, as they had left Ohio and Missouri colonies, he feared. A strong and practical leader like Brigham was needed, rather than the visionary, ailing Joseph Smith. The Pratts had many talks with Sam upon this issue. They accused the prophet's brother of personal immoralities, of spreading dissension. Even Joseph was worried about him, they said.

Sam listened to their talks attentively, more than half convinced. He liked but had no great respect for William Smith, who was a weakling, easily moved by his passions and prejudices. Maybe he was wrong. And it would be well to identify himself with the stronger faction, if there was to be a rift in Mormon power. He began to nod his head when Pratt expounded Brigham Young's good points.

And then, like a thunderclap, shaking the very foundations of Mormonism, came the news of Joseph Smith's tragic, sudden death at the hands of a butchering mob.

Civil warfare in Nauvoo had been fanned into flame by a newspaper editor who charged Joseph Smith and the governing Council of Twelve with misrule and immoral practices. They retaliated by suppressing the paper and imprisoning its editor. Outside forces made use of the Mormon conflict to arouse a rabble army against Nauvoo, and state police spirited Joseph Smith to a jail in Carthage for protection. But armed forces stormed the jail and took Smith from his cell. They riddled him with bullets.

"Good God!" cried Brannan when he heard the news. "What will happen now?"

"Nothing for the moment," Parley Pratt returned. "Governor Ford has sent militiamen to disperse the mob. Brigham Young has taken over. Joseph's widow and his brother William tried to establish a sort of regency for Joseph Junior, but the people didn't want it. They need a man, not a boy, at their head. They're surrounded by murderous enemies. They'll have to get out of there soon."

"But where will they go?"

"Hard to tell," Pratt answered soberly. "Out beyond the Rockies, probably; to Oregon, perhaps."

Sam sat silent, drumming on the table with his fingers. "Do you know what I think we ought to do?" he asked. "We ought to change *The Prophet's* name to something else. The preachers are attacking us on account of it. They say we're an immoral sect that flouts the Bible and the law. They're trying to have the government investigate us."

"God's chosen people are forever being persecuted," Parley Pratt said bitterly.

"We can stop some of the mischief by throwing them off the trail," Sam mused. "Suppose we call it, say, *The Messenger,* and put a new address on the masthead. They'll think they've put *The Prophet* out of business and let up on us. We can alter the make-up a little and no one'll know—except our own people. How about it?"

"That's not a bad idea," said Parley Pratt.

"Another thing," said Sam. "I'm planning to be married."

Pratt held out his hand. "Good for you, Sam," he replied. "I'll seal the girl to you, myself."

Sam was silent and uneasy for a moment. "She's not a member of our Church," he said at last.

"Well, that doesn't matter. We'll convert her."

"I'm afraid you can't," said Sam. "She doesn't like us Mormons. She thinks we're not respectable—and have a lot of wives. She's been reading stories——"

"We can soon convince her that it isn't true," Pratt stated gravely.

"No, you can't. . . . I've tried. . . . It isn't any use," said Sam. "You've got to let us have a Gentile preacher. . . ."

"Sam," said Parley Pratt, his eyes stormy, "this'll work against you with the Council of Twelve." He paused. "I suppose you know Brother Woodruff's already preferred charges—against William Smith primarily, but you're included. You've said some pretty harsh things about Brigham Young . . . and he's the leader now. It wouldn't be wise to provoke him, to give him fresh grounds."

"I tell you what we'll do," said Sam. "We'll have two marriages. I think I can persuade Ann Lisa into that. If she thinks she's legally married by her own minister, she won't mind the Mormon ceremony. She'll go through with it to please me—I guess."

"Does she know about Harriet Hatch?" Pratt questioned.

"No," said Sam. "She doesn't. . . . And I daren't tell her. She—she'd never marry me. . . . I'll go back and fix it with Hattie," he added hastily under Pratt's accusing gaze. "I'll give her some money and tell her to get the divorce."

"All right," said Pratt. He wasn't too hopeful about the situation. Nevertheless, he attended Sam's wedding in an Episcopal church and later "sealed" her to her husband by the Mormon rite. Sam went back to Painesville to fix matters up with Hattie, but she wasn't there. She and the child, a girl, had disappeared, his sister told him. Sam tried for days to find a clue to Hattie's whereabouts, without success. So he shrugged his shoulders resignedly and went back to Mother Corwin's boarding house and his new spouse.

He was very much in love with Ann Lisa. She was pretty and had a good figure. Smart as a whip and ambitious she was; and she had faith in him, like his mother. She believed that, one day, he'd be rich. They could give up the boarding house and live as they used to: Sam, her mother and she. Sam encouraged her dreams. He believed in them, too.

Then, moiling all his plans, came news from Nauvoo that the Council of Twelve had "withdrawn the hand of fellowship." He was excommunicated from the Church. Frantically he sought the Pratts but could not locate them. What they had written to Brigham Young about him, whether they were friends or enemies, Sam could only surmise.

He decided to take the bull by the horns. He would go to Nauvoo, face Brigham Young and demand a hearing. Without explaining his predicament or the nature of his mission to Lisa

Ann, he packed a few belongings, left his shop in charge of two Mormon youths who were his assistants and set forth posthaste for Nauvoo. He reached there early in May. The size of this Mormon colony, so recently established, amazed him. There seemed to be thousands of buildings stretching over a wide-flung region. The Temple was a truly imposing structure, half Byzantine in its architecture and housing a great domed cathedral. On the main street were stores stocked with wares worthy of a big city. He found lodgings, removed the marks of travel and presented himself at the executive office of the Church. In this large and handsomely furnished room, a big man, bearded and with hard, determined eyes, rose from a desk chair to greet him.

"Where shall I find Brigham Young?" asked Samuel Brannan.

"You have found him," said the other.

Sam smiled and held out his hand. "I'm Elder Samuel Brannan from New York," he announced. "I've come to ask a hearing on whatever charges have been made against me. I've worked hard and earnestly for Mormonism, Brother Young—and I've done nothing to deserve being kicked out."

The Mormon leader eyed him sternly. "You have sowed dissension in the Church, according to reports," he said accusingly. "You have attacked and slandered me among the brethren."

"I did what I thought was right," Sam answered. "I followed the Prophet, through his brother. . . . If he misinformed me, that was not my fault. Joseph Smith was our beloved leader. I believed you were his enemy."

"Do you still believe it?"

Brannan hesitated. "Brother Young, you've been accepted by the Church. That's good enough for me . . . and I've had cause to question William Smith's intentions, lately. I've come here to learn the truth—and ask for justice."

"You'll get it, Brannan," Brigham Young said simply. "I am favorably impressed by your defense. Tomorrow I will let you know the Council's verdict."

Sam wandered about inspecting the city. He spent a restless night. In the morning he again sought Church headquarters. He strode jauntily in, head high, his bearing confident, but inside he was quaking. If he should lose his fellowship, the whole scheme of his life would alter. He had built up a following among the Mormons; his friends, customers, social contacts, were mostly in the Church. Without its "fellowship" he would have to begin all over again. Ann Lisa would be glad, he thought grimly; but it would be a hard blow.

To his surprise a group of middle-aged men stood about the room. Young, as yesterday, sat at his desk. Twelve pairs of eyes were centered on the young Mormon as he entered. He could not determine whether their glances were friendly. They were cold but not hostile, he thought.

"Gentlemen," spoke Brigham Young, "this is our brother, Elder Samuel Brannan."

"Good morning, brothers," Sam said eagerly. He passed among them, holding out his hand, and each of them shook it gravely.

"We want to ask some questions, Elder Brannan," said one of the Council. "If you answer them to our satisfaction, the hand of fellowship may be restored. We believe your attacks on our leader were prompted by false testimony, and we have decided to excuse them. There remain two other matters. All the funds that you and William Smith collected did not reach the Church. Do you know what has become of them?"

"I turned them in to Elder Smith," said Brannan.

The questioner cleared his throat. "It has been said you have two wives," he stated.

Sam reddened. He had not suspected that the Council was informed of his domestic troubles. He told them about Hattie, her slovenly habits, her violent temper, her threat of divorce. "I assumed that she'd got it," he said. They looked sympathetic.

"Did you go back to find out?"

Sam explained that she had disappeared, that he had searched for her in vain. The councilmen nodded. They withdrew to a corner of the room and for a time talked earnestly. Sam stood near the door, perspiring. At last Brigham Young advanced.

"The hand of fellowship has been restored to Elder Brannan," he pronounced sonorously.

Early in June *The Messenger* printed a letter from Governor

Ford of Illinois to the Mormon Church, a letter that was to play
an important role in Sam's destiny. Governor Ford sympathized
with the Mormons, who had been hunted out of three states. He
had found them for the most part law-abiding and industrious
people and had ignored public protests against their so-called
"shames and immoralities." Nonetheless, he warned them that a
tide of public sentiment was rising which might end in violence
and bloodshed.

> If you get off by yourselves you can enjoy peace [he
> wrote]. I was informed by General Joseph Smith last
> summer that he contemplated a removal westward, and
> if he had lived, I think he would have begun to move by
> this time. I would suggest as a matter of confidence,
> the following:
>   California now offers a field for the prettiest enter-
> prise that has been undertaken in modern times. It is
> sparsely inhabited and by none but the Indian and the
> imbecile Mexican Spaniard. If conquered from Mexico
> the country is so physically weak and morally distracted
> that she could never reconquer it.
>   *Why would it not be a pretty operation for your
> people to go out there, take possession of and conquer a
> portion of the vacant country and establish an indepen-
> dent government of your own subject only to the law of
> nations?*

Governor Ford added the following caution:

> If you conclude to do this, your designs ought not to be
> known; otherwise it would become the duty of the
> United States to prevent your emigration. But if you
> once cross the line of the United States territories, you
> would be in no danger of being interfered with.

"That's good advice," said Sam enthusiastically. "We could
charter a ship here and take a couple of hundred converts by
sea. I've heard my brother John speak of San Francisco Bay. He
thinks it's a grand harbor, big as an inland sea and landlocked

by a narrow strait. Nobody there but a few Mexican land-owners back in the hills. We could capture it with a hundred men."

Parley Pratt considered the idea. He was opposed to fili-busters. But he knew the Mormons would have to leave Nauvoo —probably within the year. Many of them had sold their farms already. Brigham Young had written to President Polk, plead-ing for a special session of Congress to consider their dilemma and provide an asylum from persecution. But he had received no satisfaction.

Desperately, the Saints addressed Governor Thomas S. Drew of Arkansas, asking for sanctuary in his state. The Secre-tary of the Council of Twelve added the following significant postscript:

> As many communications postmarked Nauvoo have failed to reach their destinations and mails have been intercepted by our enemies, we shall send this to some distant office by the hand of a special messenger.

Governor Drew replied that he could not guarantee the Saints protection. He was friendly but powerless to control certain elements, he wrote. He advised Oregon or California.

In October Brannan and the Pratts talked matters over in the printshop. Sam had an offer to sell his place. He argued for chartering a ship at once. There were several hundred converts in New York and the New England states awaiting orders from Nauvoo to move on. If some action was not taken soon they might backslide, Sam contended.

The Saints had been warned to leave Nauvoo by the end of the year. They had addressed an answer to Colonel Levi Williams, leader of the anti-Mormon crowd and his "mob party," agreeing to vacate in the spring if not further molested. The Council had appointed a committee of five to get informa-tion about the newly discovered Salt Lake Valley. Stephen A. Douglas had advised the Mormons to occupy Vancouver Island, then claimed by the United States.

Everything was in confusion. A thousand families were preparing to abandon the colony as soon as winter was over. Mormons were trying to sell their farms and buildings in the town. It was rumored that a showman planned to make a theatre out of the Temple as soon as the Mormons were gone.

"I saw a sweet little ship in the yards today," said Brannan to the Pratts. "She's three hundred seventy tons and seaworthy. She could be done over with cabins for colonists—several hundred of 'em. And she can be chartered cheap."

Orson Pratt pursed his lips thoughtfully. He favored the sea journey, though his brother did not. "What's her name and where can she be seen?" he asked. Brannan told him and the two Pratts departed talking together in low tones. "Don't you see it's best?" said Orson. "Let this follow take the converts to California. As he says, they're getting restive. . . . And it's a fine way to be rid of the man. When he's gone we'll have the field to ourselves."

"Maybe you're right," returned Parley.

In November, 1845, Orson Pratt, who now presided over branches of the church in eastern and middle-western states, issued a farewell message to the Saints in those parts, prior to his return to Nauvoo. His brother Parley had already returned to the disturbed Mormon capital. It had been decided to discontinue publication of *The Messenger*. Its present editor, Elder Samuel Brannan, would charter a vessel to take the press, type and a company of Saints from the eastern branches, by way of Cape Horn, to California, "as the distance to travel from that point to their probable destination in the Rocky Mountains would not be so great and the trip would be attended with much less expense."

Complying with these instructions, Brannan chartered the ship *Brooklyn*. Captain Richardson, a recent convert with a master's certificate, was employed as "skipper."

Small companies of Saints from Massachusetts and New York State began to gather in New York City, awaiting the day of departure. They were directed to a certain boarding house near the docks where others were already waiting. Alterations on the *Brooklyn* proceeded feverishly. Cabins to accommodate several hundred men, women and children were being constructed. Medical supplies for the long journey were placed aboard as well as twenty-four muskets with powder and ball "to repel pirates." In the hold was packed one of the strangest and most varied cargoes any ship had ever held: plows, flour mills, sewing machines, *The Messenger* press and many cases of type, paper and ink, quantities of cooking utensils, cobbler's lasts, saddles, a blacksmith's forge, carpenters' tools, iron pipes, hammocks, tents and livestock.

Shipwrights were finishing the cabins; otherwise all was ready to make sail. Sam was jubilant and impatient. He looked forward to conquest and wealth in a new land. He had even convinced Ann Lisa and her mother that fortune awaited them in California.

"Never mind the Mormons," he said with his gusty enthusiasm. "They're good folk enough. But once we're in California we can leave them behind if we've a mind to. We'll have acres of land, me darlin'! For ourselves and the boy." He glanced at the baby fondly. "We'll be rich as Croesus, with servants to wait on us. No more cookin' and slavin' for you, Mother Corwin. You can be a lady in silks and satins, with a carriage to ride in, if ye'll wait a few years."

Mother Corwin smiled in spite of herself, though she shrewdly discounted most of her son-in-law's gay prophecies.

Each day Sam went down to the docks. The *Brooklyn* was a trim yet sturdy craft. She looked seaworthy, as he had told the apostles. Carpenters were dividing the two upper decks into small cabins each provided with four or six bunks. Even the officers' cabins were small; every inch of space was needed for two hundred or more passengers and a hold full of cargo for the colony. Besides this, by means of advertisements in *The Messenger* and personal solicitation among shippers, Sam had secured a thousand dollars' worth of freight for the Sandwich Islands, where a stop was to be made. He took Ann Lisa carrying Sam Junior in her arms down to the ship and showed her their cabin. It was one of the larger ones, and Mrs. Corwin was to share it with them. They could hang up a sheet in the center for privacy while they undressed. Ann Lisa demurred at this. "It's not respectable," she said primly.

But Sam laughed at her. "Lord love you!" he returned. "We're all one family, darlin'. Plenty others will be doin' the same. This is a ship—not a hotel."

As usual she gave in when he insisted, but not without a hint of virtuous resentment.

It was the first week in January, 1846. They were almost ready to weigh anchor. Some of the Saints had already occupied their cabins to save hotel bills. Sam was having a last look around his stripped printery, making sure nothing had been forgotten, when the door opened. A large man in a frock coat and bow tie that smelled of politics entered impressively. He removed his broad-brimmed statesman's hat with a flourish.

"Am I addressing Mr. Samuel Brannan?" he inquired unctuously.

"Sure and you are," replied Sam. He didn't like the fellow's look. He didn't like the hand his visitor extended—pudgy and soft, as if there were no bones beneath the yielding flesh. "Sit you down. . . . As you'll observe, we're movin'. Did you want printin' done?"

"I wish to talk with you, sir," said the stranger, "on a most important matter."

Sam continued his eleventh-hour survey of corners and nooks. He did not ask what the matter might be as the other evidently expected him to do. He displayed no curiosity, in fact. He waited.

The big man said, "My name is A. G. Benson. I'm from Washington." He turned a searching, calculating stare on Sam. "You've a ship loading down at the docks. You're about to set sail for California . . . with a load of men and arms."

Sam laughed, despite his apprehension. "We're bound for Oregon, my friend, as our papers'll show. We're not armed, though we've twenty-four muskets aboard to repel pirates if any show their face; and most of our passengers will be women and children."

The other smiled wisely. "That's your story, friend . . . and a very clever one. But I happen to know better. President Polk has for some time been informed of your Mormon expedition to colonize Mexican territory—by force, if necessary. The President has only to issue an order. A sloop-of-war is close by. . . ." He paused.

Sam spoke suavely but directly. "What's your proposition, Mr. Benson?"

"I represent A. G. Benson and Company. Amos Kendall, the former Postmaster General, is an active partner. He has the President's ear. The President, himself, is a silent—shall we say, sympathizer? With our help you can move your ship. You may proceed unmolested to—let us say Oregon. Do I make myself clear?"

"Deed and you do, man. . . . What's the price?"

"Ah, a very simple matter," answered Benson. "I shall come tomorrow with Mr. Kendall. We shall draw up a little agreement. You shall sign and send it to Nauvoo for the Council of Twelve to ratify. . . . Then all will be smooth sailing."

"Good day to you, then," said Sam impassively.

Benson glanced back at him furtively as he went out. He was, somehow, not quite certain of his victory.

A week later Sam wrote to Brigham Young as follows:

BROTHER YOUNG:—

I have received positive information that it is the intention of the Government to disarm you after you have taken up your line of march in the spring on the ground of the law of nations or the treaty existing between the United States and Mexico that an armed posse of men shall not be allowed to invade the territory of a foreign nation.

Amos Kendall was in the city last week and positively declared that it was the intention of the Government and I thought it my duty to let you know that you might be on your guard. I declare to all that you are not going to California but to Oregon and that my information is official. Kendall has also learned that we

have chartered the ship *Brooklyn* and that Mormons are
going out in her and it is thought she will be searched
and if found taken from us and if not an order will be
sent to Commodore Stockton on the Pacific to search our
vessel before we land.

Kendall will be in the city again next Thursday and
then an effort will be made to bring about a reconcilia-
tion. I will make you acquainted with the result before
I leave. I have it in my power to learn every movement
of the Government, which I shall make you acquainted
with from time to time. God is at work in the East and
so is the Devil but Moses' rod will be too hard for him.
I feel my weakness and inability and desire your bless-
ings and prayers that I may be successful. My cares and
labors weigh me down day and night but I trust in God
that I shall soon have a happy deliverance.

All the Saints in the East are crying for deliverance;
but I must now close by subscribing myself your brother
in the Everlasting Covenant,

                                                S. BRANNAN

He made a wry face as he added the final paragraph. If
Ann Lisa read it she would have a fit. But Brigham Young was
a stickler for form. He demanded devoutness.

Sam folded the written sheets hastily, put them in an en-
velope and sealed it. Better get it into the post and away from
his wife's sometimes prying eyes. He was in his own home now;
it was almost dismantled, only a few sticks of furniture remaining from an auction sale.

Tomorrow Benson and Kendall would bring the contract for
him to sign and send on to Nauvoo for ratification. Sam was
familiar with its terms, for he had been permitted to read it—
an infamous document, an extortionary instrument framed by
political blackguards. He did not believe that the President had
any hand it, but one could never be certain. It wasn't worth
while taking chances.

He would sign it, dispatch it to Nauvoo—and get away to
sea with the *Brooklyn*. After that he could take care of himself,
alter the ship's course if need be. . . . And Brigham Young was
no fool. *If he and the Council ratified any such agreement they
had only themselves to blame.*

On January 26 Sam wrote again to the Mormon President:

DEAR BROTHER YOUNG:—

I haste to lay before your honorable body the result
of my movements since I wrote to you last, which was
from this city stating some of my discoveries in relation
to the contemplated movements of the General Government in opposition to our removal.

I had an interview with Amos Kendall in company
with Mr. Benson which resulted in a compromise. The
conditions of which you will learn by tending the contract between them and us which I shall forward by this
mail. I shall also leave a copy of the same with Elder
Appleby who was present when it was signed. Kendall
is now our friend and will use his influence in our behalf in connection with twenty-five of the prominent
demagogues of the country. You will be permitted to
pass out of the state unmolested. Their counsel is to
go well armed but keep them secreted from the rabble.

I shall select the most suitable spot on the Bay of
San Francisco for a commercial city.

When I sail, which will be Saturday at one o'clock,
I shall hoist a flag with Oregon on it. Immediately on
the reception of this letter you must write to Messrs.
[*sic*] A. G. Benson and let him know whether you are
willing to coincide with the contract I have made for
our deliverance. I am aware that it is a covenant with
death but we know that God is able to break it.

Here Sam paused and studied carefully what he had written.
Would Young and the Council of Twelve be thick-headed

enough to miss the meaning of that final sentence? He meditated for a moment; then he underlined it heavily.

. . . but we know that God is able to break it.

And the Prophet has said, "As it is, was then, so shall it be in the last days."

He wasn't certain of the accuracy of that quotation; but it sounded biblical. He continued:

> And I have been led by a remarkable train of circumstances to say "Amen!" And I feel and hope that you will do the same. Mr. Benson thinks the Twelve should leave and get out of the country first and avoid being arrested if it is a possible thing; but if you are arrested you will find a staunch friend in him and you will find friends and that a host will deliver you from their hands. If any of you are arrested don't be tried west of the Allegheny mountains. In the East you will find friends that you little think of.
>
> The Saints in the East pray night and day for your safety and it is mine first in the morning and last in the evening. I must now bring my letter to a close. Mr. Benson's address is 39 South Street and the sooner you can give him an answer the better it will be for us. He will spend one month in Washington to sustain you; and he will do it, no mistake. But everything must be kept silent as death on our part, names of the parties in particular. I now commit this sheet to the post praying that Israel's God may prevent its falling in the hands of wicked men. You will hear from me again on the day of sailing if it it the Lord's will, Amen!
>
> Yours truly, a friend and brother in God's Kingdom,
>
> S. BRANNAN

Sam had made two duplicates of the original contracts on ruled foolscap paper. It had cost him hours of unwelcome labor, for he wrote rather slowly in a large, sprawling hand. His copies covered twice as much paper as the signed documents transcribed by Amos Kendall in his compact Spencerian script. Many of the words that Sam had misspelled, erased and written over were almost undecipherable.

The instrument was more than seven hundred words in length. It began with a tribute to the Saints, a professed belief in their high principles and good intent, a sympathetic acknowledgement of their persecution and an intimation that their hegira to a sanctuary west of the Rocky Mountains might be interfered with by the Government through misunderstanding of their purpose. Epitomized, the contract read:

> WHEREAS, A. G. Benson states he has it in his power to correct any misrepresentations which may be made to the President of the United States and prevent any unauthorized interference with them on their journey . . . *Therefore* it is covenanted and agreed between A. G. Benson on behalf of himself and such as he may hereafter associate with him on the one part and Samuel Brannan for and in behalf of the Latter-Day Saints by their principal men duly authorized on the other part, that the said A. G. Benson shall take the necessary steps to guard the said Latter-Day Saints against the effect of misapprehension and prevent interference with them by the officers or agents of the United States on their journey westward . . . *and when any of them acquire lands from the United States or from any other source . . . one half of the said lands shall belong and be conveyed to the said Benson and those whom by written contract he may have associated with him, his and their heirs and assigns. . . . And if the said Saints or any of them or the said Brannan or any of his associates, assigns or heirs shall within ten years lay off or establish any city or cities town or towns on the lands acquired by them each alternate lot in such cities and towns shall belong and be conveyed to the said Benson and his associates and assigns.*

The contract was signed by Samuel Brannan and A. G. Benson and witnessed by W. I. Appleby, in whose hands one of the original copies was to remain. Sam mailed his duplicate to Nauvoo several days later than his letter of announcement. That would afford the Council of Twelve an opportunity to digest the idea, he thought, before the actual terms of the contract were presented to them. He wrote on the margin: "This is the only copy of the original which I have filled out. It is drawn up in Kendall's own hand—but no person must be known except Mr. Benson." On a separate sheet of paper Sam inscribed a brief note to the Mormon President:

BROTHER YOUNG:—

Your letter confirming the contract I have made which I directed to you to address to A. G. Benson, must be written to me and on the outside addressed to A. G. Benson and all will go well.

Yours very respectfully and in haste,

S. BRANNAN

Deeply concerned, Brigham Young read the document Sam had conveyed to him, a puzzled frown gathering on his broad, high forehead. As he went on his brows throbbed and his eyes flashed. But it was not until he had reached the end that he made even the smallest gesture. Then he sprang from his chair trembling with anger and sought the company of his apostles. They gathered as usual in Elder Taylor's big parlor, where secret sessions were held. There, amid murmurs of indignation and astonishment from his hearers, Brigham Young read the contract aloud.

There was a momentary silence when he finished. The eyes of the twelve men were upon their leader.

"We shall put our trust in God!" the President said firmly. "We shall look to Him for our protection—not to political demagogues who plan to rob the Saints of millions. We shall not ratify this unjust and oppressive agreement nor submit to its threat of Federal bayonets."

He tore the document in two and dropped it on the floor. "Amen!" cried the twelve in one voice.

Soon afterward, the *Brooklyn* sailed from New York harbor on her long voyage round the Horn. Her decks were filled with busy men. Women in gay dresses waved farewells to friends and kin ashore. Children were everywhere, scampering and sprawling over coiled ropes, shrieking in their excited play.

At 39 South Street, A. G. Benson waited vainly for a letter.

. 3 .

The Voyage

It was winter weather, clear and crisp, when the *Brooklyn* weighed anchor—one of those cloudless and perfect days, sharp with frost and strangely stimulating. Everyone aboard was keyed to the pitch of adventure. Even Jerusha Ensign, with a sick wife and ailing father, was cheerful. Eliza Ensign, frail and ethereal, with a spot of high color in each cheek, had been brought on board by means of a stretcher. She lay in her bunk, cheerful but weak, smiling at her husband and little son. She was sure the voyage by sea would help, perhaps cure her of inherited lung disease. The doctor said it was her only chance. That was why Jerusha had sold his farm in New Hampshire and set out for the new land. If Eliza recovered, it was worth the sacrifice. His father, Ellis Ensign, tottered about the deck muttering discontentedly. He had not fancied being dragged from the hearth he had built with his own hands a generation ago. But he could not remain behind, with a sickness of the heart which caused him now and then to fall unconscious. He had never liked the sea. One of his sons had run away and been drowned.

Lucy Eagar came by and gave him one of her warm smiles. She smiled at all men, thought old Ensign sourly; none were too far advanced in years or too ill for her deviltries. A bold, handsome woman, full of life, was Lucy Eagar, a widow with three children and something in her eyes that set many men running after her wherever she went. Captain Richardson eyed her askance. She would bring trouble to his ship on their long voyage, he feared, but he said nothing. Elder Moses sidled up to Mrs. Eagar, doffing his broad, Quaker-like hat, and she took his arm. Elder Pell joined them. She put a hand on his arm also, and they strode about the deck chatting gaily until Pell, who was not a good sailor, succumbed to the ship's rolling motion and deserted them hurriedly. Orrin Smith took his place. Smith's wife, seated between her two children, watched her husband with a sardonic smile.

Janice Nichols and her squalling babe sat beside Ann Lisa Brannan. Everybody called the latter by her second name. She was a good-looking woman with attractive features and a fine slender figure. But for her prim mouth and her self-conscious virtue she might have been beautiful, thought Janice. Women resented her aloofness. Janice said with a touch of rancor, "That Eagar woman's making eyes at all the men—and they like it. . . . She'll be having your husband by the arm next."

"What's the matter with your child?" asked Lisa coldly.

"He's got the flux," said his mother. "I'm giving him paregoric." She glanced at the child harassedly. He had kept her awake two nights with his crying; but at last he was asleep—or drugged with the large dose of anodyne she had forced down his protesting throat. "There's your husband now," she said to Lisa. "Watch."

Sam Brannan strode across the deck, shouting words of good cheer right and left as he passed the groups scattered about the deck. He had a fine, robust figure, deep-chested and broad-shouldered, with shaggy hair and flashing black eyes. His speech was pleasingly bombastic, his costume dandified but masculine. Lisa thought his manners somewhat coarse, but others liked them. He was natural of manner, full of life. He stood out even among finer-looking, bigger and more cultured men. Lucy Eagar was quick to note his approach. Somehow, without rudeness, she freed herself of her two swains and came toward him smiling. "Oh, Mr. Brannan . . . I want to ask you something." He eyed her appreciatively, for he liked fine women. But he was not vanquished, like the others, by her charm. After a moment of talk he lifted his hat and passed on. Lisa smiled but Janice said acidly. "Wait till the journey's over, my dear. She'll get him yet, else I'm wrong."

She *was* wrong. Sam Brannan was no prig but he was a far-sighted man. He recognized trouble when he saw it. As religious supercargo of the *Brooklyn*, chieftain of its general affairs, he was not to be snared into a liaison which under other circumstances might have intrigued him. Lucy Eagar tried her wiles on him during the next few days in vain and then turned, angrily, elsewhere.

Just before noon on the tenth day out of New York Joseph Nichols sought Brannan hastily. He found the latter in the captain's cabin having a glass of rum with the skipper. "Come in. Have a drink," they called through the open doorway.

"I have no time nor taste for liquor, gentlemen," said Nichols. "My little boy is dying and my wife's beside herself. Is there a medical man aboard?"

"None but the captain," said Brannan, rising.

Richardson did likewise. "We'll go to your cabin, friend," he said reassuringly and took up his medicine case.

Off the Bermudas, which those with acute vision could glimpse from afar, Sam Brannan, in his best black coat, read a funeral service for Joseph Nichol's babe. He did it impressively, for he had a magnificent voice. His words boomed over the roar of the wind for a storm was brewing. The little canvas-sheeted body was lowered into the sea. It was over just in time, for a young hurricane followed by a heavy downpour drove all but the crew to shelter. The ship lurched drunkenly between huge waves.

Less than a week later Ellis Ensign died. A sailor found him prone on the afterdeck at dusk and carried him to the Ensigns' cabin. The sick woman screamed when she saw him and fell back in a faint. Jerusha Ensign lifted his father's body into the bunk above her. He did not seek medical assistance. He knew Ellis Ensign was dead.

Again Samuel Brannan put on his black coat and shouted words against the wind over a corpse. Another empty shell was given to the waves. This time the weather was pleasant enough. Men and women stood about talking in low tones or staring out to sea.

There was no laughing or playing of games that day—only a spiritless gloom. Eliza Ensign, it was whispered, could not last long. She had not eaten since her father-in-law was carried into the cabin; she coughed rackingly day and night. Several children were ill, one with scarlet fever. That was John Robbins' baby. Captain Richardson had quarantined the Robbins cabin. Food was taken to the door, but no one permitted to leave or enter.

Sam was the only dauntlessly cheerful soul aboard the *Brooklyn*. He went about spreading good humor, clapping men on the back, chucking young women under the chin and bantering older ones. He found one who had had experience as a midwife. "She'll be needed soon," he said to Captain Richardson.

"How d'ye know that, man?" the skipper asked, surprised.

"I've eyes in my head," returned Sam, laughing. "Its a good thing, too. . . . 'The Lord giveth' as well as 'taketh away.' I hope it'll be a boy."

John Robbins' baby died in mid-afternoon, February 28, a week after Ellis Ensign. The third death did not make so great a stir. On the ship they were accustomed now to the Dark Angel's visits, were half expectant of more. When John Fowler's infant son died of the flux March 6, it was scarcely noticed. Few attended the burial service, and deck games went on spiritlessly but simultaneously. On the following day Eliza Ensign's ailing spirit passed. Jerusha and his small, motherless son went about sad and lonely. Women took turns in looking after the child, but few of them tried to comfort the father, whose dour, meek face did not attract them or invoke their sympathy. Only Sam Brannan tried to console him. He bullied the bereaved man into eating his meals, taking exercise on deck, having a nip of rum now and then. Sam could stand no drooping. He hoped the calendar of deaths was closed. But John Robbins' second child died a week afterward, also of scarlet fever; and three days later Charles Burr lost his baby son.

Then, as if to turn the tide, a baby was born. Sam was playing shuffleboard with Lucy Eagar for a partner against Elders Moses and Pell when Jonathan Cade came running across the deck and whispered to him. Sam excused himself hurriedly to search for Hannah Reed. She had just put her own child to sleep and exclaimed in excited whispers when Sam told her the news. She was a big, hearty woman, strong as an ox but with a low voice and gentle ways.

"Lord's Mercy!" she cried. "I'll go right away, poor lamb! Have a pan of hot water sent in from the galley, Mr. Brannan." She rushed along the careening aisle, carrying a bag in one hand, a roll of cotton in the other, steadying herself with difficulty under the ship's sway. From the Cade cabin she heard heavy groans. She pushed open the door. "Go away—and stay away," she commanded the distracted husband. She entered, closing the door softly after her. Sam sent hot water by a sailor and rejoined the deck games.

"Another death?" they asked anxiously.

Sam laughed. "No, it's the other way round," he told them.

The boy weighed eight pounds on the galley scales. He had red hair like his father. Jonathan Cade was a proud man. He and his lady had been married several years, but this was their first— a strong, determined mite, lustily squalling and kicking when hungry or fretted, smiling like an angel between whiles.

"He's like the Atlantic Ocean—either demon or cherub," said his father, standing the drinks for all. "He'll make his name in the new country. . . . I'm wondering what we'd best call the brat."

"Why not 'Atlantic,' for the ocean he's like and was born on?" laughed Sam.

"By God, 'Atlantic' it shall be!" cried Cade, emptying his glass.

"Better consult the missus," cautioned someone longer married; but Cade would have none of that. He ordered another round of drinks from the steward. "I'm boss of my shebang," he boasted.

Apparently he was, for a day or two later Elder Brannan was again required to officiate at a public ceremony. It was held in the cabin for the weather was stormy again.

"I christen thee Atlantic Cade," announced Sam, and the child immediately set up a protesting howl, but whether against the unusual name or the trickle of water upon its head none could tell. Everyone laughed. The *Brooklyn's* passengers were in high spirits; they believed with Sam that the advent of birth had checked the tragic retinue of deaths which seemed to follow them. But the Grim Reaper had not yet abandoned his quest. On March 26 Edward Miles, a sailor who had complained for days of cramps, died in agony. And the very next afternoon the Winners' baby daughter succumbed to a cankered sore throat, despite the combined doctoring of Captain Richardson and Hannah Reed.

"Folks die on land as well as at sea," said Sam philosophically. "Let's hope these will be the last of our afflictions. All the children are well; all the older folk too, saving the poor young lady who fell and hurt her back soon after we left New York. What's her name? I've forgotten."

"She's my wife," said Isaac Goodwin dolefully. "God help us! I fear she'll never see land again."

"We'll sight land in a month at the Straits of Magellan," said Sam.

"Then 'tis like we'll bury her there," returned Goodwin. "She's a horror of being cast into the sea."

He went off shaking his head while women murmured sympathetically. "A good man and a fine-looking one he is," said one. "He'll have no trouble finding another wife."

"With six children to care for?" said another doubtfully.

Laura Goodwin had her dying wish. She was buried April 2 on Juan Fernandez Island with a stake at her head and a priest from the mission praying over her soul. Hers was the last death on the voyage. A month earlier, opposite Rio de Janiero, Silas Aldrich had died of dropsy. His wife, Prudence, and his half-grown son and daughter had long expected the end. They had brought him along because there was no place to leave him in the abandoned home. There was little sorrow for the passing of this poor, sick middle-aged man with his huge paunch and lack-luster eyes. His family was better off without him.

Other matters engrossed the *Brooklyn*'s passengers. Another baby was expected. John Horner's lady would soon be confined. Hannah Reed said it might be any day now, with the ship rolling as it did. Mathilda Horner was a robust woman, broad-hipped and young. She would have little trouble, Hannah said—much less than poor, slender little Mrs. Cade.

There was also scandal and dissension in the air. Lucy Eagar, as had been predicted, was the center of it. She was playing fast and loose with the men—not only widowers and bachelors, which could have aroused only competitive jealousy, but with the married men. Elders Moses and Pell had each a family, the former four children, the latter two; and Orrin Smith with his lady and six children presented obstacles to annexation as a swain.

Nor was mere deck flirtation charged to Lucy Eagar. Her cabin, which she shared with her children, was forward, far removed from those of Elders Moses and Pell. Yet both of them had been observed, not infrequently, near the young woman's quarters. Most of the women were down on Lucy Eagar; Orrin Smith and his wife did not speak because of Lucy. All kinds of stories were whispered about, and skirts were drawn aside when she neared.

But Lucy was not without her supporters; most of the unattached males were her champions. She had her friends among women too. Hannah Reed and Mercy Narrowmore were her allies, as well as others. The ship was rent with dissension.

Captain Richardson was most bitter in his disapproval of the woman. "She's little better than a strumpet," he said furiously one day. John Eagar, her brother, had struck him for that remark and been put in the brig. Several of the married women wanted Lucy Eagar tried for immorality, and Richardson favored an investigation.

But Sam said no. He tried to smooth matters out, and with some success, for he had the confidence and respect of both factions.

"We'll soon be in the Sandwich Islands," he argued. "Forget your troubles till then. If anyone wishes to leave the ship or make charges before a magistrate when we land there, he or she can do so. Meanwhile, let us have peace."

He had his way, though ill feeling persisted. Lucy was behaving better. Sam had given her a wigging. Some said he had threatened to debark her and her kin at Honolulu. Whatever the cause, she became more discreet. But she spread a deal of dissension and animosity, not only against Brannan—for whom she felt the hatred of a woman baffled if not scorned—but against the captain, whose public disapproval had enraged her and her friends. It was a far from united shipload of people who sighted Diamond Head June 20—just 136 days' sail out of New York. The seas had been smooth and the weather balmy for some days. Long ago the heavy winter wraps and coats of Cape Horn regions had been laid aside.

When the lush greenery of Oahu Island was visioned, women were in light, starchy summer apparel. Everyone rushed to the decks at the first news of land. Curious natives, their lithe brown bodies shining like bronze in the sun, surrounded the *Brooklyn*, paddling outrigger canoes or swimming effortlessly. Most of them were naked, causing the ladies to shrink back, embarrassed, but to steal covert glances overboard nevertheless.

The *Brooklyn* anchored at a long wooden pier crowded with people of both sexes—all decently clothed, Ann Lisa Brannan was relieved to observe. Those in the front ranks were Caucasians, but as the vessel docked a group of brown maidens carrying chains of flowers about their necks made their way forward and tossed their fragrant welcoming tokens expertly on the deck. Captain Richardson and some of his sailors slipped the flowers over their heads and signed to others to follow their example. Sam placed a gorgeous hibiscus chain about Ann Lisa's neck. She smiled and held little Sammy up in her arms to watch the crowd. Farther down the rail Lucy Eagar deftly caught and donned a chain of ginger blossoms. She was laughing happily. For the time all rancors were forgotten.

Sam was first down the gangplank, shaking hands with an impromptu reception committee, making arrangements for the accommodation of his passengers while the vessel remained in port; for it had been decided to give the *Brooklyn* a thorough cleaning and refitting after her struggle with wave and storm upon two oceans.

Sam found it delightfully easy to lodge his sea-buffeted Mormons ashore. The residents of Honolulu almost fought for the privilege of offering hospitality to the voyageurs. Scores of landaus and phaetons appeared to transport them to their whilom quarters ashore, which seemed to them vast and palatial after their cramped cabins. It was a day of rejoicing. *Luaus,* or native feasts, were planned; there were trips to Pali, the historic cliff, and jaunts to Waikiki beach, a crescent of white sand lying in the sheltered lea of Diamond Head. Tropical fruits were offered on flower-garnished trays. Most of the men went up town to drink *okalehau* with native princes and resident traders.

It was paradise, after five months of confinement in the rolling, pitching ship. Even the youngest baby, named Pacific Horner in honor of the ocean which had cradled it so roughly, was smiling and gurgling in its mother's arms, apparently conscious of more pleasing airs and solider foundations. Mary Addison, nineteen and bright-eyed with delight, cried out, "This is Heaven!"

"And you are one of its angels," retorted Henry Harris. He was the son of her hostess and her escort for a day of sightseeing. She gave him a pleased, arch look.

Lucy Eagar had gone swimming with a Kanaka prince.

It was a busy fortnight for Sam Brannan. War had been declared by the United States against Mexico, he learned soon after his arrival. The announcement pleased him. He summoned a meeting of the men, both passengers and crew of the *Brooklyn.*

"Here's our chance, boys," he told them eagerly. "We can capture a colony on San Francisco Bay—and no trouble about the law of nations. We can make our own laws and be a sovereign people. . . . No more persecution from religious bigots . . . Freedom!" he cried with a grand gesture, flinging wide his arms. "Will you stand back of me, boys?"

They cheered him vociferously.

"Listen," he said, lowering his tone, drawing them closer about him. "We'll have money to spare. It'll cost us little or nothing to stay here while the ship's being overhauled. These people will charge us no board. They're glad to have our company. . . . Why, they even give us our drinks and tobacco. Do you know what we'll do with our surplus? *We'll buy arms.*"

Again they cheered.

"I've been making inquiries," said Sam. "Guns are cheap here; so are powder and ball. We'll arm ourselves and drive the Mexicans into the sea."

They cheered a third time, crowding around him, eager and questioning.

"We'll found a big colony," Sam told them, ". . . and build the Temple," he added sanctimoniously if laggardly.

Sam lost no time. He bought one hundred fifty rifles and twenty rounds of ammunition for each. Aboard the ship were three brass six-pounders with powder and shell "to repulse pirates." Sam drilled his men daily. Enlisting the aid of a retired naval officer, he taught them the manual of arms; they had both rifle and artillery practice. The women watched them admiringly. Young Henry Harris, son of a local merchant, asked leave to join them. He was tired of the islands. Life was too easy there, he said, too soft. He wanted to go to California and make a name for himself in a man's country.

The truth was that young Henry had become romantic through love for Mary Addison. He could not bear the thought of parting from her now that the *Brooklyn*'s date of departure approached. They were engaged to be married.

Sam didn't like the plan—or Harris. The latter was not a Mormon. He was aggressive; a trouble-maker. Sam sensed in him a foreign and disturbing element. But he did not immediately or definitely refuse the boy's request. Some of his relatives were influential traders with whom the Mormons were doing business, and his parents were hosts to several families from the *Brooklyn.*

Reluctantly at last Sam granted his request and took his passage money, assigning to Harris a bunk in an already crowded cabin.

The *Brooklyn* set sail once more amid a shower of leis, loud shouts of "Aloha" from the natives and tearful farewells between womenfolk. Men shook hands heartily and regretfully. The melancholy music of a native band came to the voyageurs over miles of placid and windless blue sea. Henry Harris stood in the stern, his arm about Mary Addison's waist. Sam was in the hold checking over the arms and ammunition they had taken aboard. It was the first of July. Early in August they hoped to reach San Francisco Bay. Sam counted the rifles carefully and checked the contents of the ammunition store. He was dreaming of conquest and empire-building.

Captain Richardson sought Sam the fourth day out, his brows dark with anger.

"It's time once for all that we dealt with this Eagar woman," he shouted, careless of who heard him. "You promised me that after we left port——"

"Yes, yes," soothed Brannan. "Not so loud. What's she been doing now?"

"The same thing over again," said the skipper with an oath. "Seducin' the men and arousin' the women. We'll have mutiny yet unless something is done."

"That's strong talk," Brannan answered. "Have you proof?"

"Plenty of it. I've had my men watching her."

Brannan stood a moment, silently staring at the deck. "It'll raise the devil either way," he mused speculatively, regretfully, yet not without a certain relish, for he loved action. "Lay charges against her. . . . You're the skipper. . . . *But be sure you can prove 'em.*"

"I'll do that," Richardson replied. "By God, I'll make the shameless woman hang her head!"

Brannan laughed. "That's one thing you'll never do," he

said, "but you may get your face scratched for your pains. . . . And don't single her out for a scapegoat. Remember she's no guiltier than the men. . . . And two of 'em elders in the church!" he exclaimed, shaking his head. "Lay the same charges against *them*. You understand?"

"Yes—I understand," the captain said more soberly.

Lucy Eagar did not appear to defend herself against charges of "wicked and licentious conduct." She sent word that she would publicly horsewhip the captain and Brannan as soon as they set foot ashore. Elders Moses and Pell blustered about their innocence and the "foul minds" of their accusers. "Polygamist!" they shouted at Sam Brannan. "What about Hattie Hatch whom you deserted for a bigamous marriage, you hypocrite?"

Sam never learned where they had unearthed that story. He ignored it. The captain made good his boast. He produced sailors who had spied on Mrs. Eagar and the elders. They had seen many things. The cheeks of the elders grew red. After a time they left the cabin in which the trial was being held.

Henry Harris, who had studied law in Honolulu, defended the accused. Sam acted as prosecutor, Richardson as judge. Young Harris was bold and clever, but Brannan shouted him down. The sailors' testimony was convincing.

Lucy Eagar, Elders Moses and Pell were excommunicated from the Church. Captain Richardson warned them that further misconduct would result in more serious punishment. But the matter was by no means settled. Harris and Mrs. Eagar kept the broth of dissension stirred. They rallied many families against Brannan: the Addisons, the Hyatts and Scotts were openly his foes; others followed in their lead discreetly. One third of the passengers would not speak to the other two thirds. But the majority sided with Brannan, and few of the women recognized Lucy Eagar openly after the trial.

In such a state they neared their destination. The insurgents threatened an appeal to port authorities as soon as the ship reached California. The others were busy with plans for conquest and colonization. Sam's thoughts were of commonwealth building, homemaking—freedom from established laws and prejudices. Self-government! A new flag!

Liberty and power! He threw back his head elatedly. Once ashore—especially if there were fighting to be done—he could reunite the unruly elements of his band. Smaller companies than his shipload of Mormons had formed the nucleus of a nation.

The word "nucleus" aroused some sleeping and uneasy memory. Suddenly he remembered, frowned. He went striding to his cabin, unlocked his dispatch box and rummaged among its contents. Finally he found a folded paper, copy of the agreement between himself and Benson. Sam studied it with care. Unlike Brigham, he smiled as he did so. Where they were bound, under the authority he would set up, Benson's contract would not be worth the paper on which Amos Kendall had so neatly and explicitly transcribed it.

Like Brigham Young, Sam tore the paper in his hands contemptuously. There was no one to see him or applaud his act. Quietly he dropped the pieces through an open porthole. The wind caught them, whirled them from sight.

On the deck above a sailor was shouting, "Land ho!"

. *4* .

The New Land

Gray skies and choppy seas ushered the *Brooklyn* across the threshold of San Francisco Bay. At first eager watchers crowding the forward deck saw nothing but rolling sand knolls stretching toward higher green-clad hills in the distance. A few Indian rafts made apparently of reeds and propelled by rude paddles were the first evidences of human life. Later a small one-masted schooner was sighted. Smoke rose from Indian villages: huddles of domelike cabins built of clay.

As the vessel approached a tiny cove into which a short wooden pier jutted from the curving and littered beach, houses which apparently belonged to white men were seen. Not more than a score in all, they were of wood, adobe and cloth-covered framework. In the cove rode a number of vessels, one of which was patently a sloop-of-war. From a tall pole raised above the group of houses a stone's throw from the water floated Old Glory.

Sam Brannan, standing beside the skipper, his sharp eyes scanning the shore, was first to glimpse that bit of waving color. He seized a telescope and stared through it. Then he set the glass down roughly. "Damn that flag!" he cried.

Captain Richardson glanced at him astonished. "What might you mean by that, Mr. Brannan?" he asked truculently.

Sam turned, his eyes troubled, his hands twitching. "I mean nothing disloyal to my country, sir," he said. "But we're too late. . . ." His tone was sharp with bitter disappointment.

"Too late for what?"

"Can't you see? To conquer this land from Mexico. To make it our own as we've planned. To gain our freedom——"

"The Constitution gives us freedom," said the skipper.

"Has it given freedom to the Mormons?" Sam asked passionately.

Captain Richardson made no attempt to answer that. Brannan stood a moment staring toward the flag. Then he laughed his old, good-natured laugh and clapped Richardson on the back. "Never mind," he said philosophically. "What's done is done. We'll make the best of it."

People were gathering along the shore. They were dark-skinned for the most part, Sam observed through the glass; their clothing varied from the virtual nudity of the squat, long-haired Indians to the foppish apparel of the Spanish dandy. A sprinkling of Nordic types stood out, easily distinguishable by their lighter faces and more commonplace costume. Not a woman was to be seen, though half a dozen children ran about pointing excitedly at the ship.

From the sloop-of-war a boat put off as the *Brooklyn* came to anchor, wishing to sound the depth of water at the pier before approaching it more closely. In the warship's dinghy were half a dozen jacktars, rowing with the rhythmic precision of trained men, and two officers. Captain Richardson ordered the boarding ladder let down, and the subalterns ascended to the deck as soon as their boat was made fast.

"I am the captain, sirs," said Richardson stepping forward.

Lieutenant Misroon saluted. "Captain Montgomery's compliments," he said. "He desires information of the purpose of your landing, the character of your passengers and the nature of your cargo."

"Faith and he shall have it," said Brannan joining the group. "I'm in charge of this expedition. We're peaceful men and women seeking homes in a new land. We want to colonize this country. Our cargo is what's needed to bring civilization to the wilderness."

Lieutenant Misroon eyed him sharply and nodded. "Your papers, captain," he said to Richardson. The latter led his visitor to the captain's cabin and opened his dispatch box. Misroon glanced over the papers.

"I see you cleared New York *for Oregon*," he snapped. "This is California."

"I can explain that," Brannan again broke in.

Misroon gave him another of his searching glances. "You may explain it to Captain Montgomery—aboard the *Portsmouth*," he said succinctly. He stuck the ship's papers under his belt. "I suggest that you do so without delay." He saluted once more and, turning his back on them, made his way to the ladder and the boat. It pushed off immediately. Brannan and Richardson watched it crossing the water toward the sloop.

"Come, captain; order out the boat. We're going," Brannan said. "The young squirt!" he added under his breath.

Captain Montgomery received them affably enough and ushered them into the ward room. He was a tall, thin man, much older than Misroon, much less officiously punctilious. He gave them seats and pushed a decanter toward them on the table.

"Fill your glasses gentlemen. It's good rum—from the West Indies. We can talk better over a glass."

They thanked him and complied.

"Misroon informs me you have cannon aboard—six pounders —and that there's some mistake about your destination."

Richardson was about to answer but Brannan waved him aside. "We changed our course at Honolulu——"

"Why?"

"We heard our country was at war with Mexico and decided to fight for her."

"How—and where?"

"Here," said Brannan. "And with close to a hundred hearty countrymen . . . they could drive out a thousand Mexicans," he added a bit pompously.

"Then you're armed?"

"We've a hundred and fifty stands—bought in Honolulu," Sam answered.

"Hm! Didn't you know the United States had warships in the Pacific?"

"We heard a rumor of it in the Sandwich Islands. But we thought a landing force might help."

"I see," returned Montgomery with a smile. "And what did you hope to gain?"

"Homes for our people . . . freedom from persecution."

"Persecution?" asked Montgomery puzzled.

"We're members of the Church of Latter-Day Saints," Brannan told him.

"Ah!" Montgomery exclaimed. "You're Mormons!"

Something in his tone offended Brannan. "We're honest, industrious, God-fearing people, sir," he said stiffly.

"No doubt, no doubt," the captain returned with haste. "I believe everything can be arranged." He finished his rum, raising his glass in salute. The others followed his example.

"I'll tell you what," said Captain Montgomery after he set down his glass. "If you'll remain at anchor until Monday—that's day after tomorrow—I'll fill out your landing certificate." He rose, as did the others, and held out his hand. "I'll tell you what," he said again. "We'll hold a reception for the ladies on the *Brooklyn* tomorrow. We'll serve refreshments in the afternoon. . . . How many are there of your ladies, Mr. Brannan?"

Again Sam was disturbed by some hidden quality or thought behind Montgomery's words. "There are sixty-two, captain," he said.

"Ah, yes. Well, we shall try to entertain them. Thank you, Mr. Brannan. Good-day, Captain Richardson." He walked with them to the boarding ladder and bowed them into their boat.

"A kindly man," said Captain Richardson as they rowed toward the *Brooklyn*.

"Yes—and a sharp one," Brannan amended.

"What makes you say that?" asked the skipper.

"Why d'ye think he invited the women. To have them for tea? Not a bit of it."

"Eh? What for, then?"

"To count them and learn their names—*to discover if we've plural wives.*"

On Sunday morning the decks of the *Portsmouth* were holystoned to spotlessness and the brass fittings polished till they shone. The quarter-deck was cleared, awnings were spread and chairs brought from ward room and cabins for the visiting ladies. The men would have to sit on capstan bars, but they wouldn't mind that.

Early in the afternoon Captain Montgomery's guests arrived with a brave show of colored fabrics, laces and furbelows, many of which had been resurrected and aired for the occasion after six months in camphorated sea chests. Officers and men of the *Portsmouth* were lined up to receive the visitors, and receive them they did, with much bowing and kissing of hands. Some of the Mormon women were past their first youth, but most of them were attractive and young, eager to gush over a uniform and enjoy to the full their first social event since leaving Honolulu.

Captain Montgomery's eyes roved over them searchingly. But if he expected Mormon women to be different from others he was disappointed—agreeably disappointed, as he afterward confessed. It was some time since the men aboard the *Portsmouth* had enjoyed wholesome female companionship. In Monterey, which they had occupied without firing a shot, the women had smiled or scowled at them through the barred windows of adobe *casas* and girls in the *cantinas* had lured them shamelessly. But these visitors—whatever their religion—were their own kind, like their sisters and sweethearts at home. They made the most of Captain Montgomery's party.

As for the gallant commander himself, he was immediately annexed by Lucy Eagar. She had come to sow discord against her enemies, but she always prefaced such gestures by an effort to charm. She set her cap at once for Captain Montgomery, and being a bold, handsome piece, she gained at least his ear. Insidiously, cleverly, over tea and cakes, she revealed the secret of her sufferings on the *Brooklyn*. She managed, without apparent guile, to picture poor Sam as a monster, preying on women's virtue and misusing the colony's funds. Captain Richardson she indicated deftly as an intolerant martinet, believing the worst of everyone and a helpless tool of Brannan. She called on Mary Addison to substantiate her charges. Mary was pretty and innocent-looking. Between them they made a good case. "We'll look into this," the captain promised.

On Monday he gave the *Brooklyn* and her passengers their landing permits. He placed his boats and sailors at their disposal, and by noon the beach was strewn with an extraordinary agglomeration of odds and ends. There were innumerable chests, bags and trunks, large and small; there were hundreds of children's toys, bird cages, cats and dogs, a pet monkey, chickens in crates, a pair of white geese, a dozen pigs; there were a hundred tents, two flour mills small enough to be carried by a couple of men, cases and cases of type, the all-metal press from Sam's New York printing shop, heavy as an elephant, which had to be lightered ashore. There were a dozen plows, scores of shovels and picks, hundreds of cooking utensils, barrels of wine and cans of printing ink. There were more than a hundred rifles, bars of lead, and powder kegs for ammunition. The crews and boats of both vessels, assisted by shore help, labored through an entire day to land the *Brooklyn*'s cargo.

The Mormons at once set up their tents, and the women began housekeeping over fires of driftwood. Men from the *Portsmouth* stored the *Brooklyn*'s arms and other military equipment in an improvised arsenal—a log-and-adobe house that stood in a fenced square near the landing. It was here the American flag had been raised less than a month ago.

Sam Brannan and his ladies were invited to stay at Captain William Richardson's *casa grande,* a large house, as its Spanish title implied, that stood on the Calle de Fundación near where Washington Street intersected that unimposing, muddy thoroughfare. Captain William was not related to the skipper of the *Brooklyn.* He had come to Yerba Buena Cove almost twenty years before the Mormon vessel's arrival and was master of the port—a high-sounding title for a practically nonexistent duty.

Richardson made his living by transporting lumber and other articles across San Francisco Bay. Wood was scarce in Yerba Buena. Most of it came from the *contra costa*, or opposite shore, where oak trees grew in profusion. A heavily timbered island midway across the water from Yerba Buena had been almost denuded by wood-choppers.

Already Sam was looking about, noting these facts wondering whether a sawmill could not be rigged up to dress lumber for building. He had set up one of his flour mills under a protecting roof. His press and printing equipment had been transported by oxteams and Indian labor to the second story of a building whose ground floor housed the gristmill. He was laboriously but not inartistically lettering a sign which read:

LETTER-PRESS PRINTING

While he stood back, admiring it, Lieutenant Misroon approached.

"Captain Montgomery's compliments, sir," he said in his best manner. "He desires to see you aboard the *Portsmouth* at your earliest convenience."

"Tell him I'll be there in a jiffy," Sam returned. He stroked the excess paint out of his brush against a board and laid it carefully aside for future use. "I wonder what's up now?" he mused as he made his way down to the pier and ordered a boatman to row him to the sloop.

He found Captain Richardson already in the *Portsmouth*'s ward room. Once more Montgomery brought out a decanter and glasses. He said rather soberly, "I have here some accusations by a lady named Lucy Eagar——"

Brannan laughed. "So that's how the wind lies," he exclaimed more amused than discomfited.

But Captain Richardson spat out a round, angry oath. "That hussy——" he began, but Brannan held up his hand.

"I'll take care of this, skipper," he said and began a dispassionate recital of Mistress Lucy's exploits during the voyage.

"I knew she'd be making trouble," said Sam, "so I prepared for it. There's a record of her trial aboard ship. I had notes made of all the testimony." He winked at the commander. "You'll find it good reading, sir . . . spicier than a French novel." Montgomery smiled. "I shall be pleased to look it over. . . . Did the verdict meet with the approval of your passengers?"

"About two thirds approved it, sir," said Brannan.

"And the rest?"

"They side with her."

"That's quite a large minority, Mr. Brannan."

Sam grinned. "Well, after all, Lucy's a good-looking wench and has a way. . . . Men are men, captain; you'll have learned that in the navy."

"I've observed it, yes," the sailor said sardonically. He was silent for a time. "If you will bring your record and, say, half a dozen witnesses——"

"I'll bring a dozen if you like."

"Suppose you do," said Montgomery rising. "We'll look into the matter thoroughly."

Sam was as good as his word. Witnesses in large numbers appeared for both sides. After two days of testimony, much of it flatly contradictory and acrimonious in the extreme, Captain Montgomery dismissed Lucy Eagar's charges and washed his hands of the dispute. On the following day Brannan called an executive meeting of the Saints. He gave his enemies a taste of their own medicine by charging a number of them with fomenting trouble in the Church and bearing false witness against an elder.

He won again. Three more of the arch rebels against his authority were excommunicated: Elisha Hyatt, James Scott and Isaac Addison. Some of Mrs. Eagar's sympathizers fell away with her defeat. There was greater unanimity than before.

Presently the whole affair was forgotten in the interest aroused by Lizzie Winner's wedding. She was the second daughter of George K. Winner, who had brought his six motherless children to California on the *Brooklyn*. The groom was Basil Hall of Washington, D. C. He had accumulated a fortune as a trader in the West, and though he was much older than his little

Mormon sweetheart, people said it was a true love match. Sam announced he would perform the marriage ceremony.

And so he did. The first wedding of whites at Yerba Buena was performed by this Mormon elder, indoctrinated in a New York printing office and baptized in the Hudson River. None disputed his authority as he "sealed" Lizzie to Basil with a service he had refused to accept for his own wedding. It was an event which everyone who knew of it attended—Caucasians thronging the inside of the *casa grande;* Indians outside, peeping and listening. Even Lieutenant Misroon and some of his brother officers from the *Portsmouth* lent the grace of their presence— which made it official, as Alcalde Washington Bartlett remarked. He was a trifle piqued because he, as the temporal authority, had not been asked to officiate. Later he had revenge on Sam, whom he considered a pushing intruder. He saw to it that Sam was "initiated."

White residents of the port had a kind of fellowship for sport and rough horseplay. They initiated newcomers by blindfolding them securely, turning them about several times and bidding them to find the flagpole at one end of the Plaza. At the southeastern corner there was usually a pool of water or, at best, oozy mud, and the candidate for initiation was maneuvered into a position where, sooner or later, he would find this pool across his path. On the day of Sam's initiation it was several feet deep, and to the great delight of onlookers, especially the alcalde, Sam made straight for it with his usual impetuosity. He slipped, sprawled, tried to recover his equilibrium frantically and fell prone, wallowing in the muddy water. But to the astonishment of observers, he did not tear off his eye bandage as most of them did. He straightened his dripping, slithery attire as best he might, walked or waded through the pool and, after some floundering about, located the flagpole. The laughs which followed his misfortune turned to cheers.

"B-r-r-h!" cried Sam, removing the bandage from his eyes and shaking himself like a dog. Then he gave a great laugh and shouted to his tormentors. "Let's all have a drink."

They followed him into the tavern, crowding about him and

shaking his hand. Washington Bartlett returned to his office, disappointed. He had succeeded only in making the fellow popular —instead of ridiculous. But he laughed a little, nevertheless. Sam had looked very funny floundering in the mud. He would have something to explain to that prim-mouthed, pretty wife of his when he got home covered with dirt and smelling 'of liquor.

By the end of August the Mormons had spread far and wide from the first group of huts on the beach. Some had taken land claims in the sun-drenched hills around Mission Dolores. Others had settled in Happy Valley farther to the south, and still others had raised tents or shacks on a hill bordering the bay north of the landing place. The colony as a whole had lost its unity. But close to a hundred of the *Brooklyn's* passengers still lived within sound of a bell which Brannan rang each Sabbath evening in the Plaza. It called them to worship in the home of some member or in the open under the stars, when the weather permitted. Elder Brannan had a gift for exhortation. He kept most of his flock together by his eloquence and fervor. He even made a few converts among the older residents.

Those of the Mormons who remained in Yerba Buena were mostly artisans and craftsmen. One of them with his stock of drugs and simples opened an apothecary shop; the saddlemaker set up a bench under his canvas roof, and a blacksmith established his forge. There were few horses in Yerba Buena, but in the surrounding country were many *campaneros* from which animals were brought to be shod.

Sam's colony had made a great change in the destiny of Yerba Buena. It had more than trebled the population and brought with it a cross section of modern progress from the Atlantic States. Besides the saddler and apothecary, the *Brooklyn's* passengers included bakers, surveyors, coopers, gunsmiths, masons, carpenters and cabinetmakers, cobblers, tanners, tailors, a brewer, a cigarmaker, a silversmith, a watchmaker, a weaver and several attorneys at law.

Brannan's printshop was busy from the beginning. Alcalde Bartlett, always a stickler for form, found it gratifying to his dignity to issue ordinances and regulations in print. Through

Captain Montgomery, who had taken a liking to the Mormon leader and often came ashore to drink and chat with him at the Portsmouth House, Sam secured the official printing of the navy. Captains of trading vessels that came to Yerba Buena in increasing numbers, now that the prohibitory Mexican customs charges were abated, had manifestos of their cargos printed. They were called "broadsides" and were posted in prominent places not only in Yerba Buena but other outlying settlements so that buyers might be drummed up from near and far for the auctions announced. Sam found the Portsmouth House a good place to obtain printing orders between drinks. It was a quaint little hostelry on the edge of the Plaza, which people were now beginning to call Portsmouth Square in honor of Captain Montgomery's sloop-of-war. There was talk of naming a street on its eastern margin after the commander.

John H. Brown kept the Portsmouth House. He started it with a few bottles of grog and some mattresses filled with Spanish moss. Now these were augmented by four feather mattresses for select patrons, bought from members of Sam's colony. The barroom had a fair variety of liquors, and a little lean-to had been added for the serving of food.

Three of the *Brooklyn's* unattached women had entered Brown's employ. Sarah Kettleman, a big, comely widow in her thirties did the cooking. She had a child to care for, but she managed not to let her maternal and culinary duties interfere with one another. Mercy Narrowmore was Brown's housekeeper, an office which included the service of chambermaid. Lucy Nutting, youngest of the three, with fine eyes and a good figure but a plain face, waited on the long bench-flanked table. Each had many swains; that was not remarkable, for when the *Brooklyn* landed its Mormons, there were only two Caucasian females in the port of Yerba Buena.

Brown's most distinguished and steadiest boarder was Dr. Elbert C. Jones, a former newspaper editor from Kentucky. Undersized but fiery and gallant, he at once paid court to Mrs. Kettleman, who outweighed him by many pounds and, perhaps, for this reason, declined his offers.

Sam Brannan, however, was not deterred by Dr. Jones' abbreviated stature. He was already planning another publishing venture. "We'll start a paper together," he said to the little man. "You'll be my editor. . . . We'll do it soon."

"There's not much news here," Jones objected.

"Then we'll *make* news," returned the indomitable Sam. "We'll get reports of the battles in Mexico—and what's doing in the States."

"Where'll we get 'em?"

"From the ships that come in," Sam told him. "We'll read all the papers they bring and reprint the leading stories. We'll tell of the whalers and traders that come to port and their cargos; we'll report fiestas at the mission and ask travelers for news of Monterey and Stockton. We'll print a column in Spanish for the *Californios*. Can you write Spanish, Doc?"

"Yes—after a fashion," said Jones.

"It's settled, then. I'll hire young Kemble that was on my ship to help you. He's done typesetting in New York. And we'll start a movement for a school. We need one for the children. Can you write editorials—powerful ones?"

"Oh, yes," replied Jones modestly.

Sam plunged into the life of Yerba Buena. He and Lisa organized many of its social activities. Captain Montgomery was easily intrigued into making a social club of the *Portsmouth*, where weekly dances were held; visiting whalers made it a practice to invite settlers aboard their ships for a supper and dance while in port, and William Leidesdorff liked to give parties. He was one of the older residents, antedating the *Brooklyn*, a bachelor who had a big house on the beach. Occasionally some of the Mexican *rancheros* came to Yerba Buena's social gatherings from their *haciendas* in the hills that lay southward along the long peninsula of which the village was the point. The ladies arrived in ox-drawn *carretóns* with mounted outriders attending them. Many of the señoritas and younger señoras were beautiful and vivacious. The elder women were fat and usually moustachioed. They wore splendid displays of jeweled hair ornaments and lacy *mantillas*. The men rode prancing, long-maned horses caparisoned with silver harness and wore costumes glittering with buttons and braid.

At a ball in honor of Commodore Stockton, many of the señoritas danced with Sam. They liked his rough yet chivalrous directness. Most of them spoke a little English. Some of them had American husbands. They called Sam Señor Brannan or Don Samuel. He liked that. He told them, "I'm going to wake up this place. We'll have a school for the children; a newspaper . . . a theatre by and by."

They understood only a little of what he said; but his flashing dark eyes, his bold, sweeping gestures, his masculine, laughing arrogance—all women understood those and approved.

"Si, *señor*," they said. "*Bueno! Bueno!*"

Sometimes even Lisa looked at him proudly, but there was always calculation in her pride—calculation and ambition.

Sam had one more brush with his enemies, the Eagar faction. Henry Harris precipitated it. He had expected money from home, for his people in Honolulu were well-to-do. But they didn't like his joining the Mormons, his refusal to return, so they cast him off. He worked at odd jobs here and there; he was a clever fellow, young Harris, but he lacked stability, and for the same reason, he lacked cash. He and Mary decided to go East. Mary's father had a store in Boston. Henry would find employment there. He came to Sam's printshop with the news. "We want to draw out of the colony," he said.

"Go ahead, my boy, and God bless you!" said Sam.

"We want our share of the community funds, Mary's and mine."

"Funds?" asked Brannan. "What d'ye mean, lad? You put no money in save your steamer fare; nor has your wife. . . . Besides, there aren't any funds."

"I demand an accounting," cried Harris. "I hear you've grown rich from the colony. You've collected tithes for the Church. . . ."

"And the Church'll get 'em when the time comes; not you, my young jackanapes. Run along with you now."

"You'll hear from me. . . . You can't cheat *me*, you robber," shouted Harris furiously.

Sam turned his back.

The next day he was summoned into court—the first court to convene under American occupation. Formally and not without a certain relish, Alcalde Bartlett charged Sam with breach of contract and misappropriation of trust funds. The plaintiff was Henry Harris. Brannan laughed. "Faith," he remarked, "before you can violate a contract, you must have one mustn't you, Alcalde?"

"Naturally," said Bartlett, somewhat nonplused.

"Has the plaintiff a copy of the contract?" Sam demanded. "Has he shown that any public fund in which he has an interest *exists?*"

Bartlett said with some asperity, "Is it the purpose of the defendant to prove that there is neither contract nor fund?"

"The defendant doesn't have to prove his innocence, Alcalde. The plaintiff has to prove guilt."

Once more Alcalde Bartlett fidgeted. He knew little of law. He was a naval lieutenant holding an unfamiliar post, and he had no answer to Sam's questions. Both of them turned to Colonel W. H. Russell, who had followed Brannan into the stuffy little court room, unfloored and smelling of wet earth.

"Mr. Brannan has stated the law correctly," he declared. "I am here as his attorney. We demand a jury trial."

Once more Sam made history in Yerba Buena. The first trial by jury in California was even more largely attended than the first wedding. Standing room was at a premium, and places on the jury, if they might have been auctioned, would doubtless have brought a hundred dollars a seat. Around the open door stood scores of listeners, buffeting and pressing for points of vantage, and among them was Yerba Buena's first Chinese citizen. The trial lasted only a couple of hours. It ended in a verdict of acquittal, which the jury returned without leaving their seats. It would, in fact, have been impossible for them to leave their seats before the courtroom was cleared, so great was the press of attendance.

The result was inevitable, since no contract between Harris and Brannan was produced. None had, in fact, been made.

Harris was neither a Mormon nor a member of the communal organization formed by the colonists before he boarded the *Brooklyn*. This was known as Samuel Brannan & Company. Harris' action was brought against Brannan alone.

The defendant's claim that all passage money, tithes and other income had been absorbed by expenses of the journey was supported by figures. Sam's vindication was complete and his reaction characteristic. He invited judge, jury, plaintiff and by-standers to have a drink. Harris alone declined.

January 9, 1847, the first number of Brannan's *California Star* issued from the press. It was a four-page paper, 12 by 15 inches and three columns wide. It reprinted from the New Orleans *Delta* an item of war news almost a year old, also an undated Washington report of a presumably later military engagement. To quiet rumors that the *Star* would advocate Mormonism, Sam made the following declaration editorially:

> It shall be our purpose to invoke and defend the rights of all the people against oppression, diffuse accurate information, detect and expose tyranny and *eschew all sectarian issues.*

News in Spanish was promised as soon as a suitable person could be secured. Evidently Editor Jones, while competent in other respects, had not lived up to his promise as a linguist.

Another announcement made in the *Star* was of General Kearny's departure "last summer" on his march toward California via Sante Fe. This march included, though Sam's paper did not state the fact, one thousand members of the Mormon Batallion, recruited from Nauvoo, Illinois. There was also an anonymous communication to the editor accusing Alcalde Bartlett of the misuse of government funds and charging Second Alcalde George Hyde—virtually Bartlett's clerk—with "bad manners."

Sam took an armful of his papers to Portsmouth Square and hawked them with exclamatory shoutings in his great voice. That evening, after a canvas of the village, he returned happily and none too sober with one hundred paid annual subscriptions at six dollars each. He tossed the money on a table which served as Jones' editorial desk and began to set type for the second issue. He hummed a joyous tune to his composing stick.

Once more Sam Brannan was a publisher.

. 5 .

Growing Pains

Wherever Sam went things moved faster. Yerba Buena, which had slumbered for decades under Mexican rule, and showed little change under American occupation until the *Brooklyn* arrived, now began to seethe with new issues and movements. Most of them were Brannan's. Having established social activity as a leaven for the apathy of Yerba Buena's previous existence, he began to sow the seeds of commerce and industry. In March, 1847, the *California Star* observed prophetically:

> Our town is no doubt destined to be the Liverpool or New York of the Pacific Ocean. Her position of Commerce is unrivalled and the fertile countries watered by the Sacramento and San Joaquin rivers emptying into San Francisco Bay must when settled pour their agricultural products into this place and receive in exchange from our merchants all their supplies, luxuries and manufactures . . . the products of gold, silver, copper, iron and quicksilver in which this country abounds must be concentrated here for export.
>
> Mechanics and artisans from all over the world will flock here and we shall have the enjoyment of the

elegancies and luxuries of the oldest and most polished countries of the globe.

Most of the old residents laughed, good-naturedly, at these predictions. Alcalde Bartlett scoffed openly at Sam's "wild dreams." But Brannan's visioning was not without foundation. He had been up and down the bay on Captain Richardson's little schooner. He had explored for many miles the brush-tangled shores of the rivers that fed the bay. He had talked with hunters and trappers wherever he met them, with *Californios* and Indians through interpreters.

Sam learned that the soil of river deltas was exceedingly fertile, that the streams could be cleared of reeds and made navigable. He talked with padres at the missions who confided to the engaging "gringo" their secrets of fig and grape culture. They gave him home-grown fruits and wine from the southern missions. Sam believed these could be produced in the north. The good fathers smiled and said, "Perhaps, my son." They told him many things that were withheld from other heretics—including the mineral discoveries that Mexican prospectors had made in the California back country.

"This land will make our fortune," Sam said to his wife and mother-in-law. "California's the richest country in the world. It produces everything—even oranges. . . . A few hundred miles away they grow them—the same as in Italy and Spain."

"Are you thinking of turning farmer?" asked Lisa, apprehensively. She never could tell what this husband of hers was planning and constantly suspected him of some treason against her comfort or position in life. They had a good house now, overlooking the bay. She was expecting another child and didn't wish to go into the wilderness and make a new home as some of the Mormon women were doing. She had watched the departure of Harris and his wife with envy. Mary's father had finally sent them enough money to take a passage for Boston. If Sam ever achieved the wealth of which he was constantly boasting, they too could go back to New York.

Sam did not answer her question, which he recognized as

rhetorical rather than imperative. He stared at her thoughtfully. Perhaps he read some of her thoughts. At last he said: "I want to build up the country, to colonize it with people who'll grow crops. They'll sell us provisions and buy our merchandise. . . . That's how cities are made."

"*Cities!*" she exclaimed scornfully over her shoulder. She was standing at a window looking down at the huddle of shanties and tents that was Yerba Buena.

"All cities were like this once," Sam told her. "Wait till the New York Volunteers get in—a thousand of 'em in four transports with two sloops-of-war to convoy 'em. And Kearny's regiment is on the way. We'll have plenty of company soon—a big town."

"How are subscriptions for the paper?" she asked listlessly.

"Fine! Fine!" he answered with manifest pride. "Advertisements too. It's a good, payin' business, Lisa. The only trouble is they want to tell me what to print—and what to leave out. I've written a little squib for next Saturday's paper. Listen to this: 'The price of the *Star* is six dollars per year. But it is a mistake for people to imagine that for the sum named they buy the editor.'"

"I think it's rather silly," answered Lisa. "How could anyone expect to buy an editor for six dollars?"

Brannan made a face and put the paper back in his pocket. "You're right, my dear," he said good-naturedly. "Nevertheless, I'll print it. Perhaps it'll make someone laugh."

It did. And it made others frown, which was what Sam had intended. General Vallejo, former Mexican commandant at Sonoma, had called to confer with Sam. He planned to establish a city on the Carquinez Strait, miles inland on the site of his great Spanish grant. Dr. Robert Semple, who published the *Californian* in Monterey, favored Vallejo's scheme. "Francesca" was to be the new city's name, in honor of Vallejo's wife.

Brannan liked the old general. Despite his excessive dignity, which approached pompousness, he was kindly and well-meaning. But Sam could not approve of a plan to exploit the Vallejo acres at the expense of colonists. Carquinez Strait was too far from the ocean, inaccessible to larger vessels, unpromising commercially or industrially. Besides, it might interfere with San Francisco's trade. So Sam had opposed the venture editorially, amusedly declined to duel with Vallejo because of his stand, and with equal firmness declined to be bought.

For once Sam found himself in accord with Alcalde Bartlett, who also sensed a menace to Yerba Buena's future in the proposed city of Francesca. It was a brazen attempt to steal the name of Yerba Buena's great bay, declared Bartlett. He promised to "take measures."

Robert Semple moved his type and press from Monterey to Yerba Buena. His was the oldest paper in the state, but it did not take much of Brannan's trade. The *Californian* was a smaller sheet, not comparable to the *Star* typographically. And Semple had neither Sam's salesmanship nor energy. He was a lanky, overgrown fellow, so tall that Proprietor Brown of the Portsmouth House built a special bunk for him when Semple took up his abode there. People called him and Jones "the long and short of journalism." Their papers belabored each other—especially over the Francesca project. But Brannan, who disliked useless bickering, ordered Jones to cease his attacks. He invited the two editors to the Portsmouth House, bought drinks for the crowd and persuaded them to shake hands.

It was Alcalde Bartlett, however, who settled the dispute by a proclamation which appeared on the front page of the *California Star*. Sam set the type himself. It read:

AN ORDINANCE

WHEREAS the name of Yerba Buena as applied to the settlement or town of San Francisco is unknown beyond the district and it has been applied from the local name of the cove on which the town is built: *Therefore,* to prevent confusion and mistakes in public documents and that the town may have the advantage of the name given on the public map,

It *is hereby ordained* that the name of SAN FRANCISCO shall hereafter be used in all official communica-

tions and public documents or records appertaining to
the town.

WASHINGTON A. BARTLETT
Chief Magistrate

Published by order,
J. G. T. DUNLEAVY,
Municipal Clerk.

Thus was San Francisco christened. The act was Washington Bartlett's political swan song for he was ordered back to his ship, the *Portsmouth,* and resumed his former post of naval lieutenant.

There had, for some time, been unpleasant rumors affecting Bartlett. It was said that he commandeered cattle and horses from California ranches as a "war measure," paying for them in "notes of hand" to be redeemed by the government. It was more than whispered that, far from devoting these animals to military service, he sold them or distributed them among his friends.

A band of *Californios,* infuriated by his depredations, had captured and held him a prisoner after one of his forays, and his rescue had precipitated the battle of Santa Clara. Another much-criticized activity of Bartlett was the granting of public lands, in which he assumed the authority held by Mexican alcaldes before the American occupation. Bartlett began discreetly by granting a fifty-vara lot to his superior officer, Captain Montgomery. Having established this precedent, he granted lands right and left, pocketing, it was charged, the "considerations" involved.

It was Brannan who brought the growing antagonism to Alcalde Bartlett to a focus. He said to Captain Montgomery, over a round of drinks at the Portsmouth House: "I could make a fine story for my paper out of your man Bartlett."

Montgomery set down his glass. "Why do you call him *my* man?"

"You appointed him, didn't you? And you've winked at his doings this many a day."

"Sir!" cried Montgomery, "Do you insinuate——"

"Insinuate *nothing*," Brannan cut in. "Come off your high horse, captain. I'm your friend. . . . Before long news'll be goin' to Washington. . . . You know what that means."

Montgomery finished his drink. He was thoughtfully silent for several minutes. Then he asked, "If you've a story, why haven't you printed it, Mr. Brannan?"

"Because I wanted to talk with you first."

"And what do you wish me to do?"

"Faith," observed Brannan, refilling their glasses, "and should I be givin' orders to the navy, captain?"

Montgomery laughed. "You're a queer fellow, Brannan." He held out his hand. "But I like you. . . . I'll see what can be done."

A few days later Lieutenant Washington Bartlett was restored to duty on his ship.

George Hyde had acted under Bartlett as second alcalde, a title more honorary than authoritative. He stepped into Bartlett's shoes and followed in his footsteps—so much so that Sam called editorial attention to the fact. "Like master like man," he reminded, for Hyde had been little better than a clerical servant to the former magistrate. His tenure in office was short. On February 22—the anniversary of George Washington's birthday, which had been declared a public holiday in the United States— Edwin Bryant was installed in the dingy, moldy office which housed San Francisco's chief magistrate.

Bryant had arrived in the town almost simultaneously with Sam, though he had made the journey overland from Independence, Missouri. From him Brannan had his first news of Mormon affairs in Illinois, where matters were approaching a crisis at the time of Bryant's departure.

Not until the early part of 1847 did Sam learn of the September riots in Nauvoo, when the Saints had been driven out of their homes and across the Mississippi River, scattering throughout the eastern states. But Sam now knew from Brigham Young himself that the President with less than one hundred fifty followers would set out from Council Bluffs on April 14. Their objective was the Great Basin of western Utah, of which good reports had been received from scouts. But Sam determined to intercept the pilgrims before they reached that point, explain the superior advantages of California and bring them to the shores of San Francisco Bay.

He was pleased with his success in dictating or at least influencing local government. Bryant would make a good alcalde. And the change had been made none too soon. In a fortnight, perhaps, the four transports, bringing a thousand new residents—the volunteers of Stevenson's Regiment—would reach port. Their arrival would create fresh problems—serious ones, perhaps. Sam knew the city of New York and the kind of men who volunteered for fighting regiments. Most of them might be good fellows, honest and industrious. But there would be a large leaven of undesirables, ranging from adventurers and ne'er-do-wells to fugitives from justice who had enlisted for no other purpose than to escape capture and imprisonment. There was little or no law in San Francisco to control them—neither sheriff nor constable to arrest evildoers, and no place to confine them if there had been.

Sam discussed the situation with Bryant. "We shall have to make our own laws for a while," he declared, "and enforce them too, by the powers!"

"Well," said Bryant philosophically, "I don't doubt we can do it when the time comes." He had witnessed communal law in the wagon trains and had been a member of Fremont's California Battalion. "Do you carry a derringer, friend?"

"Lord love you, no!" cried Brannan with a laugh. "Whom should I use it against? I haven't an enemy in the village—now that Harris with his wife and the Eagar woman are gone."

"You may have plenty—as man and editor—after Stevenson's forces land," Bryant warned. "That crowd will carry knives and pistols. Best arm yourself. Can you shoot?"

"Oh, yes; I can shoot well enough," returned Sam.

He thought of Bryant's words when the *Thomas H. Perkins* arrived March 6 and debarked Colonel Stevenson with the first detachment of his New York Volunteers. Sam had never seen a more motley assortment of men in common uniforms. There were fellows who reminded him of rats and others of lions, mild-mannered clerical chaps and bold rascals. Their eyes roved with unrestrained curiosity right and left as they landed and marched through the town. Especially did they eye the women. They had seen none in months. From many a bearded face naked lust shone avidly.

There would be plenty of trouble before long, Sam decided. Neither locks nor bolts secured the doors of his house—nor of any house in San Francisco, probably. He had not even thought of locks and keys since he came ashore from the *Brooklyn*. Today he had a feeling that they might be useful.

Critically, as became an editor, Sam surveyed the passing men. Some of them had fine faces. He would find new friends— as well as the enemies Bryant had predicted. There should be plenty of news henceforth, he thought with a thrill. Some of it might not be pleasant. Editorials would be challenged, might become battle cries, he concluded excitedly.

Something militant no doubt in his glance struck immediate and hostile response to the eyes of a soldier. A great bearded fellow he was, with the shoulder straps of a subaltern and the arrogance of a savage king. As the marchers halted for a moment, he stood directly abreast of Sam and stared at him insolently. Sam returned the stare. He had a queer, intuitive conviction that he and this man would one day cross swords. When an order to resume the march was given, this fellow shifted his belt and, with studied deliberation, spat at Brannan's feet. The column moved on.

San Francisco was gay that night. The long bar of the City Hotel and the short one of the Portsmouth House were crowded. Sam making his rounds in search of news, encountered the oversized soldier at the Portsmouth bar. He reached out his long arm. A hairy hand as big as a ham grasped Brannan's shoulder. "Come 'n' have a drink."

"I will that," said the Mormon.

They had several drinks. "What's y'r name?" asked the soldier.

Sam told him. "We're both Sams, then," the other bellowed.

"I'm Sam Roberts of the Uni' States Army. . . . I c'n lick any man in the house."

Swiftly, inexplicably, his bravado withered. He seemed to diminish into lowlier dimension before some unseen power, and Sam, turning, observed the stately soldier-like figure of Colonel Stevenson.

"Save your prowess for the battlefield, lieutenant," he said good-humoredly but none the less warningly to Roberts.

The latter saluted. "A fine man, that," he said, suddenly sobered.

"And a good commander," observed someone else.

Sam left thoughtfully.

Colonel Stevenson quartered his men at the Presidio some miles away. It became, overnight, a city of tents, growing in proportions as the other transports landed their men. The old military reservation established by the Spaniards more than a century ago hummed with activity from reveille to retreat. Soldiers visited the town as frequently as leave was granted them, but not in great numbers, for the commander was wise enough to run no risk of a possible clash with residents, in which the latter might be outnumbered. Stevenson knew how to handle his men; they respected and feared him. What was better, they obeyed his orders.

Roberts and his following frequented one of the cheaper grogshops. It was known as The Shades, apropos of what, no one knew, unless its shady reputation inspired the title. It was patronized as well by residents of "Little Chili" and visiting ships. Brannan went there now and then for news; and there he learned of "The Supreme Order of the Star-Spangled Banner."

There were lodges throughout the East, Roberts informed Sam. He was organizing the first western branch. Anyone who believed in God, had been born in the United States, and was not affiliated through belief, heredity or marriage with the Catholic church might belong. One took a solemn oath to vote for none but Protestants, American-born, and pledged himself to the cause of "America for Americans." The order had secret grips and passwords, though both appeared to be common property. All this childish nonsense amused and disgusted Sam. He evaded Roberts' pressing invitation to become a member by confessing that his father had been a Catholic. He was busy supervising the preparation of a Mormon colony on the Stanislaus River for Brigham Young and his advance army of Saints soon to leave Council Bluffs for the West. This project was unauthorized by the Church, since President Young was reported to favor the Salt Lake Valley in Utah; but Sam with his usual enthusiasm and initiative promoted the California project, satisfied that its superior attractions would bring the Prophet and his followers there.

He selected a site on the northern bank of the Stanislaus River not far from the mouth of the San Joaquin—lush green, fertile, well timbered and overrun with wild game. There he sent a score of his Mormons experienced in agriculture and woodcraft aboard a launch he had bought for the purpose. He loaded the vessel with oxen, wagons, implements for putting in a crop, and a supply of wheat seed.

Guided by the chart of an old trapper named Merritt, they sailed up the reed-choked waters of the San Joaquin River—the first sailing vessel to attempt such a passage—and after two days reached the head of navigation. They christened the place New Hope and began immediately the construction of a large log house, the walls made of native timber, the roof shingles hand-cut from oak trees and the floorboards fashioned by means of an improvised sawmill. Planting was started and eighty acres fenced by the native Californian method of felling oak trees, cutting them up, rolling the butts and larger pieces into line and covering them with limbs. The surrounding forests were filled with antelope and deer; the river banks abounded in geese and ducks, so that three hours' hunting usually provided fresh meat for a week. The place was a primitive paradise. In the *Millennial Star* appeared a letter from Brannan describing New Hope as follows:

> We have commenced a settlement on the River San Joaquin, a large and beautiful stream emptying into the

Bay of San Francisco, but the families of the company are not wintering in this place. About twenty of our number are at the new settlement putting in wheat and other crops, making preparations to move their families up in the spring where they hope to meet the main body by land some time during the coming season.

Late in the spring Sam with two companions undertook the hazardous journey to Utah, where they planned to meet Brigham Young's cavalcade of Saints and lead them to California. The high sierras were covered with snow. Sam was warned that his attempt to cross them was perilous in the extreme, but he did not hesitate. With a dozen pack animals laden with food and supplies, they set out afoot from Sutter's Fort April 26.

They reached Fort Hall June 9, setting a record, for two months was considered good time to traverse this distance. Sam wrote:

> During our journey we have endured many hardships and fatigues in swimming rivers and climbing mountains, not being able to trace the regular route owing to the high waters.

From Fort Hall onward travel was easier, though by no means free from danger or hardship. Sam, browned by the sun, toughened by outdoor life and inured to stress, was enjoying the journey. He was relieved to be for a time away from home and domestic frictions. Lisa was a fine woman; but women were a bit exacting. They were apt to fret a man past all bearing sometimes.

She had her baby now. She would not miss him. The second child was, as she had wished it, a girl, so she ought to be happy. Sam smiled a trifle whimsically. He wondered whether she would ever be really happy. He feared not. She would always find something a bit out of gear in her world, something to set that pretty mouth of hers, which might have been so sweet (he sighed), in lines of discontent.

Early in June they reached the Green River country. They

were lean and haggard after weeks on horseback. They had gone hungry when game was scarce and had thirsted on waterless stretches. But on the whole they had borne the many hardships of their journey well enough, and the red savages had not troubled them, though they had glimpsed roving bands now and then. They were healthy and cheerful. And, when one morning from a high hill they perceived a line of moving dark mites in the distance, they knew the Mormons were coming. Their mission was nearing its end. On the shores of Green River they waited for Brigham Young and his pioneers.

The President's greeting to his western elder was noncommital. But Brannan was not disturbed. He expected no effusive greeting, for he suspected that both Addison and the Harrises had made reports of the trouble between them, which reflected no credit on him.

The President seemed older and more stern than when Sam had previously seen him at Nauvoo. He made a strangely impressive figure, seated astride a great roan horse, his frock coat buttoned tightly under his chin, his high, broad forehead shaded beneath a wide-brimmed hat, his great, steady eyes smoldering with some hidden power which at once attracted and disturbed those upon whom they rested.

His followers were hardy fellows, mostly young, for the journey was fraught with trials. Older members with women and children were to follow later, Brannan learned. The Mormons crowded around Sam and his companion, asking innumerable questions. Many of them were interested in California. Was it true the valleys were so fertile that three or four crops of grain might be harvested in a single year? Were the Indians friendly? And did snow never fall in the great inland valleys?

Sam gave glowing answers to these queries. Then, for a time, he rode beside Brigham Young, answering the latter's more pointed interrogations, growing a bit restive under the President's probing. Was it true the colony from New York had mingled and become a part of the general commonwealth in California? Did they observe the rituals of Mormon life and worship. Had they paid their tithes to the Church and had Elder Brannan brought them?

Sam replied to the last question that all such funds had been expended for the upkeep of the colony. Few of the members had as yet established themselves in any profitable enterprise. But, with the growth of San Francisco, he argued, they would soon be able to contribute generously.

"We need you there to hold the colony together," Sam pleaded ardently. "There have been many apostates, and there may be more from the Mormon Battalion, scattered all over the state, unless you go to California. They've been offered lands when they're discharged from the army. And many people from all over the earth will be coming to San Francisco. A fine opportunity to prosyletize, Mr. President."

Young made no answer. He rode on apparently bemused. "I am much impressed by reports of the Great Basin," he said finally.

"But that," said Brannan, "is a barren land. And the Great Salt Lake is a poisonous water, filled with alkali. Not even fish can live in it."

The President said nothing.

"Beside it California is a paradise," Sam coaxed.

"Yes, yes, Elder Brannan. Let us say no more about it. When we reach the valley, God will guide me. I shall know."

They rode on discussing more general subjects. Sam learned of the expulsion from Nauvoo of the Council and the Mormon settlers in the spring of 1846; a few that remained had been driven out in September. In their extremity the government had helped matters by enlisting a thousand of the Saints in a battalion to cross the plains with California as their destination. Most of the able-bodied male members of the Church were in it. Their families and the older men and children waited at Council Bluffs. The Mormons were scattered over the face of the land, but soon they should be united. When the place for the Temple was found they would come. They would have a new home, freedom from intolerance and molestation. Brigham Young's eyes glowed.

"You see, Elder Brannan," he explained, "if we settle afar from other human habitation, in a place where men will have to work hard for a livelihood, no one will trouble us. That is one advantage of the Salt Lake Valley."

"But——" protested Sam. "It's little better than a desert."

Brigham Young said as if in a dream: " '. . . and the desert shall rejoice and blossom as the rose. It shall blossom abundantly and rejoice even with joy and singing; the glory of Lebanon shall be given unto it, the excellency of Carmel and Sharon.' "

Sam had no reply to that. He dropped back and talked with the others, somewhat abashed. They made camp that night in a mountain pass. At dawn they were up again, summoned by a bugle. Soon after sunrise, at their leader's call they halted. A broad valley lay below.

Even Sam had to admit it was beautiful. To the east rose lofty mountain ranges, snowcapped and serene; below them timbered slopes ran down to green-robed foothills. Northward, Salt Lake shimmered in the morning rays of red and gold; all around it carpets of wild flowers lay.

Brigham Young took a deep breath as he beheld that valley. Of it he had heard many things and concerning it he had dreamed many dreams. He stretched forth his arms toward it, hands extended as if in a benediction.

"This is the place!" he cried in deep, satisfied tones.

. *6* .

Foundations of Fortune

For hours after leaving Brigham Young, Sam's world seemed out of joint.

The Mormons had chosen a barren plain in the mountains of western Utah as their "Promised Land," the site of their Temple. Like sheep they had followed their leader into that arid valley close to the great, evil water so highly charged with minerals that even birds avoided it. They had ignored Sam's arguments and pleas to come to California.

Sam was on his way home, furious and astounded, for he had met with few frustrations, and this one seemed incredible. If the Salt Lake Valley were a "land of promise," surely California must be the land of fulfillment, he assured himself in the silence of mountain and desert.

His spirts lifted with the thought. He began to realize that his predicament was not devoid of compensations. He would remain the titular head of the Church in California. And plenty of the Saints would stay there—paying him tithes. They could be invested.

San Francisco was the place for investment, he thought eagerly. With a little money he could buy land, start new enterprises. The newspaper and flour mill were well enough in their way. They made a good living for himself and the family. . . . But Sam wanted more than that. He recalled his promise to Mother Corwin: that she should ride in a carriage.

"And, by God, so she shall!" he exclaimed.

He had crossed the desert. He was in the Californian mountains. Below him lay the Sacramento Valley, where rivers crawled seaward like huge yellow snakes, meadows of incalculable length and breadth were bright with lupin, daisies and poppies, and flocks of birds and wild fowl made moving patterns against an amethyst sky.

If Brigham Young were beside him now, thought Sam, he might stretch forth his arms indeed!

But the Mormon President was right in one conclusion, Sam admitted to himself. The Saints could not achieve the isolation they desired in this great fertile plain. The world's horde would flock there in a few years. They would dot it with farms and orchards. Steamers would ply up and down the rivers, and some day a railroad might connect it with the great cities of the East.

Eager and prophetic motivations swelled and urged in Samuel Brannan. Here was Opportunity, unlimited and fallow . . . his for the taking. He rode on singing to himself; his eyes shone. He had forgotten Brigham Young.

At New Helvetia, on the Sacramento River, he stopped for the night. A Swiss named John Sutter had a huge estate there: thousands of acres and a wall around the heart of it, like a fortress. He owned mills, granaries, a distillery, herds of cattle and horses. Hundreds of Indians were his servants. Hunters and trappers brought him their wares. He was as important and powerful as the old Irish kings Sam's father had told him about— and as democratic.

They lost no time in establishing a friendship, "Cap" Sutter and his Mormon visitor. Sutter's wine was good and his hospitality boundless. He was a man after Sam's own heart. They both believed in the Sacramento Valley, though they visioned its future variantly. Sam dreamed of cities and towns, Sutter of an agricultural empire.

"You should have a store here," Sam declared, "a big trading post to buy hardware, clothing, tea and coffee from the ports . . . to sell lumber, meat and provisions to the town merchants. That's what you need, Captain Sutter."

"A good idea," agreed the Swiss, puffing at his pipe thoughtfully. "Why shouldn't *you* start it, Mr. Brannan?"

Sam hesitated. "I've little money to spare. . . . Perhaps later——"

"Now is the time for starting things," said Sutter, "while the land is young. I will give you storeroom in the fort. And I will buy from you. There are many things I need—the supplies for my sawmill, for instance. Go back to the city. Find a partner who has money. . . . We will make it pay."

Sam liked the idea; it was promising. He knew a man in San Francisco who might help to swing the deal.

"I'll see," he said. "I'll let you know—quickly. Hold your order for the mill supplies. Give me a chance at it."

"I will do so, my boy," returned Sutter. This fellow would be worth while having on his place. He was smart.

Sam reached San Francisco tired but elated. He had thought to return apologetically, explaining as best he might his failure to bring the Mormons. He had boasted of what he should do, and his boast had been vain. But now his mind was filled with the new enterprise in the Sacramento Valley. He lost no time in finding C. C. Smith, who was a good trader and had money to spare. And presently C. C. Smith & Company opened a store in Sutter's Fort. They bought a good stock of supplies, for the valley was growing. Sutter kept his promise. He gave the order for his mill supplies to the new firm. Marshall, Weimar and Bennett, three of his employes, had a contract to build the mill on the American River about thirty-five miles from the fort.

Sam and his partner made a good profit on the mill supplies. Sutter gave them all his trade, which, in itself, was enough to keep the store going until the valley was settled—and that would not be long. The men of Stevenson's regiment would be discharged when the war with Mexico was over. Then they would be seeking homes, as would the Mormon Battalion. Some of them would join Brigham Young. But most of them might be persuaded——

Lisa was nursing her baby; she looked sweet in her fresh maternity—a pretty woman and a smart one, Sam thought proudly. If only she were more tolerant. It had pleased her mightily to learn of the Mormons decision against California. She was ashamed of his connection with the Latter-Day Saints.

Well, he was branching out, thought Sam. If the store at Sutter's Fort could be developed as he and Smith hoped, he would be independent of the Mormons.

San Francisco was beset with growing pains. The Stevenson Regiment had brought fresh problems, new progress. The number of ships arriving from the States and from foreign ports increased steadily—whalers and traders, for the most part. The passenger boats brought Chileans and other South Americans. They did not mix with Americans and northern Europeans but made common cause with the lower-caste Mexicans, or *cholos*. Their settlement was north of the town.

The alcalde was a busy man, so busy that he called on half a dozen fellow citizens to aid him in administering town affairs. They were known as the Ayuntamiento—Spanish for "Town Council"—and they labored without pay or official standing until Governor Mason called an election to give them a legal standing. Sam's editor, Elbert C. Jones, was a candidate, and under the stress of electioneering he found little time to edit the *Star*. Sam, returning from the Sacramento Valley in September, found his paper neglected. He promptly retired Jones and appointed Edward Kemble to his post.

"Governor Mason's ordinance says, 'No soldier, sailor or marine, nor any person not a bona fide resident of the town, shall be allowed to vote for a member of the Town Council,'" read Sam from the official broadside he had printed. He laughed. "Faith! Stevenson's boys'll be disappointed, I'm thinkin'."

"I heard Sam Roberts boast he'd see about that," Kemble answered. "I think he means to bring a crowd of his comrades up to town and have them vote him into office. I told him it would be unlawful."

"What did he say to that?"

Kemble grimaced. "He said, 'To the devil with law! We'll make our own. Who'll stop us?' They're making bets at the Shades he'll be elected."

"Not if I can help it," Brannan returned hotly. He mounted his horse and rode to the Presidio.

Colonel Stevenson received him cordially. He listened with interest to Kemble's report and shook his head. "The man's a good enough soldier," he said, "but he's not to be trusted when drinking. He's likely to try any foolhardy thing." He pondered for a moment; then he said, "I have it. Lieutenant Roberts and his company shall go on a two-day foraging expedition for wood. That will take care of them without trouble. When they return the election will be over."

Sam nodded understandingly. "I was prepared to round up a crowd of my Mormons to maintain order," he said. "But your plan is much better." He held out his hand and Stevenson grasped it. Suddenly Sam laughed. "Lord love you, colonel! It's an angry man he'll be."

An angry man Roberts was indeed some time later when he met Sam on the street. "So," he stormed, "that's why you came to see my colonel just before election! A fine trick you played me. I'll remember it, Brannan."

He strode on muttering. That night, after leaving the Shades, Roberts and some of his companions invaded "Little Chili," as the Latin settlement was called. Shots were fired. A soldier was stabbed by a Chilean woman he tried to violate. Sam printed the story in his paper. "The time may come—and soon— when San Francisco's citizens must band themselves together to uphold law and order," he commented editorially. Sam wrote a short, pungent editorial such as this now and again. He left the long ones to Kemble.

Sam attended the first meeting of the newly elected Ayuntamiento. He was there to exact a promise. San Francisco needed a school. Too many young ones were running around unchecked, he told the councilmen, learning bad language from sailors, bad habits from gamblers and tavern-keepers. They needed direction and schooling. He held the floor, hammering home his points, obstructing other legislation until, to be rid of him, a committee on education was appointed. At the Ayuntamiento's second meeting Sam appeared to demand a report. He got it, quite a simple one: "No funds."

"Make funds then," he shouted. "I'll give a hundred dollars. Who's cheaper and stingier? Hold up your hands."

Some of the council raised theirs. Some laughed. The fund grew to six hundred dollars then and there. Soon it reached one thousand dollars. A school was opened on Portsmouth Square.

About once in a fortnight Sam journeyed to New Helvetia. He had shipped most of the materials for Sutter's mill, which was progressing as rapidly as might be hoped with Indian labor. The Indians worked slowly. Sutter had taught them industry and simple crafts, but he could not teach them speed.

Indians were good customers for C. C. Smith & Company, better than the white men at Sutter's Fort. They bought clothing, knives, guns, blankets, frying pans, and perfume—the cheaper and ranker the better. Between personal adornment and drink— which C. C. Smith & Company also sold—they spent their small wages quickly. They had learned to wear shoes in winter and were avid for the large red handkerchiefs called bandanas.

C. C. Smith & Company sold many things: powder and ball, wax candles—which some of the Indians ate—English treacle, molasses from New Orleans, Dutch schnapps, tea, coffee and spices. Sam bought them in quantities from sea captains as soon as their ships touched port—sometimes before. Often he had himself rowed out beyond the strait which locked the harbor—by a crew of stout oarsmen, for those were rough waters—and drove a hard bargain for an entire cargo while the skipper waited for a pilot. He bought cheap, though he seldom haggled. "Take it or leave it," he would say, and usually he won. C. C. Smith & Company made enormous profits.

Sam was rapidly becoming well-to-do. His printing office was a small affair compared to his other assets. He sold his flour mill and with the proceeds bought a spring wagon and a gentle horse from Sutter. The saddler made a special harness. It was not the carriage he had promised Mother Corwin, but it was an honest effort at fulfillment and it pleased her. She took the children for rides to the mission and elsewhere. But Lisa seldom accompanied her. She would rather ride a horse, she said, than drive around in a farm wagon. Lisa considered her dignity. Sometimes she rode with one of the officers on a horse borrowed from the Presidio.

One day Sam found his friend John Sutter oddly excited. It was during the first month of the new year, after the floods had subsided. All looked green and fresh and placid at New Helvetia save the master of that great domain. Sam had never seen him so distraught.

"What's wrong with you, Sutter?" he asked.

Sutter led him to an inner office where he kept his books. He closed the door. "It's gold," he said in a whisper. "They've found it at the mill."

"Gold," repeated Brannan. "Why, that's great, man. I'm delighted."

"I don't know whether I'm glad or frightened," Sutter said in a queer, disturbed tone.

"What's there to be frightened about?"

"You know what gold is: a bait for the world—for its rascals. If there's much, they will come running all over my place. They might spoil everything."

"Stuff and nonsense," cried Brannan, amused. "Why should the world know? We can keep it a secret."

Sutter shook his big head thoughtfully. "You can't keep *gold* a secret. It's like murder. It comes out."

He opened a closet door and took from it a small bottle filled with water. On the bottom lay shining flakes. Sam reached for it excitedly.

"By the powers! It *looks* like gold. Have you tested it?"

"Yes, with acids and with scales," said Sutter.

"Who—who knows about this, saving ourselves?"

"James Marshall is the one who found it . . . I have told him to keep quiet. But Marshall has a loose tongue. He cannot be secret."

"What have you done about it? Anything?"

"Yes," said Sutter. "I have bought up all the lands along the river from the Indians. The gold is on my land now. If I could forget it, I would—gladly. But Marshall will not have that. He claims the right of discovery. He wants to dig for it. He has quit work at the mill."

Sam studied silently. "I'll tell you what to do, Cap," he said presently. "Let me bring a band of my Mormons. We can trust them. They shall dig up your gold."

Sutter answered vaguely, "I have said it wrong. You do not dig. It is in the sand . . . the stream. You wash the dirt away; the gold is left. But Marshall knows about it. He shall tell us."

"Well, whatever way it is, my Mormons will find it. Are you willing?"

"Yes, yes, I suppose so. If it must be, it *will* be. You will need many pans. . . ."

Sam returned to San Francisco jubilant. "Gold!" he thought. "By the Eternal!"

On the riverboat he pondered this new tide in his affairs more calmly. What did they prove, after all, those yellow flakes in a bottle? Marshall had found them in the tailrace of his uncompleted mill and rushed in mad excitement to Sutter's home with the news. He had doubtless blabbed of his discovery to the workmen.

Perhaps Sutter was right. What would a few dollars' worth of gold mean to one who owned an inland empire? It spelled trouble. His men might desert their tasks to hunt the shining metal—and, if they succeeded, others would come from afar. They would interfere with Sutter's plans, breeding dissension— shivering his great dream into a thousand little greeds.

But with him, Sam Brannan, it was, naturally, a different matter.

Well, he would send some of his Mormons to work on the sawmill and others to the big flour mill farther up the river. He had long planned to colonize an island on the American—not far from where Marshall had found gold. He would play fair with Sutter. . . . If the gold was to be developed, his men would be on the ground; if not, they would make good workmen for the Swiss—and new customers for C. C. Smith & Company.

Every day Mormons came to him for work or to pay their tithes, for advice and aid of one sort or another. They had been a problem, the unemployed ones. Now he would know what to do about them. He would send them to New Helvetia. Later he would tell them of the gold and impose a tithe of ten per cent on all they found. But he would say nothing about Sutter's gold for the present in San Francisco.

When the Mormons paid him their tithes for the Church, Sam made special entries in a book devoted to that purpose:

| Mercy Narrowmore | Loaned to the Lord | $ 10.00 |
| Isaac Goodwin | *do.* | *do.* | $100.00 |

He kept it in a safe in the *Star* office, and no one saw it but himself. He would need a larger book soon, he reflected complacently.

In March, 1847, a couple of months after Marshall's discovery, Dr. Semple printed the first news about gold in the Sacramento Valley. No one paid it much attention. The story read:

GOLD MINE FOUND

In the newly made race-way of the saw-mill recently erected by Captain Sutter on the American fork, gold has been found in considerable quantities. One person brought $30.00 worth to New Helvetia, gathered there in a short time. California no doubt is rich in mineral wealth. Great chances here for scientific capitalists. Gold has been found in almost every part of the country.

Young Kemble read it with a frown. "What nonsense is this?" he said in disgust.

"Maybe there's some truth in it," Sam answered mildly.
"Don't believe it . . . just a cock and bull yarn of Semple's.
We ought to deny it—show him up."

"This is a wonderful country, boy," said Sam. "I wouldn't
wonder but there's some foundation for the tale." He laid a hand
on the young man's shoulder. "When I go up the river next week
I'll ask Sutter about it."

Apparently Sam forgot. Kemble heard nothing more about
gold from his employer in the month that followed. But there
were many and persistent rumors of a gold strike on the American River. Teamsters and trappers came to town with stories of
gold-laden streams. Some of them brought tobacco pouches full
of the tiny flakes—"gold dust," they were called. A Mormon who
had been mining up the valley offered to pay his subscription
with the stuff, but Kemble declined to accept it as legal tender.

Sam's visits to Sutter's Fort grew longer and more frequent.
He was opening a branch of C. C. Smith & Company at Natoma,
sometimes called Mormon's Island. Many of the Saints had gone
there to try their luck. Reports reached Sam that they were wash-
ing considerable gold from the American River.

Toward the end of May, Kemble could restrain himself no
longer. The *Californian* had printed more articles about gold-
mining and the *Star* had lost subscribers by failing to do so. Gold
was a bone of contention in San Francisco. Men came to blows
over arguments concerning it in the saloons. There were as many
scoffers as believers.

May 29 was Kemble's publication day, and he let fly at the
treasure reports: "ALL SHAM!" he screamed in bold-faced type.
"A supurb [sic] take-in as ever was got up to guzzle the gullible."
In the ferocity with which he flung type into his composing stick,
both grammar and spelling suffered. But he felt relieved when
the paper was off the press and he had uttered publicly his long-
restrained anathema. San Francisco should know that there was
one honest, outspoken paper in town.

His complacent reflections were interrupted by the sounds
of a mounting commotion on the square below. Kemble, with the
news instinct of his craft, put on his hat and hastened toward the
disturbed area. He joined a crowd whose proportions grew mo-

mentarily and whose interest centered in some object or person—he could not at first determine which. But he was not long in doubt. From the middle of the gathering a great, vibrant voice issued. It was shouting answers to a multitude of queries. "Yes, boys. Sure, and it's a fact. Gold on the American River? You can bet there is. Here's the proof, lads. I mined it myself—an ounce in three hours. Gold on the American? Faith, there's gold enough for the world."

Edward Kemble, editor of the *California Star*, did not turn away in disgust from these statements, so radically opposed to his own printed opinion of a few hours before. He felt, all at once, very foolish and young. For the voice in the crowd was that of his employer, Samuel Brannan.

It was Sam who turned the tide. "If Sam says there's gold, there *is* gold," people said to one another. They believed in this Mormon elder with a twinkle in his eye and a laughing, big-hearted comradeship in his heart for all men. Sam Brannan knew what he was about. Wherever he led they followed. . . . And now he was leading the way toward the gold fields. "Hurrah for Sam!" they cried—and went home to pack.

A few days later Semple's *Californian* voiced its farewell to journalism:

> The whole country from San Francisco to Los Angeles and from the seashore to the base of the Sierra Nevada resounds with the sordid cry of "Gold! *Gold!* GOLD!" While the field is left half-planted, the house half-built and everything neglected but the manufacture of shovels and pick-axes and the means of transportation to the spot.

Semple locked his door—which was more than some San Franciscans bothered to do in the frantic haste of departure—and started for the goldfields. Kemble stuck it out a week longer. Then he was forced to confess editorially:

> The streets no longer resound with the tread of stirring feet; everything wears a desolate and somber look; everywhere all is dull, monotonous and dead.

His statements were not exaggerated. When young Kemble mounted his horse and confided the printing shop to the care of a half-breed Indian, he left exactly seven white men in the town of San Francisco. Kemble headed for Mormon's Island. If Sam Brannan could wash an ounce of gold from the riverbed in three hours, he wanted to have a try at it. He didn't believe it; but if it were true, it was better than newspaper work. "Panning" gold, they called it. That reminded him to get a pan. He halted at a store whose proprietor had joined the stampede but whose wife carried on.

"I want an iron pan for the gold mines," he told her.

The woman laughed. "You aren't the only one," she said. "I could have sold a hundred if I'd had 'em. There hasn't been an iron pan in town for a week."

"What became of them all?"

"Sam Brannan bought them for his store in Sutter's Fort," she answered. "There's a smart one—as you probably know. C. C. Smith and Company will sell those pans for ten times what he paid for 'em . . . and pans are not the only things he's bought. He has a shipload of provisions and clothing going up the river for his three stores."

"Three?" repeated Kemble. "Why, there's only the store at the Fort and a branch at Natoma."

"He's opened a third one at Sutter's Mill," the woman told him. "He's christened the place Coloma after the Indians. He's put a German by name of Von Pfister in charge."

Kemble clucked to his horse and rode on.

"Buy a basket from the Indians," the woman called after him. "Some of 'em will hold water. Miners use 'em when they can't get pans."

That night as Kemble made camp he took from his saddle-bags a small stock of provisions wrapped in a copy of the *Star*. In the light of the campfire something caught his eye: "ALL SHAM!" he read. "A supurb take-in as ever was got up to guzzle the gullible."

Kemble lacked a sense of humor. He swore.

. 7 .

The Flood Tide

The formal ceding of California to the United States at the close of the Mexican War in February, 1848, brought to the American public its first general knowledge that such a place as San Francisco existed. The first mail packet from New York to the new Pacific port carried less than half a dozen passengers. But the *Falcon*, which sailed a fortnight later, was crowded to the gunwales. Between the two departures President Polk had received from Governor Mason of California thirty ounces of specimen gold washed out of the river sands of Sacramento County. Thereupon the President sent a special message to Congress confirming the discovery of treasure grounds "of the first importance." It aroused immediate and widespread excitement. In New York and other eastern cities newspaper editions containing the announcement were exhausted. People gathered in the streets to discuss the new Eldorado. A stampede for the West began.

The sea voyage to California was broken by an interval of land travel—unless one preferred the long and sometimes hazardous route around Cape Horn. Mail packets debarked their passengers at a Central American port on the eastern shore of the Isthmus of Panama. After the land journey across it, they re-embarked and were carried by another packet to San Francisco.

When the *Falcon*'s three hundred passengers had crossed the Isthmus, they learned that the *California*, which was to carry them the rest of the way, was already loaded, having shipped a full passenger list in South American ports. The fury of the voyagers from New York and New Orleans became so violent and threatening, however, that the *California*'s skipper finally turned his Chilean and Peruvian passengers into improvised quarters on the hurricane deck and gave North Americans the rest of the ship. The vessel's rated capacity was seventy-five. It left the Isthmus with four hundred passengers and crew. In spite of two tempests, four fires, a mutiny and a fuel shortage, the *California* managed to reach San Francisco in less than thirty days.

Sam Brannan was on the beach when she docked. The entire population was there, as a matter of fact. Most of the absentees had returned from the mines to resume their former vocations. They formed a respectable throng.

Edward Kemble was there, proud owner of the merged *Star* and *Californian*. He had made a little money in the mines, but he had soon got his fill of hard labor and returned to buy out both Semple and Brannan. The former was ill, the latter concerned with larger affairs and glad to be rid of his paper. Kemble called his merged newssheet the *Alta California*.

He saw three distinct types of passengers landing from the *California:* one group, mostly from New York, in rough clothes, carrying shovels, pickaxes, and packs on their backs; a second group, more sleek, better-clothed—the gambler type—giving orders to idlers about the dock for the bestowal of trunks and valises; they had sharp eyes and deft-looking quick-moving hands; the third group was composed of men who, by costume and manner, advertised the fact that they were foreigners. They wore wide-brimmed, conical crowned hats, gaily colored *serapes*, boots, and sashes, into most of which pistols or daggers were stuck.

Between the North American groups and that from below the equator, an odd, implacable hostility was evident in looks filled with hatred, muttered imprecations, occasional jostlings and reachings for weapons. It came to no more than that, but it told a plain story to Kemble of Nordic arrogance and Latin resentment. It must have made the voyage anything but socially pleasant, he decided.

Sam Brannan, perhaps divining his thought, spoke at Kemble's elbow: "They'll stir up a deal of trouble, lad—fighting each other. They'll divide the town into armed camps; mark my words!" He watched the South Americans on their way to "Little Chili," his brow clouding. Sam Roberts was back from the mines; he and his former soldier companions were certain to foment trouble with these Latins. Stevenson's transports had had a brush with port authorities at Rio de Janeiro; they had not forgotten it, Sam knew. Tales they would hear from New Yorkers of their clash with Chileans and Peruvians might fan the smoldering animosity into flame. Again the feeling that he and Roberts would soon become active enemies imposed itself upon Sam's consciousness. But he dismissed it: not likely, now that he had sold the paper, he concluded.

Sam mingled with the newcomers, answering their eager inquiries about the goldfields. He directed them to hotels and sold them steamship tickets to Sacramento for thirty dollars a trip. He had bought up all the reservations on the next three boats, so that even those whom he missed or who balked at the high rate of passage for a one hundred-mile journey were compelled to return to him for accommodations. Sacramento was a young, brawling city of tents and shacks near New Helvetia—the gateway to the northern mines. Sam had a store there, too. C. C. Smith & Company were branching out. He gave everyone a printed card containing the addresses of the firm's stores.

"Don't buy equipment here," he argued. "No use carrying it along and paying extra for transportation. Get your supplies when you're near the mines. Yes, C. C. Smith & Company. . . . Anyone will direct you."

Sam found interpreters and canvassed "Little Chili." Its dark-skinned residents eyed him suspiciously at first. They expected no good of a gringo. But Sam's smile was infectious; when they learned that his mission was peaceful they crowded around him, as the New Yorkers and the gamblers from New Orleans had done, eager to learn more of the mines. Sam answered some of the questions himself. He understood and spoke a little Spanish. Soon they were all his friends. The señoritas and señoras made eyes at the bold, good-looking *caballero*.

Ships kept piling in; from every seaport in the world they came, bringing pigtailed Chinamen, swarthy, brigandish Italians, swaggering, serape-clad Spaniards, Englishmen in tweeds, Germans, plump and red-cheeked, puffing at long-stemmed meerschaum pipes, and dapper Frenchmen, some of whom established bootblack stands throughout the town.

Nearly all of them were young—just past adolescence. They made Sam, in his thirtieth year, feel almost elderly. Sometimes of a morning, during the rare intervals when he could surrender his dynamic mind to reflection, Sam sat at his window on the second floor of the Alta Building in Washington Street and watched the milling, cosmopolitan crowds. It was like a costume ball, he thought, rather than a cross section of city life. He felt the stir and ardor of it in his heart. He knew San Francisco was going to be a metropolis. And he became more and more eager to take an active part in its development—a violent part, if need be, but a *big* one.

Sam seldom visited New Helvetia nowadays. There was too much to do and plan at home. Profits from the Sacramento Valley stores were almost incredible They were clearing close to $100,000 a month, which meant $50,000 for Sam. He collected no more tithes from miners. In fact, they had ceased to pay since one of them consulted Lieutenant Sherman as to the legality of the obligation. Sherman's answer was explicit if profane. Tithe payments to the Mormon elder stopped.

Nor was Sam any longer an elder of the Church. Parley Pratt had been sent by Brigham Young to get an accounting. He had failed, for Sam had misplaced his book, and the two had quarreled.

"You've got the Lord's money," Pratt accused. "The President has sent me for it. Give it to me."

"I don't trust you, Parley Pratt. I never did," said Sam.

"I'll give you a receipt for it."

"You'll give me no receipt—because you'll never get it," Brannan cried. "If it's the Lord's money, He'll show me how to use it. It's *His* receipt I want—not yours nor Brigham Young's."

"You're a thief, then," Pratt fumed, red with anger. "You shall be cast out of the Church. You shall die in agony and poverty, without a dime to buy you food."

"Good-by, Parley Pratt, and better luck to *you!*" returned Brannan. The other strode off, fuming. Several months later Sam received official notice of his removal from the Church of Latter-Day Saints. He lighted his pipe with it.

Sam bought land in Sacramento. Some day it would be valuable, for the town was growing amazingly. John Fowler and Sam were opening a hotel there—in an old gristmill they had bought from Sutter and moved to Front Street near the river. But few would guess that, while the building was being remodeled, Sam and Fowler were spending $80,000 to convert it into a first-class tavern. They would get it back in a few months if the stampede to the mines continued.

Sam had a store in San Francisco now. He and J. W. Osbourne had gone into the China trade. They dealt in tea, silks and a hundred other articles that came halfway around the world. They bought anything and everything that offered, if they could get it cheap enough. That morning a ship was coming in. Sam could see her masts from his window. He reached for his hat. Better go early and learn what she had to sell, he thought.

As soon as a vessel docked, auctions began. Skippers lost no time for they wished to put about and head back to sea again before sailors got the gold fever and deserted.

Gillespie, the auctioneer, was already on hand when Sam reached the dock. So were most of the provision merchants and brokers. Buyers for family groups were scattered through the crowd; sometimes a dozen families pooled their needs and funds, buying food in quantities and distributing it among themselves.

"Five hundred cases of tea I'm selling," shouted Gillespie in his strident auction voice. He and the captain, with the ship's manifest, were offering a cargo while the vessel was still in midstream. Gillespie, like Sam, sometimes intercepted ships outside the harbor and brought the skipper back with him as soon as a pilot took charge.

"Fine teas from China and Japan," Gillespie chanted. "Oolong and Young Hyson. Five hundred cases. What am I bid?"

Sam sat on a box and began to whittle a stick with his pocket knife. He smoked a long cheroot and seemed uninterested in the bidding. He was an expert in auctions. At first there would be spirited competition; then there would come a lull. . . . That was the time to make offers. So he whittled unconcernedly while bids flew thick and fast. They began at thirty-five cents, to which Gillespie paid no heed, for tea was worth from $1.25 to $5, according to scarcity, and there had been no recent cargoes. There might not be another China ship for months to come.

Yet bidding was slow. It progressed to sixty cents, and there it paused. Sam let the bid ride till he saw the auctioneer's hammer about to make a reluctant descent. Then he said, "Sixty-five."

Another pause. Then the hammer clumped against wood. "Sold," cried Gillespie. "How many cases, Sam?"

"The whole damned concern," replied Brannan.

There was a stir of astonishment. Five hundred cases of tea! That was unprecedented. Even the auctioneer gaped. But Sam came forward and signed the order of sale. When J. W. Osbourne, who had just heard of the transaction, ran out of the store, waving his arms and shouting expostulations, Sam silenced him with a gesture.

"We'll sell it—don't worry," he assured his partner. "We own nearly all the tea in California. . . . Don't you understand?"

"You mean we'll have a monopoly. We can fix our own price."

"I mean—with everybody coming to our store—we'll make a handsome profit, John," said Brannan mildly.

Sam Roberts and his gang had forgotten "The Supreme Order of the Star-Spangled Banner." They had formed another organization called "The Regulators," sometimes "The Hounds." A hundred or more of the town's toughest characters belonged to it. Many of them were discharged soldiers who had tried their luck at the mines; who, for lack of fortune, skill or honest effort, had failed to make a living in the goldfields. Some of them had been run out of camps in the northern mines for dishonest practices, and all of them found San Francisco a more profitable field of endeavor for their particular talents—as well as a safer one. Other members of the Hounds were escaped or released prisoners from Australia's penal colony at Botany Bay.

Roberts was their acknowledged chief; a large tent near the City Hotel served as their meeting place. They called it Tammany Hall—perhaps, to give their organization a semblance of political legitimacy—but it was recognized by the better element in San Francisco as little more than a rendezvous for thugs and thieves from which forays were made at night and where stolen loot was believed to be hidden. Their principal victims for a time were the gamblers and prostitutes of the Latin quarter, but as their depredations progressed and no punishment followed, they grew bolder.

They paraded full strength through San Francisco one Sunday morning, carrying rifles and banners behind a fife-and-drum corps. At the Parker House they ordered drinks for the crowd, and when payment was demanded, they smashed glasses, laughed and marched on. Kemble printed a story about it in the *Alta,* demanding editorially, with fiery, crusading youthfulness, that citizens combine to stop further outrages of the kind. The following day Sam Roberts stalked into the *Alta's* printshop, swept a form of type contemptuously to the floor and issued a warning.

"If you print anything more about the Regulators, your plant may catch fire," he said.

Brannan was thinking of this as he watched his tea being loaded into a warehouse. If these fellows were allowed to continue, nobody would be safe. He must see Alcalde Leavenworth. Perhaps he could round up a citizens' posse to deal with the situation.

Next month there would be another election for councilmen.

Sam had been talking with a fellow named Talbot Green about that. Both of them planned to announce their candidacy. Green had a scheme for selling city lots. There might be money in that. Green was a smart fellow. He had been a bank clerk somewhere in the Atlantic States.

Sam encountered Kemble as they entered the Alta Building. "A young fellow named Beatty was shot in 'Little Chili,'" said Kemble. "There'll be the devil to pay."

Sam nodded absently. One shooting more or less did not seem to him a matter of importance. Several times each week some luckless wight's body was found on the waterfront when the morning patrolman made his rounds. A local expressman sent regular bills to the Ayuntamiento "For removing dead bodies from the streets." It was a recognized item of expense.

Young Beatty, Sam remembered, was a pleasant, weak-willed fellow who couldn't hold his liquor—and wouldn't let it alone. He had been drinking around with Roberts and his gang for some time. He had courted trouble and, apparently, had found it.

Sam dismissed the matter for a contemplation of personal affairs. His brother, Captain John, had written from New York that he might come to San Francisco and give up the sea. He was to command the first steamer to make a voyage around the Horn, and would arrive in San Francisco within a few months. If he could find a land berth to his liking, his wife and baby son would follow.

"I can give him a job looking after my business," thought Sam. His affairs were becoming too complex for his own management. So many investments! The Sacramento Hotel would open in September. He and W. D. M. Howard had ordered thirty houses from China. They were to be shipped in sections and Chinese artisans, accompanying them, would put them together. . . . And there was his plan to sell city lots through the Ayuntamiento . . . to say nothing of getting himself elected to that body. Yes, he needed a manager. He would send Captain John an immediate letter.

Another family matter engrossed his thought. Sam's nephew,

Alexander Badlam, Jr., was driving a team from the Missouri River to California, though he was only fifteen. Mary Ann's boy. It seemed incredible that Mary Ann should have a grown son. Why, it was only "yesterday" she had called him "child" and warned him against land speculation in Painesville, Ohio. He thought of her fondly. Mary and her husband had stayed in Cleveland instead of coming to California as they had planned. They would follow the boy, perhaps. He must look out for Alex Junior.

Lisa was becoming more and more difficult to please. Now that they had money, she was forever urging a return to New York—to "civilization," she called it. "On account of your children," she flung at him almost daily. "You can't let them be brought up here—in this raw, rough place where they can't get decent schooling." She kept harping on that till at times Sam almost hated her. . . . He would have to let her go, probably. She would give him no peace otherwise. . . . Perhaps next year. He might go with her then on a journey to New York, or even to Europe, if Captain John would look after his affairs. C. C. Smith was going to Europe with his share of the firm's profits, so why shouldn't he? Smith had sold out to Sam. The Sacramento Valley stores had made them both rich, but Sam, because of his purchase of his partner's interest, lacked ready cash. Lisa must wait awhile, confound it! If only she wouldn't nag so, he thought moodily.

Sunday morning Sam announced his candidacy for the Town Council in Portsmouth Square. Only Brannan with his resonant voice could have made himself heard in that babble of sounds: hurdy-gurdies from the Melodeon and Living Picture theatres, shouts and songs from the taverns, a blacksmith's forge near by and the raucous cries of peddlers hawking wares of every kind to Sunday crowds.

Sam spoke of the needs of the town and its evils. He did not mention the Hounds by name, but everyone understood what he meant. "How many of you will stand by me, shoulder to shoulder, to uphold the right? To strike down the hosts of Satan?" There was a touch of his old Mormon exhortation in his plea.

"Put up your hands," he cried, "if you're with me to down the rascals."

That was more explicit, closer to their understanding. Hands popped up throughout the crowd. There were shouts of "Aye," "You bet!" "We're with ye, Sam." Men gathered about him, shook his hands and slapped his back. But there were murmurings and threats as well.

Sam was content. He had sounded his first note for law and order and got his response. The will was there to put down lawlessness. It could be developed later. Sam wiped his face with his red bandana handkerchief and got down from the box. He turned homeward shaking hands as he went. Many of those to press round him, offering support, were the old Mormon crowd. Sam's apostasy, if they had learned of it, had not estranged them. Roberts and some of his companions glared at Sam as he passed, but he ignored them.

That afternoon he would put on his frock coat and go driving with the family. They had a phaeton now, imported from Honolulu, and a pair of matched bays with clipped tails. Lisa wasn't ashamed of this equipage, though she wanted a carriage and coachman. She was ambitious—for the children, she said. She didn't wish them to grow up rough and ill-mannered, like the men on the streets. Sammy was beginning to repeat things which did not sound well to Lisa's cultured ears, though his father laughed at them sometimes and even Mother Corwin smiled. "That's dirty talk," Lisa would tell her child sternly. She threatened to wash out his mouth with soap. "I must take them away from here," she would say distressedly. "You can see for yourself."

"Yes, yes; perhaps next year," Sam answered soothingly.

They returned late from their drive past the mission, down the peninsula road, which the padres had named El Camino Real generations ago. The children were asleep when they reached home. By the time Sam had unhitched and fed the horses, the short Californian twilight had deepened into darkness.

"Looks like a fire downtown," remarked Sam as he entered the house.

"Where?" asked Lisa.

"Down near the Chilean quarter, I shouldn't wonder."

"I hope it is," said Lisa righteously.

"Now, now, child!" admonished her mother. "That's no way to talk."

Lisa said nothing. She stared through the open window toward the town, her eyes furious with resentment. Sam knew she hated the place. He sighed.

In the morning Kemble met Sam at the door of the *Alta* office. "They—they've gone and done it. . . . I told you they would." His eyes blazed.

"Gone and done what?" asked Sam.

"Burned 'Little Chili' . . . shot men and beat women and children. One's dead; two more are dying. . . ."

"By God!" Sam shouted. He didn't ask who was responsible. He knew. He turned and made for the alcalde's office with swift strides.

"The time's come," he shouted at Alcalde Leavenworth. "This is the last straw. The time's come to *act*."

Leavenworth, a former navy chaplain, looked worried. He was a peaceful man. "You mean about the Hounds and 'Little Chili'?" His eyes were baffled, uncertain. "But what can I do? We haven't enough police to subdue this Roberts gang——"

"I'll tell you what you *must* do," Sam commanded, "Call a meeting of the people. Sign an order summoning all honest men to the square this afternoon. I'll have Kemble print it, and before the ink's dry I'll have broadsides all over town. Here, I'll word it for you. Then you can put your name at the bottom." He sat down to write.

By mid-afternoon Portsmouth Square was packed. Close to a thousand men were there and all eyes were in one direction. Sam Brannan stood on the roof of the old adobe customhouse, swaying precariously as he shouted down at them. He flailed his arms; he beat his breast in a frenzy of exhortation.

"Are we cowards?" he demanded passionately. "Are we worms? Shall we let a parcel of dirty rascals from the slums of New York set their feet on our necks and spit upon us? Are

thieves and murderers spewed out of Australian prison dens to
butcher our women and children—and then parade the streets
with flags and drums? Good God! Are we *men* or aren't we?
Answer me if you've got tongues. If you aren't *afraid!*"
   A roar went up. "Yes, yes. We're with ye, Sam," they cried.
"Lead the way. We'll follow," others shouted.
   But the voices were not unanimous. Epithets were flung at
Sam. Someone fired a shot.
   "Ye'd best have a care," cried a voice. "Ye might stop a
bullet."
   Another called, "Yes—and yer house might burn down."
   For a moment Sam was daunted. He thought of his wife,
the two children. But he conquered vicarious fears. For himself
he had none. The eyes of the crowd were on him. Dramatically
he tore at his shirt, bared his breast.
   "Shoot! I dare you to, you cowards."
   A hush followed.
   "There's my house," Sam pointed, "with my womenfolk and
children in it. So you'd burn that, you scum! Like you burned
'Little Chili' . . . How about it, men?"
   This time the response was thunderous. "Get ropes," yelled
the crowd. "Hang the rascals."
   Sam held up a hand. "Not so fast, friends. Let's do it orderly.
This is a meeting of lawful citizens. Don't forget that."
   He pointed at W. D. M. Howard, respected merchant. "I
name Mr. Howard as chairman of the committee-at-large for law
and order. Who'll second the nomination?"
   "I, I, I," called scores of voices.
   Sam descended from his "rostrum." Some of the crowd had
drifted away, among them Roberts with a group of companions.
They had made a hurried exit from the square, halting at a safe
distance to watch proceedings.
   Howard came forward. Sam held up his hand once more.
"We should organize a force of military police," said Howard, "if
we can get volunteers."
   "We'll do that right enough," said Sam, "but first let's take
up a collection for the poor devils in 'Little Chili' who've lost

their homes." He took off his hat and tossed a gold piece into it. "Pass it around, friends. Give what you can."

Sam's hat passed with amazing quickness through the crowd. Gold and silver clinked into the crown. When it was handed back to him full to the brim, Sam passed it to Adams the banker. "Put that in your safe and come back," he said. "We'll be getting a posse together."

Two hundred and thirty men enrolled in Howard's constabulary. A marshal and ten captains, chosen for their military experience, were appointed. Most of the volunteers had weapons of their own, and Captain Hiram Webb, whose firm dealt in arms, pledged sixty muskets to the organization.

Within an hour the citizens' posse was headed for Tammany Hall. But it was empty and undefended, and an intensive search for members of the Hounds began. Twenty were discovered in various hiding places disclosed by citizens. But Roberts could not be found. It was Sam who supplied the clue that led to his discovery. "Search the riverboats," he advised. And in the hold of a vessel bound for Stockton, Roberts was unearthed, hidden behind bags of flour.

The prisoners were placed in the "brig" of the war sloop *Warren*. Two days later the trials began. Sam was not interested in them. He had done his work arousing the populace, disbanding the Hounds. Such deeds appealed to him. He originated movements, got them started; but all minutiae bored him—a quality which was to militate heavily against his success in later years.

Vaguely he was conscious of a grand jury of twenty-four prominent San Franciscans—much *too* grand, he thought—like a double-ring circus—with a trio of judges sitting *en banc*, the alcalde presiding, an impromptu prosecutor with associate counsel, two attorneys for the defense. All this theatrical rubbish to try a gang of hoodlums whom everyone concerned knew to be guilty of arson, theft, murder and rape!

Most of them escaped conviction on technicalities or through perjured alibis. Only Roberts was convicted on all counts and sentenced to ten years at hard labor "in whatever penitentiary the Governor of California might direct." Eight others, found guilty of one or more charges, received shorter terms of imprisonment.

"It's all nonsense," muttered Sam disgustedly. "You can't borrow another state's penitentiary . . . and, if you could, it would be two thousand miles away. California hasn't even got a calaboose."

After much discussion of the problem Sam had stated so tersely, the prisoners, perforce, were freed. The navy wouldn't undertake to feed and incarcerate them; the town had no prison except a broken-down guardhouse in the deserted Presidio. But a popular sentence of exile was none the less clearly imposed on Sam Roberts and his followers, a threat of the noose if they violated it. San Francisco was rid of them. "Little Chili" breathed easier and returned to its minor iniquities; its burned huts and tents were restored almost overnight, its losses recouped by Sam's shower of gold.

Dark-skinned women on the hill said prayers for Sam's good health and fortune; the men, freed of Roberts' persecutions, made a belated peace with their Nordic brothers. "The Señor Brannan has saved us," they said. "His people shall be our people."

. 8 .

Public Office—and Opportunity

On the night of July 31, 1849—the third anniversary of Sam's arrival in San Francisco—three men sat in Brannan's office smoking and conversing in guarded tones. They were candidates for the office of city councilmen, and tomorrow the election would be held. All were certain of success. They had met at the suggestion of Talbot H. Green.

Green was a newcomer, a clever, soft-spoken individual. Sometimes when one called him "Mr. Green" he did not immediately answer; then he said, "Ah—oh, yes. Beg your pardon." He was well versed in banking, politics and real estate.

He said now, in his quiet but determined way, "Gentlemen: the city needs improvements. Let's remember, in our common interest, when the council meets, that improvements are required." He closed one eye and gazed in turn at each of his companions.

"What sort of improvements?" asked Robert Price.

"Well, now, let me see. . . . I might suggest a public wharf —say at the end of California Street. The city needs wharves." He looked at Sam; once more a mobile eyelid hid one eye. *"It would increase the price of lots along that street,"* he added.

Sam blinked. So this was what Green had been hinting. "But improvements cost money," he objected. "I understand there's not a dollar in the city treasury. . . ."

"Pooh!" Green's exclamation was contemptuous. "This town's a gold mine; it's rolling in wealth. High time we had taxes— big taxes that bring in a thousand a month. The gamblers make that in a night; they'll pay most of it and never say a word. We'll pass an ordinance." He laughed. "Besides—there's city property to sell."

"I want to buy some city lots myself," said Sam. "But you'll be jumpin' up the price with your improvements, Green."

Price said suddenly, "We'll let improvements wait until we've had our pick."

"Exactly!" Green said smiling. "I—I think we understand each other, gentlemen." He rose and shook hands with the others. "Good-by"—he smiled again—"until tomorrow."

Brannan was elected. So were Green and Price. One of the successful candidates was a representative of the old Spanish residents, but most of them had arrived within the past year. John W. Geary, the former postmaster of San Francisco, was elected alcalde. Horace Hawes was prefect or chairman of the Town Council. He had power to veto its ordinances, though they could be passed over his head. Sam didn't like Hawes. He was too punctilious—a political martinet. He was one of the prosecutors in the theatrical trial of the Hounds. He neither drank nor smoked. Sam couldn't understand that breed.

Hawes and the council clashed almost at once. He picked their tax ordinance to pieces. He vetoed it as unjust and un- equal in its impositions, and most people had to admit he was right. Only after considerable delay and severe amendment did it receive the governor's endorsement. Sam didn't mind so much, because he felt that the amended ordinance was better than the original. It would be easier to enforce; but it delayed one revenue: the sale of city lots.

Meanwhile San Francisco was suffering. It had no public service and no income to provide it. Offal and garbage littered the public streets—if one might call them that; in summer they were rutted and deep with dust, in winter mud sloughs—almost impassable. There were no police, and crime, though the Hounds had been suppressed, was more plentiful than ever—more difficult to check, since it presented, now, no focused or organized aspect.

The amended tariff ordinance, when it finally became operative, gave no immediate relief. Collectors had to be appointed and machinery set up for appraisal and assessment. Sam took the bull by the horns. On October 3, he moved that all water lots belonging to the town should be sold at auction after public notice of the sale had been given out.

Sam wanted to set the town on its feet, and he wanted to make money. Therefore he named the water lots as the first to be sold. They had their advantages and defects. At high tide they were submerged. But they could be bought at low prices, and later they could be reclaimed by filling in. Enough of them should be sold, thought Sam, to finance the municipal organization until taxes began to come in. Afterward, when things got going and the wharf was built, these lots would be valuable.

The sale attracted a crowd, as did all public affairs in San Francisco. Investment brokers dealing in futures, red-shirted and booted miners with pokes full of gold dust ready to spend it for anything, South Americans from "Little Chili" in picturesque costumes, curiosity-seekers, pickpockets, Chinese and gamblers mingled around the hastily erected auctioneer's stand making bids on property which for fully half of the twenty-four hours each day was submerged by the tides.

Sam Brannan was not present, but by a happy coincidence his partner, J. W. Osbourne was greatly in evidence. Talbot Green, who was among the first to arrive and one of the most active bidders, found Osbourne an annoying and too-often-successful competitor.

The sale achieved its purpose. San Francisco's empty coffers were replenished. The machinery of government progressed. Presently the tax collectors poured their take into the city treasury. Gamblers paid at the rate of six hundred dollars a year, wholesale merchants four hundred and retailers three hundred.

Auctioneers contributed a percentage on their sales; peddlers, boatmen, teamsters paid their quota. Plenty of dollars flowed into the municipal strongbox.

The problem of a jail was solved. It was Sam who found an answer: the brigantine *Euphemia*. For months she had been lying off Washington Street, empty and useless. Her crew had long ago deserted to the mines; her owners, despairing of fresh manpower, had abandoned her. She might be bought for almost nothing, Sam pointed out to the council. A comparatively small sum would convert her into a prison-ship.

The suggestion was hailed with delight. It presented humorous and dramatic possibilities besides solving one of the town's great needs. Myron Norton, appointed chief of police, had a gold star and half a dozen uniformed officers, but he had no jail in which to house potential prisoners. Consequently he made no arrests.

After the *Euphemia* had been purchased and made into a place of confinement, Norton and his men justified their office. They filled it with petty offenders and sent the council a whopping big expense account: food for city prisoners, wood to keep them warm, and doctors to cure their distempers. Sam rose in the council meeting and bellowed his disapproval. "Why, damn them! They're guests of the town!" he shouted. "We're keeping a hotel for hoodlums and thieves."

Chief Norton protested mildly. "What else can I do?" he asked.

"Make them work, by God!" roared Sam. "Establish a chain gang. Our roads are in terrible condition. Let these lazy galoots repair them, Norton. Put a ball and chain on their legs and shovels in their hands. What do you say, boys?"

"I second the motion," said Talbot H. Green.

"Aye! Aye!" cried the council enthusiastically.

Sam was not a regular attendant at council meetings. He had many other fish to fry. His stores in the Sacramento Valley were paying immense profits; he had to replenish their stocks, audit accounts and invest his returns. He had in mind an office building on Montgomery Street—the first stone building in San

Francisco. Granite slabs could be brought from China cheaper than bricks from the Atlantic coast or Honolulu; and Chinese masons made good builders at low wages. American labor was almost prohibitive in its wage demands.

Poor old Sutter lived on what remained of his kingdom with a few faithful servants; all the others had gone to the goldfields. Squatters had stolen much of his land. He could not drive them off. He was growing timid and resentful.

"It is terrible," he said to Sam. "Why, they even hate me—after they have robbed me. It is unbelievable."

"Hate you? Why that's nonsense," Sam returned.

"It is true, my boy," insisted Sutter. "Those who buy my land are angry when they see others take it for nothing. And the ones who steal my property call me a monopolist, a 'land hog.'"

"By the Lord Harry," laughed Brannan, "that's rich!"

"It is not funny, though," protested Sutter. "I am afraid to go out on the streets—in this new town of Sacramento, made from my land! They shout names at me. . . . Sometimes the children throw mud. I am no longer safe."

"Come with me," cried Sam. "We'll see who dares to bother you."

But he discovered that Sutter was right. The streets were not safe for him. "Plutocrat! Bloodsucker!" they yelled at his bent, shambling figure. And when Sam had cuffed a young hoodlum for mud-slinging and faced a crowd of angry men defending the boy, he realized that Sutter's day was over. There were shanties by the hundreds on his once-well-ordered farmland. It was now a part of the riotous young town called Sacramento.

Sutter and his son were trying to establish a rival town called Sutterville, but without much success. The Swiss, so recently a dominant figure in western America, seemed broken and baffled by his misfortunes. Sam believed he must soon surrender New Helvetia and retire to his place, called Hock Farm, on the Feather River.

Sam made it a point to accompany him, to act in a measure

as his bodyguard, whenever possible. Sam did not fear the bullies and "shoulder strikers" who moved about in truculent groups threatening violence to all who opposed their methods of lawless pre-emption. Sam wore rough clothes in Sacramento. He tied a length of Manila rope about his middle and stuck a brace of derringers through his improvised belt. He outshouted the desperadoes and exchanged shots with one or two. He "winged" a big English convict who drew a knife on him. After that they ceased to annoy Sam and Sutter was safe in his company.

An urgent letter from Green recalled Sam to San Francisco. More city lots would have to be sold. The city was "broke" again. So many men to bury out of the public purse! So many sick sailors to care for! It cost a fortune to have offal hauled from the streets and provide for the *Euphemia's* inmates—irrespective of leg irons for prisoners and muskets for guards. Much of the tax money trickled away through the fingers of collectors. Something must be done.

Sam looked into the matter. November 5 it was "*Resolved,* That 150 of the town lots of 50 varas each and 20 lots of 100 varas each as laid down and numbered on the map recently made under the survey of William M. Eddy and not heretofore granted and disposed of, shall be sold at public auction November 19th."

November 22 Brannan moved "that the city surveyor be instructed to survey immediately all the balance of the water property granted to the town by General Kearny to the depth of 12 feet at low water and place the same on the map of the town for the next sale."

On December 1 Sam resolved that 200 more 50-vara lots be sold nine days later. Green had urged making a virtue of necessity. The rainy season approached. There was no time to waste.

Sam agreed with Green and Price not to repeat the error of competitive bidding which had operated to their disadvantage at the opening sale of city lots. They pored over the map one evening in Sam's office, and after some dispute allotted certain numbers to each. No middlemen purchasers this time. Each was to do his own bidding and respect the others' territory. Sam, with more foresight than his companions, had selected lots on Market Street. Price and Green laughed at him. Market Street was little better than a broad channel of mud, but Sam, looking ahead, visioned it as the main artery of San Francisco. Straight as an arrow it ran from the bay to the foot of Twin Peaks, a great hill eight miles to the west. Any street 120 feet wide and traversing a city's center was bound to become a boulevard, Sam reasoned. He bought thirty Market Street lots near the water-line. But he did not put all his eggs in one basket. He bought lots near the square as well—an entire block, bounded by Montgomery, Sacramento, Sansome and California streets.

Selling public lands had become a mania with the council. On December 10 another sale was ordered:

> INASMUCH AS, A large number of lots have been sold already at public auction and still leaving a large number not granted or sold, therefore:
>
> *Resolved,* That the Alcalde may be and is hereby authorized to grant to any and all applicants lots of 100 varas at $500 and lots of 50 varas at $200 and that such grants be continued for thirty days from December 15th.

"That ought to clean 'em up," said Green to Brannan in an undertone. "Hawes is cutting in on our game. His justice of the peace, Colton, is selling grants right and left for whatever he can get—dividing with Hawes, most likely."

"I doubt that," said Sam. "Horace Hawes is a pest, but he's honest."

"Well, it'll be a good thing to remember this Colton business—in case Hawes gets nasty again." He leaned closer. "I'm afraid he's learned about our little conference."

"What conference?" asked Sam. He had long since forgotten the incident.

Talbot Green looked pained. "Our pre-election caucus, Sam. The little matter of *improvements.*"

"Oh—oh, yes," Sam answered thoughtfully. "Well let him find out. What can he do?"

"He can make a deal of trouble," Green replied. "We've been

a little careless of the law with all this sale of public property—especially in buying it ourselves."

Sam laughed. "What law? We make the law. We're the city council." He slapped the other's shoulder reassuringly. "Don't worry, Talbot."

Green's answering smile was dubious. "He can go to the governor."

"So can we," returned Sam, dismissing the matter. There were times when he distrusted Green and was sorry he had been lured into what smacked of conspiracy. But Green was a smart fellow. His program of selling the city's lands with one hand and buying them with the other would soon make them rich.

It might be a dangerous game elsewhere, Sam mused. But here everything was new. Every day established fresh and daring precedents. Mexican law was a back number—an emergency holdover because Congress had not yet officially recognized California, spoil of war, as an American possession. There was Peter Burnett, of course: a civil governor without power to enforce his mandates.

What if San Francisco chose to defy him?

The ship Sam had long expected came in a week before Christmas. It brought new silk dresses for Lisa and Mother Corwin from modish shops in the East; a hobbyhorse with a real mane for Sammy, now five years old, and smaller toys for the girl baby.

Sam had dispatched an Indian to the hills for red *toyon* berries and California holly. His house, like many another, was brave with holiday trimmings. A turkey from one of the California *ranchos* was ready for the oven. The two women were baking pies. Sam had brought his packages home by stealth and hidden them in the stable. He was reading an old copy of the New York *Journal of Commerce* and chuckling—his bootless feet close to the fire, to Lisa's annoyance. She didn't like his free and easy manners, which had become even more free of late. "What are you laughing about?" she asked crossly.

"It says here that we Californians are running around grubbing for gold like a lot of hogs let loose in a forest and rooting up ground nuts."

"And—aren't you?" she asked.

"Oh, come, now, darlin'——"

"Put on your shoes or slippers and come to supper," said Lisa. The little girl was crying. Lisa set down the dish she was carrying and ran to the child. Sam rose and put on his shoes with a grimace. He was about to enter the adjoining room, which was kitchen and dining room at once, when something caught his eye. He ran to the window. "A fire! Looks like a big one," he cried.

"Come to supper, Sam," called Mother Corwin.

But Sam was halfway down the hill that led to Portsmouth Square. By God! It was Dennison's Exchange. Its flimsy walls were already burned through and toppling. The Parker House was doomed, Sam thought. And Booker's store. And the U.S. Restaurant.

From all directions figures came running. When Sam reached the square, flames were already thrusting hungry tongues across Washington Street. He heard a boom of explosives and guessed that they were blowing up buildings to halt the fire.

"Give me a bucket," he yelled.

It was close to midnight when he returned, his face blackened with soot, his eyebrows scorched, clothes dirty and shoes dragging mud over Lisa's clean carpet. But there was something in his eyes which checked her petulance. "It's burned the whole south side of Washington, between Kearny and Montgomery," he said. "Done half a million damage, I guess." He pulled off his muddy boots and sat down wearily. "Oh, well. *We can build it up again.*"

Horace Hawes had gone into action. Following another public sale of city lots by order of the council January 3, the prefect addressed a sharp protest to Governor Burnett. The sale had brought $635,130 to the municipal treasury, according to Hawes' check on the sales, but no public accounting of this or of previous sales had been made by the council. Hawes' letter stated the facts bluntly. He warned the governor of a "high state of alarm" on the part of San Francisco's public, "who have sought in vain to know what has become of the large sums already raised and now see all that remains of the public property of the city is about to be swallowed up and dissipated as if it was sunk at the bottom of the sea."

Governor Burnett issued, forthwith, an injunction against further sales of city lands.

"I told you he'd do it," Green said angrily to Sam at the next council meeting. "The dirty hound! He's written us an open letter, published in the paper, *about that pre-election caucus*. He wants to know whether we didn't agree to appropriate money for a wharf *before we were elected*. And then he asks pointedly whether the same councilmen who bid in most of the lots along the waterfront *didn't vote for the wharf appropriation*."

"The town's stirred up," said Price uneasily. "Those who aren't laughing at us say we ought to be ousted from office."

"And—what have you answered?" asked Sam.

"Nothing, damn it!" Green exploded. "He—he has us up a tree."

Sam went home to think about the matter. He said to Lisa that evening, "I'd better be going to Sacramento, my dear. The squatters are getting obstreperous there. They'll need looking after."

She gave him the level, shrewd look which sometimes infuriated Sam. "Your council is in trouble, isn't it?"

"Yes," he said. "It's Green. The fellow's sharp. But there's a limit to sharpness."

Green was leader in the council now. Sam had become inactive. He had no part in the defiance of Governor Burnett or in the announcement of further land sales in March despite Burnett's prohibition. He listened to denunciations of Hawes in thoughtful silence; he heard the plan to frame countercharges against the prefect in connection with Colton's land grants. Colton had departed for the East with approximately $200,000.

"It's plain stealing," Green shouted in meeting. "And Horace

Hawes is to blame. He's got his share of the loot, I'll warrant." Sam didn't believe that but he held his peace. City Attorney Peachy was instructed to investigate "charges that had been made" and, if found true, to prepare an indictment against Prefect Hawes. Sam, accustomed as he was to rough methods when necessity or emergency prompted them, did not approve of Green's plan. Much as he disliked Hawes, he respected honesty and courage.

He made a trip to Sacramento. Conditions were bad there. Flood waters, which had inundated most of the city, were receding. But the squatters who had found temporary safety on the levees and other elevated points were refusing to leave them. They were so thick on the riverfront that steamers found little room to land their cargoes.

Sam returned the day before a council meeting, February 24. State and city were at loggerheads, he learned. Governor Burnett had ordered Attorney General Kewen to file a bill in chancery against the city council. There was talk of another meeting in Portsmouth Square. A citizens' committee was suggested to inquire into local affairs.

That evening Sam sat staring at the fire, trying to formulate his course of action at tomorrow's meeting. He answered Lisa's questions tersely and absently until she withdrew in a huff. Presently he sat down at his desk to write. When Lisa, much later, appeared to ask whether he was going to sit up all night, he answered her more sharply than was his habit.

"Don't bother me," he said, "I'm writing a report."

Before the council meeting was well under way, it became evident that a rift between leaders had occurred. Green and Brannan, both members of the committee on finance, were not seated together, chatting friendly-wise as usual. Before long Brannan rose. He presented a report. The committee was convinced, he read, that the town was unable to sustain its present expenses either through reasonable taxation or by selling more city lots in the face of the governor's displeasure. Therefore the committee recommended a reduction of the police department from fifty to thirty officers and the elimination of all foreigners from public benefits—also the immediate suspension of street improvements except by special appropriation.

The report was signed "Samuel Brannan, Chairman."

A buzz of talk followed. Talbot Green arose. "I wish to present a minority report," he announced. "We recommend that in order to get funds with which to meet current expenses of this municipality, the town lots ordered to be sold March fourth, next, *shall* be sold and that all lots in the town not surveyed and not heretofore granted be included in the sale."

"Aye! Aye!" called several voices. "That's the stuff."

Someone called for a vote. Amid considerable discussion, Brannan's report was rejected. By a second vote Green's was endorsed.

Sam jumped to his feet. "And now you can accept my resignation, gentlemen," he thundered. "I'll not stand for this. I'm an easy going fellow, as you all know. But it's too roughshod for me." He looked straight at Green. "I'll bid you all good day."

He strode out majestically amid murmurs of surprise. The occasion had not seemed to justify such an outburst.

At the offices of the *Alta* and of the *Pacific News*—a recently established paper—Sam paused to impart the news of his bolt from the council. He was pleased with himself. He had cleared his skirts of the local row. Green would not find it so easy to emerge with honor, for Sam, as he had carefully planned, had placed the onus of public suspicion squarely where it belonged. He was free now to prosecute other affairs.

After a few hours of congenial intercourse with fellow citizens in front of mahogany bars, Sam returned home to pack. He was going to Sacramento on the morning boat, which left at dawn. He took two pistols. There might be trouble along the levee.

He met Horace Hawes at the boat landing. Somewhat to his surprise the latter accosted him. "I see you've resigned from the council."

"Ah! Was it in the paper, then, Mr. Hawes?" asked Sam innocently.

Hawes chuckled. "Yes. I can't imagine how they got the story so soon. They give you much the best of it. . . . Green is furious."

"He's an easily angered man, more's the pity," said Sam with apparent regret.

Hawes looked him straight in the eyes. "There's talk of a public meeting to discuss the council—perhaps to take action. It's a good thing you're out."

Sam laughed. "Oh, that's not it at all," he said demurely.

"You're a very clever fellow, Brannan," said the prefect.

Mary Ann Brannan Bedlam
Courtesy of the Sharpsteen Museum

Illustrations

Alexander Bedlam

Courtesy of the Sharpsteen Museum

Alexander Bedlam, Jr.

Courtesy of the Sharpsteen Museum

Illustrations

San Francisco, from the Bay, in 1847

From the *Annals of San Francisco*, 1855

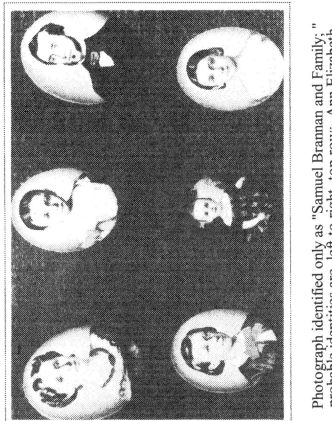

Photograph identified only as "Samuel Brannan and Family;" probable identities are, left to right, top row: Ann Elizabeth, Fanny Kemble and Samuel; bottom row: Samuel Jr., Annette, and Adelaide. *Sharpsteen Museum Reprints* (Photograph - Courtesy of California Section, Photographic Collection, California State Library.)

Residence of Samuel Brannan, Esq., in 1847

From the *Annals of San Francisco*, 1855

The Hounds

From the *Annals of San Francisco*, 1855

Illustrations

The City Hall, February 22d, 1851

Aroused citizens, following an attack on Janson - a merchant
From the *Annals of San Francisco*, 1855

Hanging of Jenkins on the Plaza

From the *Annals of San Francisco*, 1855

Illustrations

Jonathan D. Stevenson

From the *Annals of San Francisco*, 1855

John A. Sutter

From the *Annals of San Francisco*, 1855

Illustrations

William D. M. Howard

From the *Annals of San Francisco*, 1855

William M. Gwin

From the *Annals of San Francisco*, 1855

Ann Eliza Brannan
in later years following divorce from Sam
Courtesy Sharpsteen Museum

Bath and pavilion of Sam Brannan's resort in Calistoga

Courtesty of the Sharpsteen Museum

Illustrations

A cottage built by Sam Brannan
for the Calistoga Hot Springs Resort, now a registered state
landmark and a part of the Sharpsteen Museum at 1311
Washington Street,
Calistoga, California

Calistoga Springs, looking west

From *Historical and Descriptive Sketchbook of Napa, Sonoma, Lake and Mendocino, 1873* by C. A. Menefee (reprinted 1994 by James Stevenson Publisher)

. 9 .

Factions and Violence

Sacramento was a sea of drying mud out of which rose man-crowded islands of habitable terrain unsubmerged by the recent, now receding flood waters. There were three of these "islands": the high ground of Sutter's Fort, the Plaza between Eighth and Ninth streets, and the river embankment. All were covered with tents and shacks. Sutter had at last deserted the fort and retired to Hock Farm, a much smaller but safer possession on the Feather River. He had endeavored to drive the squatters off his larger property without success; had, in the end, been driven off himself.

The squatters recognized no law but force. They seized land where they fancied it or where necessity—such as the flood danger—dictated. They built ramshackle huts in defensive clusters anywhere and everywhere, defying expulsion.

Sam found the property owners of Sacramento in an excited state. Violence was in the air. Along the river levee huts were so thick and so near the water that shippers were denied proper space to unload their goods. Nor were the cargoes safe when landed. At first they were plundered by stealth and later looted openly by armed groups of squatters. A man named Robinson

had formed the Squatters' League. Its members talked loudly of
their rights. They were ready to fight for the locations they had
pre-empted.

"The gang meets at Kelly's fandango, Front and J street,"
John Rodgers told Sam. "Most of them are discharged soldiers
from Stevenson's Regiment and Sydney Ducks from Australia."

"They call us monopolists and grasping speculators," said
Dewitt Burnett, another landowner. He laughed mirthlessly. "It's
truly a ridiculous situation, but it's serious enough. Something's
got to be done . . . and right away, if we're to recover our land."

"Yes, that's plain enough," agreed Sam. "They've picked the
best places in town, and they're trying to hold 'em."

"*Trying* to? They're *doing* it," said Rodgers morosely. "I tell
you, Sam——"

"Don't tell me any more," said Brannan. "Talk's no good.
Let's get a crowd together. How many upstanding boys who're
not afraid of a fight can you muster?"

"Plenty," Burnett answered with alacrity. "Any man with the
heart of a cockroach will fight for his land."

Rodgers nodded. "Yes, that's true," he agreed.

"Round 'em up, then," ordered Brannan. "I'll do what I can,
boys. We'll meet tonight."

"Where?" Rodgers asked.

"At my hotel. The lower floor's been flooded, but they've
cleaned it up. We can compare notes. Tomorrow we'll act."

James Robinson had built the skeleton of his home on the
river embankment at the foot of I street. It projected dizzily
over the stream, makeshift piles supporting the overhang. Jim
McClatchy's shack was under way. Both occupied land owned
by Sam, but this fact disturbed neither of the squatters. "If that
Mormon plutocrat tries to collect rent for his ground or raises
any other objection, let him see how far he'll get." Robinson
patted his shotgun suggestively. "One man's law is as good as
another's."

McClatchy laughed and spat into the stream. Suddenly his
eyes stared up the river. "What's *that*?" he cried.

"Look's like a crowd—headed this way," returned Robinson uneasily. He stood back, partly sheltered by the framework of his house, cocking the gun.

The crowd advanced. A stocky, roughly clad fellow at the head of the invading host engaged the squatters' attention. He wore high boots spattered with mud, a broadbrimmed black hat pulled low on his forehead. A belt of Manila rope encircled his middle. Through it were thrust a brace of derringers.

"Come on, boys," he yelled. "Clean out this nest of rats." His followers approached at "double quick" now, a score of determined-looking fellows. Some of them carried ropes, others sledge hammers. Most of the squatters snatched up handfuls of their belongings and fled. Robinson and McClatchy were of sterner stuff.

"Touch this house at your peril," the former shouted theatrically. "It's mine and I'm going to defend it."

Sam ignored his warning. He tore a loose board from the side of Robinson's hut and tossed it into the river. Robinson raised his gun. A man called, "Look out for that fellow. He's going to shoot."

"Here, Warbass," Sam shouted to one of his followers, "cover this man. If he makes another move with the gun, shoot hell out of him. Rodgers, bring your rope."

A big fellow knocked Robinson's gun from his hands just as it exploded. Rodgers fastened a rope end around one of the supports of his hut. Half a dozen men tugged at the rope; others employed a log as a battering ram against the piles. Slowly, while the "doctor" foamed imprecations and struggled with those who held him, the house collapsed into a nondescript heap; odds and ends of lumber floated down the river.

McClatchy's house offered more resistance. The supports remained upright, though they gave slightly under efforts to raze them. The squatter watched with disdainful silence. Brannan, red and furious with frustration, turned to observe a horseman, evidently a *vaquero* from a neighboring ranch; he was surveying the scene with amused curiosity.

"Damn you!" Brannan shouted. "Don't sit there laughing at

us. Pitch in and do your share—*or get out.*" He pulled one of the pistols from his belt.

"*Si, señor,*" the horseman answered, unruffled. He uncoiled a riata from his saddle and tossed the looped end to Sam. "Make heem fast," he pointed to the prop at which men were tugging ineffectually. "I help you pull."

Sam laughed and did so. The horseman gave spurs to his steed. There was a shock as the riata tightened. The support of McClatchy's house vibrated, trembled, gave. The structure collapsed. McClatchy jumped clear just in time.

Other squatters gave Sam's regulators less trouble. By dusk they had cleared the levee. Men were left for a patrol, but no effort was made at reprisal. Sam took the rest of the crowd to his hotel and bought them drinks. Some of them remembered the opening a few months before the flood. Sam's hotel stood on Front Street a stone's throw from the river.

There had been a grand housewarming: whisky and wine for all. A basket of champagne had been tossed from the balcony to overflow crowds in the street. The hotel was paying now, as all of Sam's ventures did. Rates were high but gold dust was plentiful.

"We haven't heard the last of those squatters," prophesied Burnett, shaking his head. Drink always made him dour.

But the others were gay. "I hope *I've* heard the last of 'em," cried Brannan, raising his glass. "Here's to their confusion and damnation. We've cleaned 'em off the levee, and I'm going back to San Francisco. But my agent, Bruce, will face them in court if need be."

John Fowler, part-owner of the hotel, entered hurriedly. He took Sam aside.

"I wish you'd go with me to Sutter's Fort tomorrow, Sam," he said. "There's trouble. . . . Pickett's killed a man."

"What! 'Philosopher' Pickett?"

"Aye, none other. He had a row with some trader in his store. Pickett claims the fellow tried to knife him and he shot to save himself. But he ought to be tried."

"Well, why don't you try him, man?" asked Brannan.

Fowler flushed. "He's a bad one when he's drinkin'. Alcalde Bates was afraid to arrest him. . . . He's resigned the job."

"Well?"

"Bates named me as his successor," Fowler added hastily.

Brannan roared. "A fine, brave lot of lads you are up there. What d'ye want *me* to do?"

"We'd like ye to reason with Pickett——"

Brannan laughed again. "All right," he said. "I'll ride on over with you in the morning."

Sam found Philosopher Pickett, a tall, lanky, bearded Kentuckian, nicknamed for his studious habits, seated in his trading post. A book, a glass, a bottle of grog and a gun were on the table before him. His brow was moody and his eyes bloodshot; the bottle was nearly empty. As Sam entered he looked up, startled, and grasped the weapon.

"Good morning, friend," said Sam. Pickett laid down his gun. Sam took a seat at the table and, reaching for the glass, poured himself a drink. They talked.

In the afternoon, the sheriff of Sutter County served a warrant on Pickett. The latter followed him peacefully into the meetinghall of the fort. On a rostrum sat Samuel Brannan. "Sit down, 'philosopher,'" he said genially. "There's whisky and water on the table for any that want it. . . . Let the court come to order."

"Who's the judge?" asked Pickett.

"I am," answered Sam. "Pickett, in the name of law and order, are you guilty or not?"

"Not guilty," said Pickett, helping himself to a drink.

"Let a jury be drawn," Sam instructed the sheriff. The latter strode about the room, touching first one man and then another on the shoulder until he had selected twelve. He shifted chairs until he had assembled them in a group. Then Sam descended from the bench. "Your Honor and Gentlemen of the Jury——" he began addressing the vacated rostrum.

"My God!" cried Pickett rising. "Is he prosecutor too?"

Sam turned apologetically. "I had to be 'philosopher.' There was nobody else to take the job."

Witnesses were called. At five o'clock Sam remounted his

bench and dismissed court until tomorrow. "What shall I do with the prisoner?" the sheriff asked.

"Put him in jail," returned the Court.

"But we have no jail, Your Honor."

"In irons, then."

"No irons, either," said the sheriff.

"Pickett, will you put up bail for your appearance?" Brannan asked. The prisoner nodded. "Get out, then, all of you," Sam ordered.

Eventually, to the relief of everyone, the prisoner was freed. Sam hunted up Joe Bruce, his Sacramento representative. They had a long talk with John A. Sutter, Jr., about land and land values. Both Brannan and his agent believed in the future of Sacramento. But Sutterville was developing as a rival town. Young Sutter, after his father's departure, had relinquished his interest in Sutterville. He was promoting Sacramento, trying to dispose of the captain's extensive but disputed interests.

"The Sutterville people have offered us eighty lots free if we'll transfer our business there," Bruce told him. He looked at Brannan questioningly.

Young Sutter laid a hand on Brannan's knee. "I know you, Mr. Brannan. And my father knows you. In San Francisco, where you lead the people follow. . . . We can't let you go away from Sacramento."

Sam said, pleased but wary, "What's your proposition?"

"We have so much land, my father and I; and so little money. Here is what I shall do: I sell you half our Sacramento land for a hundred twenty-five thousand dollars. And——wait!" he went on hastily as Brannan made a gesture. "That isn't all. . . . I give you, free, for nothing, half a thousand lots in Sutterville."

"By God!" said Bruce excitedly, "I call that fair. . . . But it's a lot of money, Mr. Brannan," he appended. Bruce knew something of Sam's complex finances. His investments were enormous, his income large; but he gambled on everything from Hawaiian sugar plantations to three-card monte. Bruce had seen him lose $80,000 at the Eldorado Saloon in one night's play. His available resources, as a consequence, were slight.

Perhaps Sam read the other's thought. He frowned, and turned to Sutter. "Never mind the money. . . . It's a bargain." He held out his hand.

"We'll put it down on paper, Mr. Brannan," said young Sutter hastily. He produced pen and ink and foolscap paper. "Here, you write it, Mr. Bruce."

"By God!" said Bruce as Brannan stepped aboard the boat for San Francisco. "You own a fourth of Sacramento and the surrounding country. Do you realize that?"

"And I owe an eighth of a million dollars," said Sam soberly.

On the dock at San Francisco Sam met Theo Shillaber. The latter grasped his hand. "I hear you drove out the squatters in Sacramento," he said excitedly. Shillaber, too, had suffered from the land-grabbers. He had leased land from the government on Rincon Point, only to find it pre-empted by Sydney Ducks. Their hastily constructed tents and huts completely covered it, and they refused to vacate or pay rent. Shillaber, a choleric man, had threatened and finally denounced the squatters. "I never saw a viler crew," he told Sam. "The women cursed and spit at me; the children threw stones. I was lucky to get away with a whole skin."

"Yes, but the troops cleared your land," returned Sam. "You're in luck. We had to be our own soldiers. And the trouble's not over yet—by a hell of a sight—here or in Sacramento."

Shillaber nodded. "What I fear is that they'll try revenge——"

"What d'ye mean?" asked Sam.

"We've had two fires already this year," Shillaber said darkly. "And a deal of loot was found in Sydney Town near 'Little Chili,' where these rogues gather." He walked away, shaking his head, leaving Sam thoughtful, somewhat disturbed. The town was ready for another clean-up, he decided.

Since the affair of the Hounds, conditions, after a reform, had become worse than ever before. There were no open demonstrations now, no defiant parades of lawlessness; but for that very reason crime had assumed a more sinister aspect. Instead of "Tammany Hall" and less than a hundred blustering rascals, there was Sydney Town at the foot of Broadway, in the districts known as Five Points and Seven Dials. A dozen taverns and resorts of vice were rendezvous for half a thousand scoundrels: French stranglers, Spanish knife-throwers, Sicilian bandits, and English as well as American criminals from pickpockets to murderers. They held their own court in their own quarter, which honest men never entered and which policemen feared to invade.

"Set the town afire, will they?" Brannan muttered to himself. "We'll put a stop to that."

He talked with William Howard about fire hazards. There were three fire engines in town; two ordered by the city council at one of their early meetings. Sam had suggested that, but the engines had failed to arrive in time for the Christmas Eve blaze. Howard had brought the other engine with him from Boston on his ship *Windsor Fay*. He had given it to San Francisco, and the Howard Engine Company was named in his honor.

All of San Francisco's engines were obsolete and inadequate. Sam decided that, after he had cashed in on some of his investments, he would give the town a real fire-fighter—like the ones they had in New York. It meant social prestige to have an engine company named for you. Lisa would be pleased.

Sam plunged back into his digressive speculations. He sold some of his water lots and made a payment to Sutter. He won $20,000 at faro and paid his overdue taxes; but he lost twice the amount at monte again. The threat of Sydney Town had been almost erased from his memory when Howard recalled it sharply. "We may need another posse of regulators, Sam," Bill Howard told him gravely. "The police are worthless; those who aren't afraid of the foreign criminals are in cahoots with them and get a share of their stealings. And the courts are no better. . . . We need a man like you to lead a citizens' committee."

"What about yourself, sir?" asked Brannan modestly.

Howard shook his head. "I'm not well enough," he said regretfully. Sam noticed that his cheeks were hollow. "I'll help—but I can't lead the fighting. A few years ago I'd have liked nothing better."

"Well, let's hope there'll be no fight," said Brannan. "It's bad for business"—he smiled—"and I must get rich. . . . I've an ambitious wife, Mr. Howard."

Howard nodded. He thought that Sam's wife must have her

hands full looking after that human volcano. His inner fires were so active, his eruptions so inevitable. He hoped Lisa would stay with Sam. There were rumors that she wished to give the children a European education.

Sam wasn't the sort of fellow to be left alone. Women weren't very scarce now in California. There were plenty, Howard thought, who'd give their eyes for a man like Sam Brannan— and most of them weren't the right sort.

Sam walked back to his store. He talked with Osbourne about this and that. Rents were steadying, though they were still exorbitant. There was competition in the China trade. San Francisco had four daily papers now. New stores were opening everywhere. And almost every night there was a robbery. Somebody would have to wipe out the rat's nest of crime they called Sydney Town. The police couldn't, or wouldn't. Everytime an officer went there with a warrant he was bribed or manhandled or shot.

Sam listened absently to his partner's talk, his mind still on personal affairs. He must build on his lots. A business block at Sacramento and Montgomery would bring a fortune in rentals. . . . He could borrow the money in New York. Here one had to pay crazy rates of interest. . . . He could take Lisa and the children for a trip. Perhaps that would bring her content. . . . And he must go to Honolulu. One could buy land cheap in the Sandwich Islands. . . . And, if anything happened—if the United States, for instance, should take them over—— His old dream of conquest flamed again. A few men had taken California from Mexico. . . .

"Yes, yes," he said belatedly to Osbourne. "But the time's not ripe for a citizens' committee. There are so many other things."

"I hear you've pledged yourself to Sutter for quarter of a million."

"You've heard double, then," Sam laughed. "But I've bought a quarter of the town—for a song."

Osbourne laughed. "You must have learned to sing better than you used to, Sam."

The fire of September 17 seemed to justify Shillaber's suspicions. Definite evidence of arson was found, and some of the loot was traced direct to Sydney Town. Newspapers printed fiery editorials denouncing the police. Citizens gathered in groups here and there, angrily discussing the situation. An informal patrol was organized to assist the city authorities. Sam, trudging through the mud on a night patrol, spied a dark figure igniting a pile of shavings. He pounced on the fellow and dragged him under the light of a streetlamp. "Haven't I seen you before?" he asked.

"Leave me alone. I'm a Mormon like yourself. I was only lighting my pipe."

"You're no Mormon," Sam told him. "And you lie. Where's your pipe?"

The man felt in his pockets. "I—I must have lost it," he stammered.

"You're one of Roberts' thievin' friends," Sam accused. "I remember you now."

In an agony of fear, the man squirmed his captor's grasp and ran off into the darkness. Sam pursued him, firing a shot, but the fellow escaped.

Others reported attempts at arson. A number of blazes were extinguished before they could do much harm. Winter came; a noisy, roistering winter with a population almost doubled by miners, come to town to spend their clean-ups, or to wait for steamers to take them home.

Sam opened a real-estate office. He sold many of his water lots, still submerged except at low tide, though sand hills were being leveled and dumped into the bay. They had cost him well under a hundred each, and some of them brought thousands. One lot, clear of the tide and in a strategic location, brought $40,000; another $16,000. All of his buildings were rented.

For the block on Montgomery, which ran from California to Sacramento streets, Sam turned down an offer which, even in those days of inflated values, seemed generous to most of his friends. Sam wanted to keep that property. He planned to erect a stone building there, *four stories high.*

Concurrently with Sam's commercial dreams ran the consciousness of political crisis. Editors fumed about Sydney Town daily. Pastors denounced it from their pulpits. Clubs made resolutions condemning the inactivity of the police. One or two public meetings were held at which speakers expressed indignation and urged drastic measures. But nothing was done.

Sam knew the time was ripe. Ever since the American occupation, San Francisco had been an emotional tinderbox. It brooked wrongs and abuses patiently until some spark of circumstance struck home; then it flared into sudden flame—like its rickety, combustible houses. Sam felt that another outburst—more violent perhaps than any preceding one—was due. He was ready to lead it as he had led others. He went on, attending to business, biding his time, but watchful.

February 19, shortly after eight in the evening, a man ran out of Charles J. Janson & Company's store on Montgomery Street. "Get a doctor," he shouted. A crowd gathered round him. He had found old Charlie Janson lying prone across his counter, his white hair red with blood. A doctor was found. He revived the old merchant.

Two men had come in at dusk, Janson told inquirers. He was closing his store, but they begged him to wait. They needed blankets for a journey, an immediate journey. Janson thought that was queer, but he turned to get some from an inner shelf. He had an instinctive fear of the men. He looked over his shoulder to observe what they were doing. He saw a bludgeon upraised. He knew nothing more.

One of the men was tall and stooped with piercing eyes—dark, he thought—and a scar on his cheek. What else? Let him think. . . . A hooked nose, long, black hair. That was all he could remember.

"That's enough," cried a voice, a ringing, furious voice. "We'll find him . . . and, by God, we'll hang him!"

An uproar of approval greeted him.

"Who's going with me, boys? I'm off for Sydney Town," said Brannan.

A score of bystanders followed him. Most of them were armed. Others, after swift questioning, joined along the route.

At the foot of Broadway more than fifty were in march. They pushed in the doors of a dozen taverns. Men stopped drinking and fingered their weapons. Women shrank into corners. Sam and his followers stamped their way through the dens of thievery, examining every inmate, but the man they sought was not there. From Sydney Town they swept down the waterfront, seizing men roughly as they encountered them, examining their faces in the light of lanterns.

Not until they reached Long Wharf did success attend their quest. "Here's a big one," cried Sam grasping the arm of a man about to leap into a boat. "Here, you; turn around. . . . Bring a lantern," he shouted.

"What d'ye want?" the man snarled. He was tall; he had bright eyes—one could see that, even in the lantern light. His dark hair fell close to his shoulders. His nose was a parrot's beak. "Let's see if he has a scar," cried Sam. "Hold the lantern closer. . . . *Yes, By God!*"

They took him as well as a companion seated in the boat back with them. The police identified one of them—the tall fellow—as James Stuart. "He's a bad one," they said, and they placed the ill-favored couple in jail.

Old Janson came from the hospital next morning to look them over. "That's the one," he identified the big fellow. He was not so certain of the other man.

Before noon five thousand people gathered around the city hall. Men came out on the balconies at intervals to report what was happening in court. "He says his name's Burdue—not Stuart," someone shouted to the crowd. "The other fellow's name is Windred. Of course they're innocent." He laughed.

"Let's hang them," a voice cried. "String 'em up, damn their souls!"

"We can't trust the police," yelled another. "Let's be our own judge and jury."

"Sure thing! That's the stuff!" Words came in a roar; the crowd stirred, pressed forward.

Brannan, mounting a rain barrel, shouted at them. "Boys! Boys! Hear me. Wait. I've something to say."

They listened, as they always did to Sam. He gathered about

him respected William Howard, Joe Folsom, Henry Tesche-
macher, Frank Macondray and Theodore Payne. "Look," he
cried, "we'll pledge our word that justice is done. Will you trust
us?"

"Yes! Yes! Yes!" they called back.

"Then disperse . . . Here's Bill Coleman. You can trust him,
if you can't the rest of us. . . ."

"Come on; let's be moving," urged someone in the crowd.
Slowly it disintegrated.

Brannan wiped his face with a bandana. "Whew!" he remarked breathlessly. "That was a close shave."

"The crowd's aroused," said Folsom. "It'll come to hanging
yet I fear."

Sam turned on him. "And maybe that'll be the best way
out of it. Who knows?" he answered. "Now let's meet together
in my office and consider a plan. We made the boys a promise,
and we've got to keep it."

They followed him, joined by several others—steady reli-
able men. They sat around the stove in Sam's office, talking sol-
emnly, strangely agreed, wasting few words. They formed the
Committee of Vigilance. Howard suggested the name. Sam was
chosen the chief.

News of the committee spread. There were many volunteers.
Men trooped into Sam's office. "We've come to join," they said.
"We want law and order."

"You'll get it," said Sam. "Put your name on that list." He
pointed to some sheets of foolscap almost covered with sig-
natures.

"What else'll we do?"

"Go on about your business. But when you hear the Monumental Engine bell ring 'one, two, three' over and over, grab a
rifle and come to the square—*day or night.*"

A hundred and fifty citizens enrolled during the first few
days. No effort was made to organize. Word spread from mouth
to mouth. The volunteers continued to come. "All the decent men
in town are back of us," said Sam proudly—and that was almost
true. But rascals and crooked officials had not been idle. They

formed an actively opposing faction, a curious hodgepodge of good and bad. Leading it were politicians who feared exposure and a clan called the Chivalry Party or "Chivs." They were Southerners, proud of their lineage, arrogant and often unscrupulous. Supporting these two elements were numerous well-meaning persons who feared what they termed "mob rule" even more than the prevailing lawlessness.

Sam called their bluff. He held a trial of the prisoners before his committee in the Monumental Engine House. It was a model of decorum and justice—much more so than the city courts. Stuart, alias Burdue, and Windred were well defended—so well indeed that, to Sam's disgust, the jury disagreed. Having no jail of its own, the committee was forced to return both suspects to the police. The little prisoner sawed his way out of prison. The other, owing to a lingering doubt of his identity, was at last released.

Sydney Town resumed its interrupted activities.

But Sam did not disband his committee; nor was he discouraged by the turn of events. "We've proved we're no mob," he contended. And in this he was right. Wavering elements that had supported the opposition or remained quiescent swung to the committee's support. It had the confidence of all honest men now. Some hesitated to join it for business reasons. The "Chiv's" included some powerful figures in San Francisco's commercial world. Their wives were arbiters of society. After Lisa had received a few snubs, she demanded that Sam withdraw from his "rabble." But he only laughed indulgently. "Wait awhile, darlin'," he told her. "They'll be takin' off their hats to us and curryin' favor before we get through."

"Through with what?" asked Lisa sarcastically.

"Hangin' some of 'em, perhaps," her husband answered.

The days grew busier for Sam. Bruce was laying out the Sacramento land into town lots; he wanted money for surveying and improvements. And young Sutter was threatening to sue if payments were not made more promptly. Sam thought harassedly that they would both have to wait till he had a chance to

go to New York and borrow on his securities. He must make the
eastern journey before winter. . . . And there was the Honolulu
trip to consider. Well, it would all work out, somehow, if he
kept his head. He was drinking more than usual. It worried him
now and then. His father had gone that way—and an elder
brother.

"Oh, well! Set 'em up for the crowd, bartender. . . . What'll
you have, fellows?"

The committee held regular meetings. It was recognized
now as a formidable body not to be trifled with. Crime had de-
creased somewhat. But on June 10 John Jenkins was bold enough
to steal a safe from Virgin & Company's shipping office on Long
Wharf. He was caught with the loot and identified as an English
ex-convict. Within half an hour after his capture the Monumental Fire bell tolled its assembly signal. Within an hour Jenkins
was on trial before the Committee of Vigilance. Before midnight
he was convicted and sentenced to be hanged.

Outside the Monumental Engine House thousands of citizens gathered. Finally Sam emerged. He climbed upon a sand-
bank where all could see him, shouting, "Listen, boys: We've
tried John Jenkins fairly accordin' to law. We found him guilty
and we're goin' to hang him. What d'ye say, boys? Are we right?"

A thunder of approval rose from the gathering. Mayor Brenham tried to make himself heard in protest, but he was shouted
down. The crowd formed an escort of armed men surrounding
the prisoner on his way to the improvised gallows. A rope had
been thrown over a protruding rafter of the old adobe building
on the square. The looped end was placed around Jenkins' neck
and tightened. The crowd fought for a chance to pull. At the first
tug of the rope, the prisoner was jerked high into the air. He
made a grotesque jumping-jack figure in the light of a hundred
torches as he dangled squirming above the heads of the crowd.
Sheriff Hayes rode into the square on his famous black horse.
He was a fearless and honest official whom San Franciscans
respected. But they paid him no heed that night. He could not
penetrate the tightly packed throng. It was daylight before the
square was cleared. John Jenkins body was freed of the rope

and taken to the morgue. The Committee of Vigilance had showed its teeth and Sydney Town shivered.

Edgar Wakeman told Sam about the coroner's jury. "They've brought in a verdict accusing nine of us of murder. You and I are included, Sam." He looked worried.

"Only nine of us!" cried Sam and laughed. He set down his drink. "Come along, Ed. Let's talk with Coleman and Bluxome. I've got an idea. If it works, it'll spike their guns."

That evening Mayor Brenham, complacent over the jury verdict, picked up his copy of the *Journal of Commerce*. A "scarehead" on the front page attracted his attention. He read it and sprang up with an exclamation. "Get the city attorney," he called to a servant. "Bring him here."

The city attorney was a young man, but he was, for all that, a clever lawyer and an able one. "What's the matter now?" he asked of the evidently disturbed mayor.

Brenham laughed harshly. "You thought you *had* them, didn't you?" he cried. "You persuaded the coroner's jury to name nine of the ringleaders. You thought you could cut off the committee's head. . . . Well, you're checkmated. Look here!"

He tossed the paper. It contained a statement signed by every member of the Committee of Vigilance, admitting equal responsibility with the nine men charged at the inquest. It included most of the prominent merchants and professional men in San Francisco.

"What are we going to do now?" asked the mayor.

"Nothing," the city attorney answered. "I'll warrant this is some of Sam Brannan's work, confound him."

The committee went on. Its work broadened. Sydney Town was patrolled and most of its evil spirits persuaded to seek other fields. Incoming ships were inspected with care. Passengers who could not show a clean bill of moral health were refused a landing. Captains fumed but accepted return passage money and placed unwelcome passengers in the brig until they left port. Local officials talked of "piracy" but were helpless. Sam's vigilantes, several hundred strong, ruled the town.

A month after Jenkins' execution, a strange event occurred.

The real James Stuart was found, exonerating the man previously arrested. They were almost identical in appearance. No wonder old Janson, fuddled by the blow on his head and nearsighted as an owl, had identified Burdue as his assailant.

Stuart had long been sought by the police of various towns for an assortment of felonies, including murder. He saved the committee the trouble of trying him. He not only confessed but boasted of his crimes. He was sentenced to death, and the verdict was once more submitted to public approval. It was endorsed even more ardently and noisily than the previous one. A second committee hanging took place, this time on Long Wharf.

The committee had not finished its work. It had promised to clean up Sydney Town, and did so. Many known criminals had gone into hiding with the Stuart hanging, but Sam and his vigilantes pursued them and either drove them away or imprisoned them. They established and maintained their right of search, ignoring court injunctions.

Clashes occurred with state authorities. A habeas corpus writ signed by the governor and served by Sheriff Hayes in a surprise attack despoiled the committee of two prisoners condemned to death. But Sam was not to be outdone. He organized a counter-surprise and recaptured the men. They were hanged within an hour.

At last Brannan turned over his leadership to Bill Coleman. Demands for payment from Sutter and other creditors had become so insistent that Sam had to hasten his New York journey. To borrow at local interest rates would have ruined him.

In his New York hotel Sam read of the committee's disbanding. Well, it had done its work, he thought. San Francisco would be a law-abiding city for a while at least. And he had helped to make it so, Sam reflected with pride.

He had been somewhat disappointed in his quest for borrowed funds. Money was tight and financiers cautious. To them his great schemes, whose outcome he saw so clearly, were visionary, unsecured dreams. Dismayed, Sam Brannan shifted his attack. He would go to Washington, where Senator Gwin needed help to promote his land bill. If Congress could be induced to pass it, Sam's securities and his prestige with New York bankers would be greatly enhanced.

He ought to be back in San Francisco. A recent scandal in which he was involved might provide his enemies with weapons —unless he was there to spike them. He had made an ill-considered, hasty journey to Hawaii with notions of a possible filibuster, and it had backfired. His own fault, he thought, morosely. Too much liquor in his stateroom. Quarrels and loose talk aboard the steamer *Gamecock* had resulted in the accusation by a fellow passenger that Sam and his cronies had "borrowed" the steward's mail sack and removed letters informing the authorities of Sam's predatory plans. Nothing came of the charge, fortunately. But it had cost Sam high to hush it up—and he had not entirely succeeded. News of it had reached the mainland.

Captain John Brannan, an elder brother, was looking after Sam's business at home, but he was no politician; much too honest to be tactful, forever shaking his gray head over Sam's fantastic bookkeeping. Not long ago he had pulled out an old ledger lettered "Tithes from Mormon Brethren." Covered with dust, from the back of the safe it had come like a ghost. "What about this, Sam?" he had asked, and Brannan had answered hastily, "Burn it." Captain John's family would have joined him by now, Sam decided. His niece and nephew would be growing up; they were older than his own children.

John Brannan has been more like a father than a brother to the unruly Sam in earlier years: the only one in all his family who could discipline him. Sam recalled, with a grim smile, that sometimes it had required a cane.

"God bless the old boy!" he mused as he packed for the Washington journey. "I'm lucky to have a brother like that to shape up my tangled affairs."

. *10* .

Politics and Enchantment

San Francisco was the lodestone of Sam Brannan's purpose. He
seldom returned to it from any journey, long or short, but a sen-
sation, namelessly elating, rose in him, a magically deep sense
of satisfaction. He had known it when the *Brooklyn* had poked
her nose through the gray mists of the Golden Gate seven years
before. Even when he came back from a trip to Sacramento or
his farm on the San Joaquin River delta, he experienced that
lifting of his thoughts.

Today as the steamer *Northerner* slid into the Long Wharf
landing Sam felt it more keenly than ever before, because his
visions were so close to fulfillment. He was a personage now.
He had always believed that one day he should be. And the
thing, almost imperceptibly, had taken place. The day was come.
It was May 21, 1853.

Sam had lobbied an act through Congress. It was William
Gwin's bill, but Sam's brains were behind it; his money and
indefatigable efforts had found votes for it—enough to pass it
over the opposition of Senator Benton and his powerful clique.
Senator Benton was the President's confidential adviser. His
daughter had married Fremont the Pathfinder. Benton had

snubbed Sam in the Senate's antechamber and orated against Gwin's measure to appoint a land commission—so that California's tangled land titles might be cleared. Benton had argued in favor of a substitute more favorable to his son-in-law's vast Mariposa claim.

But Sam Brannan, the ex-Mormon-elder, the western clodhopper with a red bandana in his pocket, had outgeneraled the President's friend.

Gwin took the credit, of course. But what did that matter? Sam would get the cash. He had at first found New York bankers anything but cordial. Even when confronted with deeds to a hundred or more of San Francisco's best business and residence lots, a quarter interest in the town of Sacramento, they had remained coldly suspicious. They feared the squatter element and clouded titles. But with Gwin's influence backing Sam's judgment in the selection of federal land commissioners everything was changed. Sam went back to New York to be courted and dined. He left it with half a million dollars, borrowed at one fourth the current San Francisco interest rate.

He would build his business block as soon as plans were drawn, four stories of fireproof construction. Sam closed his eyes and visualised it—iron-balconied, many-windowed, massive. He would make his own bricks, establishing kilns on the peninsula to bake native clay.

He noted with satisfaction that more of his water lots had been reclaimed from the bay. Before the year was out he would be a millionaire.

The *Northerner* carried distinguished passengers. Senator Gwin and Congressman Weller had crowded their full-bodied shapes to the rail and were raising their hats in response to cheering. Sam was about to take a strategic position between them when he felt a small detaining hand on his arm and turned to meet the gay, impudent eyes of Lola Montez to whom everyone of consequence aboard had made love since the voyage began. She had been a king's favorite, report said, and had cost him his throne. Liszt, the German composer, and Dumas, the French novelist, had been her lovers, according to ship gossip.

Sam liked her. Lola had been cordial, understanding. He considered for a moment the gesture of appearing with her at the rail—diverting popular attention from the two pompous politicians. But he decided, reluctantly, against it. Lisa and her mother would be there to observe . . . and his brother, Captain John. He thought he could make out the latter's tall, rather solemn figure among the waiting crowd.

"The voyage is over," sighed Lola, her eyes holding his, "and this is your San Francisco!" Her right arm made a graceful gesture.

He caught her hand and kissed it gallantly. "Yes, Lola, my San Francisco . . . the city I love." He stared at her for an instant. "Yet a poor place for the woman I—admire."

"Perhaps I, too, shall learn to love it," she said softly.

Sam hoped so. . . . Life, he thought, was going to be gay.

Lisa and her mother greeted Sam at the gangplank. A lace-capped, uniformed nursemaid with the four children lingered behind. They waved at him, all but little Don Francisco, less than a year old, asleep in the perambulator Sam had sent on from New York. Sam kissed his family boisterously and affectionately. He was glad to be home again—glad to feel the young ones tugging at him, asking questions. The baby didn't look well, he thought. But Sammy was eight now and tall for his age.

His brother, Captain John, came up and shook hands with Sam gravely. The loose gait of the quarter-deck was still in his walk, but his eyes had lost the steady, peering look of his long years at sea. Captain John wore spectacles now, and his once-straight figure was a trifle bent from setting down in ledgers the figures and minutiae of Sam's multifarious investments.

Townsmen and business associates shouted welcomes, pumping Sam's arm up and down with vociferous handclasps. Most of the crowd was around Gwin and Weller, asking about the new land act or cadging introductions to Lola Montez, who had joined them after Sam's defection. She was rather aloof, nodding only brief acknowledgments and making no effort in most cases to pursue the acquaintance. She gave little screams of dismay at the roughness with which her baggage was handled and held her skirts up from the dust. Finally she was ushered into a carriage by the gallant but ponderous Gwin and drove off between him and her dapper, moustachioed business manager. She waved a farewell to the crowd from the receding vehicle. The crowd cheered.

Lisa eyed her suspiciously. "Who's that woman?" she asked.

"The Countess of Lansfeld," Sam answered impressively. Such was her Bavarian, if somewhat-clouded, title. He turned to his brother, discussing business affairs. Everything was going well, Captain John assured him. And the affair of Tanner's Honolulu broadside had almost blown over. The *Alta* had mentioned it briefly without comment. The other papers had ignored it. Most people considered it the attack of an irresponsible person, since no investigation of the fellow's charges had been made by Polynesian authorities.

"What'll they be accusin' me of next?" asked Sam with a rueful smile. "Robbin' Uncle Sam's mail—to find out if someone wrote ill of me! A fine lot of nonsense indeed!"

"It was all because of boasting in your cups," his brother answered.

"My—what?"

"You told it round that the Sandwich Islands could be captured by a hundred men," said Captain John accusingly. "And Tanner claims he saw your stateroom full of opened letters. . . . Your cabinmates told him they had the steward's mail bag and were going through it."

"Yes, yes; I know. They were drunk," returned Sam impatiently. "Forget it—as everyone else has."

"It won't be forgot if you run for office—mark my words," retorted Captain John. "And, as you grow richer, Sam, there'll be more said against you. There's trouble ahead, if you don't——"

"Go easy on the liquor? Right you are," Sam interrupted heartily.

"The carriage is waiting to take us home, Sam," said Lisa.

He turned to her smiling, a hand on Captain John's shoulder. "Get on with you all," he urged. "I'll be followin' later. I see the boys from the engine company, and I must talk with 'em."

"Drink with them, you mean," returned his wife with irritation. But she knew there was no use waiting. She bundled her family into the equipage and told the driver to go on. Sam owned a fine home now, with stables and grounds, on Mission Street. He watched Lisa and the young ones drive away, his hat in his hand. A fine family! One to be proud of, he thought. He must send them abroad. Lisa had wept and stormed when he had refused to let her accompany him on the hasty and altogether unfortunate voyage to Honolulu, the emergency trip to New York, the Washington visit, at Gwin's urgent request. Thank God the latter two had been successful! He had enough money to send her in style now. She could go to Paris and buy clothes. That was what women wanted.

He turned to a welcoming delegation from Howard Engine Company, known as Social No. 3. "I've bought you a brand-new engine, boys," he shouted.

They crowded around him, asking questions. "It's a Hunneman from Boston. . . . They're the best that's made—and this'll be the finest in the land. . . . Ten thousand dollars it's costing me, and a year it'll take to build."

They pounded his back and shook his hand enthusiastically.

"We'll call Social Number Three the Brannan Engine," one of them said, but Sam shook his head. "You'll be offending the old man—and a grand fella he is—Bill Howard."

Someone suggested a drink. Sam caught his brother by the arm. "Come along to the Rassette House, John; I want to see the new bar."

But Captain John declined almost roughly. "It's not good for me, boy, and it's not good for you—but that's your own business—if you won't take a brother's advice." He trudged off shaking his head. He was a tall, spare bearded man with high color in his cheeks, a stern, uncompromising man, as unlike Sam as possible. But Sam loved him and feared him a little—a thing no other man could say of him.

Rather thoughtfully in the midst of his garrulous friends Sam walked to the Rassette House. Its new barroom glittered with mirrors and prism-studded chandeliers which a man was lighting by means of a polelike contrivance equipped to raise lamp chimneys and to light wicks from a slender burning taper. A new burning fluid called "naphthene," much brighter than whale oil, was employed for lighting the big room with its long mahogany bar and resplendent brass fittings. Behind it worked half a dozen white-coated bartenders. A group of young bloods from the Monumental Engine Company were discussing Lola Montez.

"The king set her up in a chateau and gave her a title," one of them was saying, "but he neglected to pay for the furniture. When the head of the Upholsterers' Guild insisted on getting his money, Lola broke a vase over his head." A laugh followed.

"She struck one of the hotel porters with her parasol for dropping a trunk," said another. He spied Sam and shouted, "Hi, Brannan; you came on the boat with Lola. What's she like?"

"She's a good enough sort—if you don't cross her," he said and added thoughtfully, "—like any other woman." He turned to the grinning, expectant bartender.

"Champagne for the house," he ordered.

Lola Montez was San Francisco's latest excitement. Its people must always focus their tense, unrestrainable emotions on something or someone, Sam reflected, as he met her driving around town flanked by outriders of the town's dandies, like a queen with her guard of honor. She ordered the driver to halt and gave Sam her really exquisite hand to kiss. He did it with aplomb, though he looked a bit sheepish when a bystander laughed. He declined an invitation to ride with her because he was on the way to an important business meeting, and he feared his brother's disapproval even more than he valued this woman's favors. He asked, "Where did you get this rig—this equipage?"

"From the livery stable," Lola answered, following his disdainful glance at the ungroomed hacks and their tarnished harness.

"Not fit for you, my dear," Sam deplored, shaking his head. "I'll send my own pair of bays and my carriage to you tomorrow

. . . the best to be had in the country. Use them whenever you like." He lifted his hat and went on. He must stop at the theatre and buy tickets for her *Lady Teazle*. And a bouquet—as big as any usher could carry down the aisle.

To his consternation Sam learned that the house was sold out. The box-office man was one of his former parishioners, a passenger on the *Brooklyn*. He said, "I can get you a box from a friend—but it'll cost high, I'm afraid. Even the gallery gods are paying a dollar a seat tonight."

Sam took out his wallet. "There's five hundred: a hundred for each of my crowd. Will that be enough?"

"Oh, yes, Mr. Brannan——"

"If there's anything left, keep the change." He went on. At the florist's shop he threw five "double eagles" on the counter. "For Lola Montez . . . the best in the house—tonight."

"Yes, indeed, Mr. Brannan."

Sam felt big, spacious. Eight years ago he had arrived in San Francisco with a few silver dollars and his printing press. Now he could throw money around. People honored him, bowed to him, followed his lead. A gracious lady, the toast of the town, had invited him to ride with her. Life was expanding. He lighted a Cuban cigar. . . . A dollar apiece, he thought complacently.

At his office a number of men were assembled. One of them glanced at his watch. "You're late, Sam," reproved Captain John. "You've kept us waiting."

Sam felt suddenly small, like a schoolboy scolded by his teacher. "I'm sorry," he returned meekly.

No bandana kerchief for Samuel Brannan as he sat in a proscenium box the opening night of *Lady Teazle*. Lisa had seen to that. Only a moderate-sized square of pure linen reposed in the almost inaccessible pocket of his swallow-tail coat. Lisa herself was resplendent in dove-colored silk with a string of pearls around her neck. They had cost Sam as much as the Hunneman fire engine.

Erect and unbending, with a touch of benignance in her manner, Lisa sat between her husband and Captain John. She was pleasantly conscious of envious glances at her jewels, her new clothes; her smile as she greeted acquaintances was gracious—worthy of the wife of San Francisco's foremost citizen. There was a great chatter in the pit, shouts of "Hello, Sam!" which annoyed her as much as his boisterously cordial responses. She tugged at Sam's coattails. "*Bow* to them," she admonished, but Sam only smiled tolerantly at her. He thought she was lovely in her new dress. If she'd only loosen up like other women. . . . And yet, in a sense, he was proud of her prim aloofness.

He liked Mary, his brother's wife, a big fine woman with few conscious artifices—the right one for John, who was a trifle too set in his ways.

Finally, after hand-clapping and stamping, the curtain rose, half an hour late. Lola Montez took the stage amid frantic applause.

A gorgeous woman, Sam thought as he applauded again and again for curtain calls at the close of the first act. She appealed to the crowd by her femininity, her abandon. She wasn't so much an actress, he thought, but no matter. She gave you something . . . something—he thought with whimsical regret and a disturbing consciousness of disloyalty—which women like Lisa could never give men.

Half a dozen ushers staggered down the aisles burdened with flowers. One bouquet was larger than all the others. Sam hoped it was his. Lola exclaimed over it. She blew a kiss in his direction.

Later she tossed a rose into the Brannan box. Sam was slightly embarrassed. Lisa gave him a sharp look, his brother a quizzical one. But it was a pleasant evening.

Lola's vogue increased. She played Charlotte Corday in a drama of the French revolution. Sam liked her better in that than in *Lady Teazle*. She put fire into Charlotte's role and Marat died magnificently by her hand. Even Lisa admitted she had talent "of a kind."

But San Francisco wanted something livelier from its idol. She was restrained by her roles, the critics objected. "Give us the real Lola," one of them demanded. She consulted Sam about the matter. They managed to see each other often. Here and there about the countryside and through the town she rode behind Sam's prancing bays. Whenever she spied him she stopped the equipage and called him to her side.

"What shall I do, Sam?" she pleaded. "They want something *daring*, my manager says."

Sam patted her hand. "Always humor the crowd . . . that's what I do. They love you for it."

"The crowd!" She raised her eyes. "They adore you, Sam. . . . Everywhere I see signs: 'Buy this or that. *Sam Brannan uses it*.' You are a great man—too great for poor Lola."

"Never!" He laughed deploringly. "But I daren't be too ardent. Pat Hull would shoot me. I'm afraid of my life."

"You are afraid of your wife, my dear Samuel," she pouted. "Perhaps you are wise. . . . But what must I do for a play—a daring one?"

"Why not have one written about yourself: *The Fair Revolutionist; or, Lola Montez in Bavaria?*"

She clapped her hands. "Will you help me, Sam?"

"I can't write plays, Lola," he said rather bruskly.

She laid a hand on his arm. "Will you come tomorrow afternoon and talk it over with me? Just the two of us. I shall order champagne—and we'll not be disturbed."

"Tomorrow?" he considered. "Yes, I'll come," he said at length.

"Good!" She smiled ravishingly and blew him a kiss as her carriage drove on. Sam stood a moment gazing after her holding his hat. Then he restored it to his head rather grimly and set out for the office of the *Whig*.

Pat Hull was not there. Sam sat down to wait, smoking one of his dollar Havanas and scowling a little as if in troubled calculation. When Hull at last returned, Sam had solved his problem.

"Can you write a play, Pat?"

The other laughed constrainedly. "I don't know, Sam. I've never tried. What sort of play?"

"*Lola Montez in Bavaria; or, the Fair Revolutionist.*"

"Oh!" exclaimed Pat Hull.

"'Oh,' nothing! You're the man to do it, Pat. See here: I want you to go to the Rassette House tomorrow afternoon and talk with her about it. Say I sent you; that I couldn't come. D'ye understand?"

"No," said Hull, "but I'll do it. . . . I'll do anything for Lola —confound her!"

"Pat," asked Sam suddenly, "why don't you marry the gal?"

Hull flushed. "Maybe I'll do that, too," he said stiffly.

"Well, good-by to you, then—and good luck. I'm off for Sacramento . . . won't be back for a week."

Lola was furious with Sam when he returned. She sent back his horses and carriage. She ignored him on the street. But Pat Hull wrote her a play with a dance number in it: the spider dance. That was her own idea. She portrayed a young peasant girl who discovers a spider under her skirts. Lola made much of the part, the situation, leaping in horror, raising and shaking her skirts in a frenzy of revealing gestures, stamping on the supposedly dislodged insect with convulsive malevolence. It stunned, amazed or delighted her audience according to type.

There were loud bravos, a few subdued hisses. "A spirited performance," wrote one of the critics in his notebook as the first curtain fell. "A disgusting exhibition," said Lisa loud enough for others to hear her. She sat once more in a box with Sam and her mother. Captain John and his wife had declined an invitation to join them.

Lola tossed no rose into the Brannan box, nor did she kiss her hand to Sam. But the new play was a great success and the spider dance aroused a furore of comment.

Howard Engine Company was given a benefit performance by the theatre management. Its members attended en masse in full regimentals. They tossed their fire helmets filled with flowers on the stage. They stood up and cheered, electing Lola to honorary membership by a viva voce vote. It was in many ways a grand occasion. But Sam's box was unoccupied.

Not long afterward a rumor reached him that Lola was engaged to Pat Hull. Pat had been in Washington, a member of the San Francisco delegation and representative of the *Whig* when Gwin's land bill was passed. And he had been on the boat which brought Lola to California. Hull made no effort to conceal his love for the actress, but she had given small response until recently. Sam wished him luck. Lola was a fine woman, but a handful. There was talk of nominating Sam for the state legislature. Senator Brannan! That would have a good sound. It would please Lisa. She was getting a bit out of hand with her plans for the young ones. He would have to send her East next spring; to Europe, possibly. Oh, well, he could afford it now. He would board with Mary, his sister-in-law, who was a fine cook. Sam liked her children. They were better behaved than his own, he concluded regretfully.

In September Sam laid the cornerstone for his new Express Building on the northeast corner of California and Montgomery streets. This was a site he had purchased in 1849 among half a hundred other lots when a member of the city council. It was one of the lots over which Horace Hawes and the council had their acrimonious controversy. It had cost Sam less than one hundred dollars and was valued at a thousand times that sum today. The contractor's estimate on the building was $180,000. Wells Fargo & Company, bankers and express agents, and Pollard & Company, real-estate and money brokers, had leased the entire ground floor before the foundation was laid. It would be four stories high, of brick faced with plaster, and the uppermost story was promised to the Society of California Pioneers, of which Sam was the president.

"The tallest building in town," he said to himself proudly as he wiped a dab of mortar from his trousers. "And one of the finest!"

"We'll soon be millionaires," he told his brother after the cornerstone-laying.

Captain John eyed him disturbedly. "You've too many irons in the fire, Sammy, boy," he returned. "Do you never stop to count 'em? Among other things, you've a lumber mill on Yerba

Buena Island, a biscuit factory near the mission, and a bookstore on Clay Street. Here's the advertisement. Have you read it yourself, I wonder? 'Bibles cheap for cash. Primers for children; 168 volumes Harpers' Family Library. Dr. Johnston, Washington Irving, Francis Bacon, Oliver Goldsmith, Benjamin Franklin. *Letters on Demonology and Witchcraft.*' "

Sam laughed. "I've always wanted to read those last, but I haven't had time. Sell them at auction, John. They're small potatoes. We're dealing with big things now."

He strode off puffing his big cigar. Captain John shook his head. The boy was a case, he said to himself. Smart as a steel trap, young Sammy was, but he needed watching. . . . The Montez woman was out of the running, thank Heaven! She'd married Pat Hull and gone on a tour. But this political game was the devil. Sam knew only one way to electioneer. Wherever he went he bought champagne for the crowd. He told bartenders to put the corks of empty bottles in his pocket and Captain John would pay for them. Or else he signed tags and the liquor men came collecting next day. It was a fantastic system—but better than letting Sam run loose with his pockets full of gold. Captain John had changed that. He took charge of the revenues and made Sam an allowance of cash. Sometimes a day's bar bill came close to a thousand dollars.

Pray God there'd always be someone like himself to look after Sam! He was good as gold, but improvident as the wind— a bad combination, thought Captain John worriedly.

. 11 .

High Finance

In 1856 Samuel Brannan was called the richest and best known citizen of California. His income was estimated at between $250,000 and $500,000 a year. No more "small potatoes" for Sam; gone from his horizon were lumber mills, biscuit factories, and bookstores. He owned a dozen business blocks in San Francisco and Sacramento, houses and lots in Honolulu. His two-hundred-acre tract in the western addition was being allotted and placed on the market. On his eighteen-hundred-acre ranch on the Feather River roamed hundreds of choice horses and cattle.

Sam was traveling in Europe. Wherever he roved he sent products for transplantation to his beloved California: grape stocks from Italy, France, Spain and the Rhineland, often accompanied by colonist peasants who understood the secrets of their growth; prize cattle from the British Isles; Scottish sheep from the Grampian hills; curly-horned rams and ewes, historic merinos of southern Europe. They arrived on almost every boat and kept Captain John on tenterhooks following instructions for their disposition.

Lisa Brannan, Mother Corwin and the children had shaken the dust of California joyously and disdainfully from their feet two years before. They had a chateau in Geneva. Sam's children were attending the best schools, and Professor Kuhne was perfecting the girls in music. Little Don Francisco Brannan had not lived to see this glory. His frail infant body lay beneath a handsome headstone in Laurel Hill Cemetery.

The big house on Mission Street was shuttered and closed. Captain John had an offer to sell it for a theatre site. Commerce had swarmed into the old residence sections. San Francisco was no longer the raw, scrambled town of a few years ago. It was becoming one of the urban centers of America and one of the world's noted ports. Overland stages made the journey to St. Louis in less than twenty-four days.

The principal downtown streets were lighted by naphthene and paved. There were a dozen first-class hotels, and certain restaurants had achieved international fame among gourmands. Jewelry stores presented display windows excelling those of New York. They contained $4,000 snuffboxes and watches worth $1,000.

Captain John sighed as he read Sam's brief scrawled letter from Paris:

> I have just returned from Geneva. I leave Liverpool on the 12th of July and shall be home as fast as possible. Lisa and the family are beautifully located and Sammy is perfectly delighted with his school and so are we all. I bless the day I took this journey for my children's sake if nothing more. They gave me a handsome reception in the Lodge at Geneva although I could not speak a word of French or German which I would say nothing about.
>
> Give my respects to Mary and all my old friends. The day after tomorrow I go to Hamburg. All well.
>
> Yours in haste after a hard day's work,
>
> SAM BRANNAN

He would be home very soon, reflected Captain John; and he would be footloose and lonely without domestic restraints or anchorage. Mary and he would take him in, do all they could to make him feel at home. But Sam would be restless. He would drink too much and gamble in everything that intrigued him. As long as his health and luck lasted there was little to be feared. But the turn was bound to come. And then, Lord help ·the boy! Lisa was a fool to let him go unchecked, to take away his home and children. If ever a man needed them, it was Sam, thought Captain John.

There had been a property settlement before Lisa left. Sam had made over to her a good deal of property so that, in the matter of income, she was more or less independent. Captain John had advised against this. But she could do anything she chose with her husband, this prim, pretty woman. Some day she would break him—strip him bare and go on her way, smugly and heartlessly self-justified—some day after he, Captain John, was dead. And he hated her with a sudden, baffled fury, while he loved with a brooding tenderness his wayward, dynamic younger brother.

When Sam returned Captain John was going to talk with him more seriously than he had ever done before. Perhaps he could beat some discipline into the boy's head and teach him to take care of himself. There wasn't much time, because in ten years Captain John would be dead. The doctors had told him so quite definitely. Even now he coughed more than he should.

About two weeks after his letter, Sam Brannan arrived. Captain John observed, approvingly, an almost indefinable change. Sam had a certain poise supplanting the crude aplomb of earlier days. Travel had given him that—and meeting the right people. Lisa would see that he met the right people, with axes to grind and culture to sell a western millionaire. Lisa had had an autograph album even before she left San Francisco. There would be famous names in it by now, Captain John reflected with a wry smile.

But, besides Sam's smack of larger sophistication, there was another new quality in him: restraint. He had never bothered with restraint before. But now he did. If you asked about the family he smiled a bit grimly and said they were very well, thank you. The children attended the best schools. Mrs. Brannan (not ·Lisa, as previously) loved Switzerland. And Lake Geneva was a fine body of water, with the majestic mountains as background. All of which concealed unspoken thoughts and feelings. He bought "drinks for the house" as lavishly as ever, but a little of the old gay spontaneity was missing. He seldom, any longer, clapped you on the back, unless he was far gone in liquor. And he was truculent sometimes, never far from an edge of emotional uncontrol, which now and then exploded in reasonless angers.

He had a fight with Jim Garvitt about nothing at all. It was really a dispute between Garvitt and the elder Brannan regarding a business transaction. Captain John had said yes and Garvitt said no. It did not concern Sam directly, but he elbowed his way into the controversy. "Shut up, Jim," he shouted. "Don't go calling my brother a liar."

"Who's calling him one?" asked Garvitt, puzzled and annoyed.

"*You!*" cried Sam flourishing his fists. "You're a liar yourself, Jim Garvitt."

"And you're a drunken fool. . . . Go away and let us alone."

Sam's clenched fist hit him hard. Sam's raised foot kicked him viciously. Captain John pulled him back. "Behave yourself." he cried. "Behave yourself."

Sam's anger went out like a puff of wind. He looked sorry, ashamed. He walked off muttering what might have been apologies. Captain John looked after him, shaking his gray head. That was Lisa's doing, damn her! he thought miserably.

Sam's mind was more than ever full of plans—bigger and more daring plans. His dealings with bankers in New York had given him ideas. Banking in San Francisco was still rudimentary compared with that of the Atlantic States and Europe. "Why not start a modern banking house and issue our own currency?" he said to Volney Howard. Howard was one of the southern crowd—the "Chivs." He and Sam had been enemies during the vigilante days, but they were friendly enough now. Howard had immense social influence and a little money. He understood banking. He liked the idea.

Sam Hensley and Eli Cook were consulted. They agreed that

Sam's scheme was a good one. But it would take money. It must be done right. There would have to be established securities, close to half a million. The burden would fall on Sam.

Captain John said it couldn't be done; he couldn't detach so large an amount from their tangled resources. "If you hadn't given Lisa the moon—then it might have been different," he reproached.

"By God! Then I'll get her to help me," said Sam. "Yes, I'll write her today."

Captain John smiled at that; but for once he was mistaken. Lisa Brannan fell in with the scheme. Whether it was Sam's persuasion or her good business judgment, nobody knew. But she pledged the property Sam had deeded to her. Between them they made over $450,000 in joint holdings to a trust. Howard, Hensley and Cook were the trustees.

The papers made a great hurrah about Sam's bank—all of them, that is, except the *Bulletin*. Tom King, brother of the martyred James King of William, whose murder the vigilantes had avenged, was no friend of the new financier. Despite Sam's leadership in the vigilante movement and other reforms, King distrusted him. He warned the people against "shin-plasters," as he derisively termed private currency. When the new bank flooded San Francisco and the mining towns with its notes, King denounced the whole scheme:

> When Mr. Brannan attempts to violate the constitution of the state and to fasten upon the community that most pernicious of all evils, a "shin-plaster" currency, he attempts to perpetuate a great public wrong and it becomes our duty as a public journalist to warn the laboring classes and others who are most likely to become his dupes against him and his illegal, wily designs.
>
> It has been the policy of rotten banking institutions who heretofore brought distress and ruin by flooding the land with an inflated paper currency, to either make their small notes payable at some place so distant that they would not be likely to reach their destination or to

send an agent from the place of issue to make purchases or otherwise put them in circulation so that in the usual wear and tear of this flimsy trash a considerable amount would never reach home to be redeemed. On this latter plan we presume Mr. Brannan has acted or intends to act as the public pulse will bear the gross imposition. We have seen a notice in an interior paper some days since of this Brannan currency but until this morning have not been able to get possession of a specimen.

For the benefit of our readers who have not been so fortunate as to get hold of what is intended as an entering wedge to sap the prosperity of our state and drive out of circulation the pure and only currency, specie, we publish what appears on the already tattered and half obliterated face of this paper bantling.

In this strain the editorial continued, more than a column in length. It ended as follows:

Space will not permit us to allude to a tithe of the evils which will follow if Mr. Brannan's scheme is tolerated. Let the danger then be nipped in the bud. Let the people refuse to receive or circulate the notes and the District Attorney prosecute the man who thus boldly, in defiance of all law, thrusts upon us such a miserable currency. The note before us is the first we have handled in many a long day and even in its short existence of six days seems, from its greasy and fingered appearance, to be the harbinger of the smallpox or some other contagious disease.

Sam laughed at the closing line as his brother, stormy of mien, read it to him out of the day's paper.

"Poor Tom!" he remarked. "I'm thinking he'd take a chance on the smallpox if he could get a handful of my notes. I understand the *Bulletin's* in trouble."

"You've got good ground for libel," said Captain John.

"And a poor chance to collect any damages but a broken-down newspaper shop," returned Sam. "I know a better way than that."

At the Rassette House he ordered drinks for all hands and tossed some of his currency on the counter.

"Is that good here—in spite of the *Bulletin?*"

"Good as gold—with your name on it, sir," said the bartender heartily. Men gathered close around Sam, drinking his health, slapping him on the back. Many leading merchants were among them. One said, "You ought to horsewhip King." Others muttered assent. But to their consternation Sam raised his glass and shouted, "Here's to Tom King, boys! A damned fool, if you like. But an honest man, afraid of nobody!"

A few set down their glasses and walked out. But most of the crowd drank, with a great roar of appreciation. The story was told about town. It spread to the mining camps. It accomplished more toward vindicating Brannan's currency than a dozen libel suits could have done.

Another bit of newspaper notoriety came to Sam with the arrival of his long-awaited fire engine on the fast clipper ship *Bostonian.* Sam had ordered it four years before, and it was to have been completed, ready for shipment, in twelve months. But so elaborate was the apparatus that Hunneman & Company, the largest and most famous builders of fire apparatus in America, found their machinery inadequate to the purpose. They wrote to Sam, suggesting changes. But he wouldn't have that. "Get new machinery," he answered. "Charge it to me."

So Hunneman & Company installed fresh equipment, specially made. The time was extended a year. But at the end of that time Sam's engine was still unfinished. The work was of such elaborate character and quality that its duration was difficult to estimate. Delay followed delay. But at last it was in San Francisco, after a voyage of 142 days from Boston.

The engine is one of the most complete and beautiful pieces of mechanism we have ever seen [rhapsodized the *Alta*'s editor]. Every portion of the steel and iron work is richly plated with silver and at the first glance it would appear too brilliant, too elegant for common service or efficiency. But on closer inspection, there is nothing gaudy nor superfluous about it—nothing but what is substantial and serviceable; and imposing as the tout ensemble is, yet in detail all is plain and in perfect taste. There are but three colors of paint upon the woodwork: green, gold and the richest shade of carmine, and these are so happily blended as to harmonize with the silver work of the remainder and produce a charming effect.

Even the mechanical detail was described by the *Alta*'s editor in ecstatic terms, including such sentences as "The beam is not straight like ordinary engines but curves gracefully to correspond with the goose-necks and adds greatly to the symmetry of the whole." The writer, however, did not attain the full flight of his poesy until a description of the engine's decorations was reached. Of these he wrote:

The woodwork of the box is of the finest mahogany. In the rear, on each side of the coupling is a griffin's head finely carved and gilded.

On the left side of the box is a landscape painting with horses, trees and a lake with a boating party; above it on the same side of the air-chamber is an exquisite painting on copper said to have been copied from an old English engraving for which Mr. Hunneman paid $60.00. We were not quite satisfied as to what the painting was intended to represent. There are four female figures in the foreground dancing to the music of Old Father Time who sits playing upon a harp; his scythe lying at his feet and a child beside him with an hourglass. Beyond the dancers is a monument with carved busts upon it wreathed with ivy; and above, on a cloud in his golden chariot sits Phoebus reigning [sic] the bold chargers of the Sun. On the right of the box is a beautifully correct view of Niagara Falls on the Canada side; above on the same side is a painting copied from a French picture and representing three females at the bath, one of them dallying with a swan upon the stream. To complete the beauty and symmetry of the engine there are four richly painted fire buckets hanging upon the scroll work, one at each corner. The paintings upon them represent the four seasons and are beautiful in conception and execution.

Its curiosity whetted by this alluring description, San Francisco waited impatiently for a sight of this king of all fire engines. But it was some time before the public desire was gratified. The new engine was housed in a bonded warehouse on Market Street below the Oriental Hotel. Day after day it remained there, an enticing and mysterious object of which sectional glimpses might be had through cracks in the warehouse door. Only the press, members of the Brannan Fire Association and an additional privileged few were enabled to pass the vigilant watchman. Sam's enemies and critics—who, to do him credit, did not include Tom King—hinted that Sam's mechanical marvel was proving to be a white elephant. And this, in a measure, was true. It embarrassed him in a variety of ways. Everyone wanted a pass to see it in the warehouse. Why wasn't it installed in the engine house where no rent for its storage would have to be paid and where it might serve the purpose for which it was intended? There were jocular threats to start a blaze near the warehouse and force a demonstration.

The fact was that when Sam had ordered his $10,000 gift in 1853 he had much more available cash than at present. He had barely finished financing the bank venture, which involved all his available resources. But he managed at last to "bail out" his engine, as one of his critics phrased it, by sacrificing some of his surburban lots at a quick sale.

"We'll have a big parade and show it to the town," said William Howard. "It's a proud day, Sam. Just think of it! Of all the world's big cities, San Francisco, the youngest, has the finest engine."

Sam laughed deprecatingly. "Perhaps it's the finest, Bill

Howard. But yours was the first. You gave San Francisco an engine when the town was four years old. That's when we needed 'em." He flung his arms about the little group that stood near him.

"Come with me, boys," he cried. "We'll drink a toast to Social Number Three."

They headed for the Bank Exchange. Captain John looked after them smiling. "Sam's a generous young devil," he thought. "If only he'd leave liquor alone."

Sam's new engine continued to be a topic of popular interest for weeks after the great parade at which San Francisco lined the roped-off sidewalks along the triumphal route from warehouse to engine house and cheered itself hoarse. Several demonstrations of its fire-fighting prowess followed. The Brannan Fire Association gave a public ball followed by a banquet at which Sam was toasted by the town's notables. He made a speech in his old rollicking style, full of bombast and good will. The next thing San Francisco needed, he said, was artificial gas lamps for lighting its streets and better express facilities. He, Sam Brannan, pledged his word that San Francisco should have them, if he had to organize his own companies with his own money. There were cheers.

"We have everything here," he cried. "We can grow all the fruits of the tropics; we can make the finest wines in the world; we can raise the best cattle. We've even got medicinal springs in Napa Valley that'll beat Saratoga, New York. I've drunk the waters of both, and I like ours better." There were more cheers.

"Give me time," he said, raising his glass, "and I'll show you. I'll show the whole world what California can do—with San Francisco behind it. . . . Here's to God's chosen land!"

He drank amid roars of applause. "Here's to Sam Brannan," someone shouted, "California's Moses."

It was a grand evening. Captain John fumed when he received the bill.

Sam resumed, more or less, his old habits. Captain John and his wife made him welcome in their home. But he had quarters

as well in the Express Building—a suite of rooms to which he
retired, or was conducted, as the case might be, when he lingered too long over wine. He often gave supper parties there to
visiting actresses; women of less distinction were occasionally
his guests. Mrs. John Brannan shrugged her ample shoulders
when reports of Sam's "goings-on" reached her. Captain John
said nothing. He could not justify his brother's acts, but he
blamed Lisa Brannan, who should have been where she belonged, making a home for her husband instead of gadding about
in foreign lands. San Francisco wasn't good enough for her. And
who the devil was she? A boarding-house keeper's daughter,
poor as a church mouse when Sam married her!

Sam was always sober when he came to eat or sleep at his
brother's home. He never was profane while Mary and the children were present. Sophie, age six, was his favorite. She had the
Brannan spirit, he used to say. Tommy, aged eleven, was more
quiet—too sedate for Sam, although he loved them both. He
bought them expensive toys, told them stories of the days when
he was a tramp printer, legends of old Ireland he had learned
from his father. He promised Sophie to buy her a piano when
she was older. She could sing any tune after hearing it once.
Sometimes Sam took her with him to the opera.

He was cheerful and irritable unpredictably. To some situations however vexing—such as King's denunciation of his currency—he could adjust himself valiantly. He could see both sides
of more-important issues: his own and the other fellow's. But for
small provocations—sometimes for purely fancied insults—he
had no defense. He exploded like a firecracker and was later
repentant, ashamed. It was the champagne he drank so constantly, people said, a dangerous liquor when used to excess. . . .
If he would stick to straight whisky he might get decently drunk
if need be without fizzing and fulminating.

But Sam stuck to his champagne. By mid-afternoon he was
quarrelsome and his friends avoided him; strangers were usually
steered off until from sheer loneliness he quit drinking and staggered or was taken home. Cab-drivers, policemen, letter-carriers,
sometimes milkmen or casual pedestrians, gave him a hand when

he needed it—occasionally some woman of the streets whom he had befriended. He knew them all and showered grateful gold upon them, but most of them would have given him aid without hope of reward.

Once Captain John stalked angrily into the Bank Exchange, after sending for Sam half a dozen times. He was needed, drunk or sober, at an important conference. But Sam was in one of his truculent moods. He paid no attention to his brother's messengers, save to buy them drinks and forget them. Nor would he heed Captain John when the latter appeared in person. Finally the elder brother lost his temper. Frail as he was, he caught Sam by his coat collar and, amid the laughter of all, dragged him out of the saloon, belaboring him with the light cane he always carried. Sam went meekly, like a schoolboy. There was not another man in California who could have treated him like that. And there was not one who dared to twit him about it afterward.

For a time after that Sam behaved. He made several journeys to Napa Valley and brought back bottled samples of the mineral waters. He turned them over to a chemist for analysis.

"They're better than Saratoga waters," he told his friends, the report in his hands. "Some day I'll buy the springs and build a hotel there."

He wrote to Lisa about the new plan. San Francisco was a big city now, with fine schools and good teachers, he informed her enthusiastically. Didn't she want to come home? He missed her and the children.

When her answer came he was dining with Captain John and his family. He read it in silence and gave Tommy the foreign stamp for his collection. Then he crumpled the doubled sheet of perfumed paper savagely and walked out of the house without a word.

Next morning the *Alta* reported a rough-and-tumble fight between three men. One was Sam Brannan. Each accused the other of starting the combat. Witnesses admitted, reluctantly, that Sam had been drunk and belligerent. In spite of his prominence he was arrested and held for a hearing. But before the date of his trial, he was off for Europe.

The case was dismissed, much to the disgust of Benjamin Moulton, who had a very black eye. He and Sam were rivals for the distinction of being the richest man in California. People laughed about it. "If that was what they were quarreling about," observed Doc Hayden, the third man in the melee, "Sam certainly proved his claim."

"How did you get mixed up in it, Doc?" someone asked him. The physician laughed. "I tried to be a peacemaker—with the usual result. . . . Poor Sam, he didn't know what he was doing. He was blind, crazy drunk."

"I hope to God he learns some sense," said Captain John to his wife. "And, little as I like that woman, I hope she comes back with him. Anything's better than having Sam footloose and moody."

"Why doesn't he divorce her, I wonder?" asked Mary Brannan. "He can do it, can't he, if she refuses to come back and keep house for him? That's desertion."

"She might come back if Sam took the pledge—but I doubt it."

"Doubt what? His taking the pledge? Or her——"

"Both," said Captain John.

. *12* .

The Great Project

Sam returned from Europe in 1859. He was more reticent than ever concerning domestic affairs. He had evidently been wandering the Continent. More rooted grapevines reached Captain John from time to time during his absence. All sorts of horticultural specimens came from overseas: citrus and olive trees, rare shrubs and plants, more varieties of sheep. Captain John sent them all to the Marysville ranch.

When Sam returned, sunburned and thinner, he asked a hundred questions. Were the new grapes growing? Had the sheep been bred? Was the climate right, so far north, for his olive trees? He was more full of enterprise than ever. He had scarcely unpacked before he was off to Napa Valley.

Just beyond the little town of Napa were the springs and geysers that attracted Sam. He compared his chemist's report of their waters with those of European spas. He showed his reports to physicians. Daily he became more enthusiastic about his new project.

The geyserlands belonged to an old settler, Captain Ritchie. Sam and he had many visits together. They drank and had long talks. Captain Ritchie was aging and wanted to visit his folks in the Atlantic States. He had talked of doing this for years, but, finally, to everyone's surprise, he did.

Sam entertained the old fellow at his quarters in San Francisco. Sam put him on the stage for Wichita. Then he burst in on his brother, excited and proud as a schoolboy who has won a prize. "I've done it, Captain John," he cried. "I've bought 'em."

John Brannan took off his spectacles and surveyed his younger brother. "Sit down and cool off, Sam," he advised. "Now tell me what deviltry you've been up to."

"Deviltry!" Sam laughed. "I've closed the greatest deal in California's history. . . . I've bought Ritchie's holdings—a square mile of geysers and springs. I'll make it the greatest health resort in Christendom!"

Captain John polished his glasses in silence.

"Can't you see it's a grand scheme, you old doubter?" asked Sam, aggrieved.

"Sammy," said the elder Brannan, "I'm afraid for you and for your future. You've made a big pile out of little or nothing; I grant you that . . . and I'm proud of you. The trouble is that you can't keep the money you've made. . . . It's time you learned to husband your resources—instead of finding new holes to pour them into. . . ."

"I've never been much good at husbanding," said Sam a trifle bitterly. "But don't you worry, Captain John. I'll make a million out of the springs. They're the best investment of all."

John Brannan shook his head. He was about to speak but Sam cut in tumultuously: "Listen! We'll build a big hotel there—and baths. The sick will come there in droves to be cured——"

"How'll they get there, Sammy?"

"By stage, at first . . . and later on we'll build a railroad."

"You haven't the money for that."

"It won't be *my* money," said Sam impatiently. "The county'll pay for it. They'll issue bonds. They'll be glad enough to build up the region. . . . We'll plant vineyards; it's an elegant climate for that. We'll build wineries and distilleries. . . . I've grape stocks growing from all over the world. We can make **California's vintages famous."**

He left Captain John half dazed with his glories of anticipation. Maybe he was right, the elder thought. But he was uneasy; his health was failing. Who would steady that whirlwind young brother of his—after he was gone?

Captain John saw little of Sam for a time. He was in Napa County developing his plan. Bills came in aplenty, huge bills for lumber to build bathhouses at the springs, to fence scores of small farms where grapes were transplanted from the Marysville ranch. There were bills for farming machinery, wine presses. One day Sam burst in on his brother, a roll of blueprints under his arm.

"Plans for the hotel at Calistoga," he announced. "What do you think of the name: California and Saratoga combined? I've brought you a bottle of the water for your health, Captain John. And in the fall I'll have a keg of wine for your family."

Captain John smiled. He was no more immune than others to the charm of his younger brother. "I wish you luck, Sam," he said, adding a trifle grimly. "You'll *need* it to pay your bills."

Perhaps it was worth while after all, this new venture of Sam's. The "boy" was looking better. He was too busy to drink excessively or brood about his family. Few letters came from Geneva, but a good deal of Sam's money still went there. The family was traveling in style that summer. Sam Junior was attending an expensive school of engineering in Germany. He made many extra demands, and Sam never denied him.

Sam had to raise money by forced sales; he often had to borrow large amounts, and although rates of interest in San Francisco had diminished, the drain on his purse was heavy. His local property, though valuable, was encumbered. His Sacramento holdings were almost sold out. He was putting all his eggs in one basket: Calistoga. "The sink," Captain John called it harassedly sometimes. But, if it kept Sam happy and busy, as it seemed to be doing, he didn't mind so much. What disturbed Captain John was a dread that he should not see the end of the project. He was coughing more than ever now. And often the handkerchief he pressed to his lips to check the paroxysms was spotted with red.

The doctor wanted him to take a rest, a sea voyage, perhaps. If he waited much longer even that would not save him. Even now it was dubious. But Captain John wouldn't go. Not until Sam's venture was well launched—on the way to success. Then, perhaps, it might take care of itself. If he could hold out a couple of years longer . . .

Sam wanted to build the hotel. He sold his Marysville ranch and the rest of his Sacramento property. Finally the hotel was finished, a small one intended as an annex for the big hostelry Sam planned for the future. People came to the baths; physicians sent them. Sam paid a commission on such customers. The curative fame of the waters grew. Indians and Mexicans had long ago known of their magic, but they had kept the knowledge to themselves. Sam spread the information far and wide. He even sent advertisements to eastern newspapers. He established a stage line. Calistoga became his passion. There was something almost religious about it, a recrudescence of his old Mormon fervors.

He spent much time on a high knoll—which he named Mount Lincoln after the new President—gazing down into the valley. At a point in line with this eminence and the setting sun he built a tomb which resembled that of Calvary. There he brought the body of his father exhumed from its grave in Saco, Maine; and there he laid the body of his second son, little Don, who died in infancy.

Sam spent hours on top of Mount Lincoln, staring at fertile reaches of foothill country, some of it patterned with orderly rows of grapevines and dotted with small farms, all of which he had established.

Sometimes his eyes were lifted to the heights of Mount St. Helena. At his feet were the geysers and springs, from which vapors rose constantly with intermittent spouts of boiling water. People in the new little town of Calistoga, mostly his employees, used to watch the solitary figure of Sam Brannan standing on the hilltop, motionless, bareheaded as if at some devotion, and wonder, half superstitiously, what it portended.

As a matter of fact, Sam's thoughts were a naïve mixture of nature worship and empirical ambition. His little hill, less than a hundred feet high, was a botanical garden covered with plants from all over the world. At its crest would be a reservoir to supply with water the great rambling hotel with spreading verandas and far-flung gardens which his anticipations painted. The spa of the West!

Such was Sam's dream. Calistoga was to become a pastoral principality and a curative mecca in one. The rich should come there, leaving their money and their ailments; the poor should enrich the land. It combined altruism and profits. It was the Perfect Enterprise.

Perhaps, as he stood on his hilltop, Sam visioned his children playing in the green meadows and groves below instead of imbibing in Swiss academies an alien culture for which he had no sympathy. Perhaps he pictured Lisa queening it over broad acres and tree-shaded lawns in a pillared mansion. Whatever were his thoughts, the solitary hours on Mount Lincoln brought him a new peace. He was tired of cities and taverns and whilom affairs with women. He reverted, perhaps traditionally, to the soil.

But the interval was short. Presently he was off to New York again to borrow more money. And in New York, with a war between North and South approaching, money was tight. Sam met disappointments. He was not used to that, and he had only one panacea. Captain John learned he was drinking heavily. He spent a night in a police station because of a fracas in the Knickerbocker Hotel bar with a slave captain.

The latter escaped when police were called to stop the fight, in which pistols were drawn. Sam's antagonist was the notorious Captain Farnham of the *Wanderer,* recently out of jail at Savannah. There had been horrid tales of these slave ships. In one of them, boarded by navy men, had been found hatches only four feet high packed with nude Negro women and children imprisoned amid unspeakable filth and stench.

Sam, who hated slavery, was in one of his belligerent moods when he encountered Captain Farnham in the barroom of his hotel and refused to drink with him. When the slaver demanded an apology Sam denounced him as a scoundrel, and the two sprang at each other. A policeman had separated them and had taken Sam to jail, while Farnham, assisted by friends, escaped. Sam was released next morning, but the newspapers were filled with his exploit. Evidently Lisa, half-persuaded to return by Sam's glowing accounts of Calistoga, learned of the fracas. She would stay, she wrote to Sam, in a country where men knew how to behave.

The trip to New York had profited Sam little. When he returned to San Francisco he was moody and resentful—drinking harder than ever. But Calistoga's development went on. Flowered patterns were being gardened about the hotel. There were croquet grounds, tennis courts, tenpin alleys, billiard rooms, a swimming pool of naturally warmed mineral water, a mile trotting park where thoroughbreds from all parts of the country ran seasonal races.

Sam sent to Asia for plants and established a tea garden. He proved that tea could be grown in California. He conducted extensive experiments with silkworms in a mulberry orchard and built a feeding room for worms. But he was too restless to carry all of his projects to successful conclusions. He abandoned many in the halfway stage. This, however, was not true of viticulture. The brandy from his distillery was declared equal to French cognac. Better-class restaurants throughout California served it. Large quantities were sent East for storage and distribution. Wine from Napa County grapes was being bottled and shipped throughout the United States. California wine was in demand.

Sam was promoting a railroad. He had brought thousands of voters to Napa Valley. Presently one began to hear about railway bonds. In the state legislature a subsidy bill was pending. Sam maintained a suite of rooms at the leading Sacramento hotel. There was champagne for legislators—and Havana cigars. There were wine suppers and excursions to the springs. California lawmakers took "the cure" at Sam's expense. Sam brought the choruses of "variety" shows from San Francisco or Sacramento on special stages for a night of merriment. Townspeople spoke of "wild goings-on" but with sly pride rather than protest.

Almost everybody in Calistoga was an employee or beneficiary
of Sam Brannan.

The Napa Valley Railroad became a reality. Chartered by
the state with a clause leaving the matter of subsidies to the
people, it moved swiftly from projection to realization. The
county passed a bond issue providing a bonus of $5,000 a mile
from Calistoga to Napa and $10,000 between Napa and Socol.
Chinese laborers by the hundreds were brought from San Francisco with native foremen to interpret and Irish bosses over them.

The first trains, flag-and-bunting trimmed, rolled into Calistoga bearing three thousand visitors. Among them were the
state's big men and their ladies, and many important easterners
too, some of them New York bankers with a stake in the enterprise, and plenty of potential settlers. And a sprinkling of better-
class courtesans to make things gay.

At each and every station on the road reception committees
waited with refreshments and drinks. Sam stood on the back
platform and made speeches, waving his arms amid cheers. And
at the end of the road a banquet was spread for the notables,
free drinks and food for all.

There was only one fly in Sam's ointment: Captain John was
not there to witness his triumph, the greatest in Sam's career.
Captain John had succumbed to the lung fever people were
calling consumption. He had died at sea.

Finally, when he could stay at his task no longer, Captain
John had taken the long voyage which might have saved him
years ago. But it was too late. In Shanghai he had been taken
ashore, desperately ill, and transferred to a ship bound for home.
He wanted to see his family again, but three days out he died
after exacting a promise from his friend Captain Coburn of the
Washington not to cast his body into the sea. Captain Coburn
had promised and kept his pledge. He had bound his old friend's
body tightly in strips of linen, winding even the fingers sepa-
rately. And then he had broken the top of a hogshead of Chinese
liquor called *samshu*. Into the hogshead went John Brannan's

body. On went the top of the hogshead. Captain Coburn had learned that trick for preserving bodies from a Chinese sailor.

In San Francisco, months later, Captain John had lain in his coffin as natural to look upon as if he had been embalmed a few days previously. And Sam, weeping, unashamed, through the service, had followed the hearse to Laurel Hill Cemetery at the head of an impressive funeral cortège.

But what was done was done, thought Sam, as he lifted a champagne glass in response to a toast from the governor. He couldn't bring back Captain John to sit beside him, more was the pity, so there was no use sorrowing about it.

"Friends and fellow citizens!" he began a bit thickly, for he had lifted many previous glasses this day. . . .

Hours later, when he could no longer talk, or even stand, he was carried to bed and undressed by servitors who shook their heads but smiled as they did so. They all loved him. It had been a great day for Calistoga.

In 1863 Sam bought more land in Napa Valley. He now owned more than two thousand acres. He made gifts of town lots to his nieces and nephews; on each he built a dwelling house of rococo, almost Byzantine design. They were square and surrounded by porches of arched scrollwork. He spent much of his time at the springs.

Sam had a new manager now, even more efficient than his much mourned elder brother. Alexander Badlam, Jr., son of his sister Mary, had attracted Sam's attention by enterprise and ability. Only a few years ago it seemed to Sam, Alex had driven his own team from Cleveland to California. Sam had offered to aid him, but the boy was independent. "I'll make my own way, Uncle Sam," he said. And Alex had. He was a member of the legislature when Sam, needing a manager for his great holdings after Captain John's death, had persuaded his nephew to take the job. Sam left everything to him. He grumbled a little when Alex vetoed some reckless expenditure. But he trusted the younger man's judgment.

What Sam enjoyed most was to have important people visit

the springs. He liked to talk big and tell tall stories. When P. T. Barnum, the circus man, came to the Calistoga Hotel, seeking a cure for his rheumatism, he and Sam regaled each other with Gargantuan yarns. Among them was Sam's boiled fish story.

"Do you like fresh fish?" he asked the circus magnate.

"Yes, I love them," Barnum answered.

"Well, we serve the freshest fish here in the world," Sam told him. "They come from an underground stream and the geysers boil them. They shoot out of the earth and we catch them on plates, ready to eat."

"By God!" cried Barnum. "That must be a sight. Let's go and watch them."

Sam was not to be daunted. He excused himself and entered the kitchen. "Tell one of the boys to go out to the big geyser with some boiled fish," he ordered. "Have three or four on a plate. Pretend they came out of the pipe. Understand?"

One of the kitchen boys nodded. He carried out the orders, and when Barnum, conducted by Sam, approached, he was holding a steaming fish by the tail. "They ain't comin' up very fast, Mr. Brannan," he said apologetically. "This is all I could get——"

"Maybe the pipe's plugged," said Sam. "Have the plumber look at it. We've got to have fish for our guests."

"Yes, sir," the boy returned.

"Well I'll be damned!" said Barnum.

Another of Sam's pranks was the legend of the "soup spring." It emitted a milky solution containing soda and magnesia which bubbled from a three-inch pipe. A visitor whom Sam was showing over the grounds one day remarked that it tasted like thin oyster soup. And Sam, intrigued by the remark, labeled it "The Soup Spring." He heightened the effect by providing salt, pepper and crackers on a table near by, and later he added another improvement by having the cook drop bits of meat into the pipe between eruptions.

The Soup Spring became one of the marvels of Northern California and received newspaper mention even in eastern cities. Its waters were avidly sampled by visitors to Calistoga until a local wag spread the report that the remarkable flavor of the Soup Spring waters was that of live bull frogs surreptitiously dropped down the pipe. The story, absurd as it was, gained wide credence and the popularity of the Soup Spring diminished.

The Brannan properties at this time—the middle '60's—included 2,200 acres of valley and more than 800 acres of hill land. Close to a thousand horses, many of blooded stock, ran practically wild over the great domain, and five hundred imported merino sheep cropped the grasses of the upper Napa Valley. Sam's distillery used 2,500 tons of grapes in a season and turned out 90,000 gallons of brandy. A dozen carloads of grapes sometimes arrived in a single day, and most of the farmers thereabouts turned their hayfields into vineyards because grapes paid them better.

It was the sheep that gained Sam the enmity of certain settlers on the lower banks of the stream which watered the valley. They roiled its waters farther up, and farmers complained that their water supply was being polluted. Sam made sporadic efforts to remedy the situation, but without success. His sheep still waded and drank in the stream, and threats succeeded protests. A sheepherder was killed, perhaps in a quarrel, though the facts were never established. And one night a crowd of unidentified persons with their dogs drove Brannan's sheep away from the stream. During the drive scores were stampeded over a precipice and killed.

Sam was furious. He invoked the law, but it accomplished little. A couple of rough fellows, believed to have been allies of the squatter element with whom Sam had clashed in Sacramento, were suspected. Strong circumstantial evidence connected them with the sheep drive, but not enough to convict them. Public disfavor finally forced them to leave the county.

Angry and hurt by the treatment he had received in Napa County, which he had done so much to promote, Sam returned to San Francisco. And it was high time he did, for creditors were pressing him on every side. Calistoga was yielding a fair return, but he had assumed extraordinarily heavy obligations in its behalf. His resources were sadly diminished and his expenditures, except for Badlam's restraints, would have been more reckless than ever. He had contributed huge sums to the Union's war chest in the Civil War; his personal charities were legion. A beggar hailing him on the street was as likely to receive a gold piece as a silver coin.

Sam's former wife, Hattie, had come to California and married again. She had made no demands on Sam, but he had bought her a ranch in Petaluma. But her husband, a ne'er-do-well, had mortgaged and lost this. He was dead now and Sam was supporting his widow. His daughter by Hattie was being raised by Mary Brannan in her own home. She was attending an expensive academy.

Sam drank a great deal nowadays. He was, in fact, becoming an inebriate, a trial to his friends, some of whom looked the other way when they met on the street. People made fun of him behind his back. When an aggravated piece of his drunken buffoonery startled the town, Alex kept it out of the San Francisco papers, but the Sacramento *Union* of February 27, 1865, printed the following:

> Sam Brannan got up a private celebration in San Francisco Saturday night and included in his program the firing of a battery on Montgomery Street which broke glass altogether valued at $2500.
>
> Brannan thought that Charleston had been taken.

Alex paid the bills and Sam, sincerely repentant, promised to keep a better hold on himself. He engaged in no more drunken orgies. But presently it was whispered about town that he was carrying on a shameless liaison with the wife of a friend.

Perhaps Lisa Brannan in faraway Geneva learned of these rumors through friends in San Francisco with whom she corresponded. At any rate, her letters took on a suspicious tinge. Sam showed some of them to his sister-in-law. He went more and more to the home of his brother's widow for comfort and advice. He liked little Sophie, his niece, now approaching fifteen. She sang for him and played pieces on the thousand-dollar piano he had bought for Lisa, who had never liked it. But Sophie loved the instrument; it had been specially made by a famous piano firm and had mother-of-pearl keys, inlays of colored shell-work and other unusual decorations. Because Lisa had found it "gaudy" in spite of its fine tone, Sam had it sent over to Captain John's when his own family left for Europe.

"I think she mistrusts me," said Sam when Mary had read Lisa's letter.

Mary nodded her head. "Is it true—what they say of you, Sam?"

He did not answer, but rose and picked up his hat. "Good night, Mary," he said at the door.

She looked after him puzzled. "Even if it is true, it's *her* fault," she thought.

Alex had ill news for Sam. A man named Warner Buck, to whom Sam had leased a sawmill and pumping plant at Calistoga, wasn't keeping his contract. He had paid no rent and defied Badlam when the latter threatened suit to terminate the lease. "Sue and be damned," he had told Brannan's agent.

"They're a tough crowd," Sam said angrily, "part of the old squatter gang that hates me. . . . We'll have trouble with 'em yet."

. *13* .

Lisa Brannan Returns

San Francisco was in the throes of an interval of civic virtue such as now and then overtook it when Sam Brannan felt the severity of its displeasure. Gambling—perhaps the town's most naïvely robust passion—was for the moment being frowned upon. And the City Council, with a more than usually depleted treasury, seized the opportunity to double taxes on all games of chance. Saloon licenses, likewise, brought fancy figures, and saloonkeepers were warned to close at midnight. Policemen disguised as sailors or miners visited the book and art shops, demanding "something spicy" in an undertone. When they received it, which they usually did, the dealer was arrested for "vending obscene matter." Temperance societies operated liquorless hotels and restaurants, proselyting actively among incoming travelers. Under such conditions it was inevitable that Sam Brannan, the city's most distinguished inebriate, should be frowned upon in private and censured in public, especially by pulpit orators.

Though by no means a vindictive man, Sam found a certain consolation in the fact that Thomas King was in the same boat. The *Bulletin's* editors had been arrested and fined for printing the "confession" of a notorious woman criminal. The charge was "publishing indecent matter." Each was fined a hundred dollars and received a scathing reprimand as well. Sam was mean enough to chuckle when he heard about it. He said to Judge Hudson who had tried the case, "Will Your Honor permit an old reprobate to buy you a drink?"

Judge Hudson grinned. "Yes—if you're the old reprobate, Sam."

The bartender opened champagne. "Here's to Morality, Judge!"

"May it never trouble you, sir," said His Honor.

But it was troubling Sam more than a little. Lisa was coming back.

Sam Junior was twenty-two and soon would graduate as a mining engineer. He wanted to study the great copper deposits of Arizona; it was partly that and partly Sam's financial condition which caused Lisa's decision to return. Sam could no longer bear the drain of supporting separate households and juggling his many investments. He was still a rich man, but he had to write his wife decisively at last that she must come home or live less expensively.

Lisa might have consented to that if she had believed Sam's statements concerning financial affairs. But she mistrusted her husband. She felt herself wronged and deceived. . . . If she could verify what her friends had written of his doings she would have a hold on Sam that would make her independent.

She wrote they would return as soon as Sam Junior received his degree.

Sam had fallen asleep over her letter in the parlor of the Russ House. Most of the good folk of San Francisco were abed, and the bad had retired to secret and shrouded rendezvous of pleasure, when sounds of sudden and mysterious revelry smote the post-midnight stillness of Montgomery Street. Down the sidewalks came a tramp of marching feet and the strains of Schultz's "Fireman's March." It drew nearer. Sam rose and rubbed his eyes.

"I wonder what's going on?" he muttered drowsily.

Volney Howard standing beside him said, "Straighten your tie, Sam and button your vest. . . . It's a serenade."

"Serenade! For whom?"

"For you," returned the other laughing. "It's the Musical Fund Society and the Howard Engine Company. They want to show the town that someone still approves of you, I guess."

Hurriedly Sam reassembled his costume before a mirror. He still wore good clothes, but by late evening he was apt to forget, to become disheveled.

"By God, that's good of them," he cried. "Bartender: break out champagne for my friends—for everybody."

"It's all arranged for, Mr. Brannan," said the barman. "Set down. Don't you worry. There's supper and wine all laid out."

In front of the hotel the procession halted: members of the Musical Fund Society sixty strong and bearing lanterns, behind them their escort of fire boys resplendent in capes and helmets. The band played a piece. Then the fire boys called. "Hey, Sam Brannan, come out!"

Sam came with alacrity, grinning, shaking hands, thanking them vociferously. They formed a hollow square about him chanting: "For he's a jolly good fellow——" A crowd gathered. They took up the chant.

"You're all right, Sam," they shouted.

"Speech! Speech!" others called.

So Sam made a speech. He told them about Calistoga and the joke he had played on Barnum. He spoke of Union victories in the South. "It's our gold that's winning the war boys," he cried, "California's gold." They cheered.

"We're freeing the slaves," he went on, enlarging his subject. "And some day we'll free Mexico from the French puppet, Maximilian."

"Hurray!" the fire boys shouted. "Lead the way, Sam, we're behind you."

Sam laughed his robust laugh. "Come on, then, I'll be leadin' you to dinner."

They followed him, the musicians playing, the others laughing and joking as they entered the big dining hall where Hardenberg and Dyer, the proprietors, had spread cold meats and relishes. Bottles of champagne stood in coolers ready to serve, and waiters with corkscrews were ready for action beside them.

Corks began to pop. Everyone fell to with enthusiasm. There were other speeches, growing freer, more disjointed as the feast proceeded. Daylight found Sam asleep in his chair at the head of the table, clutching a roll of vellum bound with red ribbon. It was a certificate of honorary membership in the Musical Fund Society.

Another organization treated Sam less gently. He belonged to most of the fraternal orders that had lodges in San Francisco. He had given the Odd Fellows a plot of ground for a cemetery, and they had honored him for it. In the lodgerooms of the California Pioneers a life-sized portrait in oils of their first president looked out from a heavy gold frame. But Sam had no affiliation with the Masons—perhaps because so many of his enemies of vigilante days, the Southerners or "Chivs," were members of that order. But California Lodge No. 1 at last considered his application—and blackballed him.

Sam laughed about it, but the town was shocked. A number of Masons resigned from the lodge. It seemed, indeed, an inexplicable proceeding, for Sam Brannan with all his loose habits, was no worse than many other pioneers. His sponsor made matters worse. He waited for a time, perhaps for sentiment to change, did a little electioneering and presented Sam's name again. The result was the same as before.

This time Sam was furious. "They can't do that to me," he shouted at Alex, who tried to calm him. "I'm going to New York. I'll see about it."

He took passage on the next boat. People said he couldn't face the town after a second blackballing; but Alex and most of his friends knew better than that.

Sam made a protracted stay in New York. He returned with a smile on his face and a Masonic insignia in his buttonhole. He mentioned casually during the next few days to persons including both Masons and newspaper men that he had joined Lafayette Lodge No. 64 of New York under the jurisdiction of the Grand Lodge of the state. He had been initiated, passed and raised to a Master Mason.

He made no further effort to affiliate with the San Francisco lodge. It was his answer to his foes in California Lodge No. 1 San Francisco smiled and deemed him vindicated, but California Masons felt themselves aggrieved. Soon after his return the Grand Lodge warned all members against Masonic intercourse with Samuel Brannan. The latter continued to smile. He attended Odd Fellows' meetings and Pioneer Society banquets; he gave more contributions to the Musical Fund Society and foregathered with the boys of Howard Engine Company. He promoted new enterprises, escorted distinguished visitors to Calistoga and engaged in less creditable activities. The Masonic insignia remained in his buttonhole but the subject of Masonry he ignored.

At the following session, California's Grand Lodge, F. & A. M., rescinded its previous action. Some time later Sam was invited to become a member of Occidental Lodge. He accepted the invitation and was passed.

Sam made another journey to New York a few years later. It had no special cause or purpose beyond the restlessness, the need for diversion which at intervals drove Sam across the continent. Much of his brandy, distilled at Calistoga, was stored in an Eastern warehouse and disposed of through New York agents, and many of his supplies were bought through them on the Atlantic Coast. Sam always had a valid-enough excuse to pack his trunk and follow it across the country for an indefinite stay. This particular trip boded nothing more important than any other. But it was destined to exert an unsuspected influence on his future and perhaps—who knows?—to change the history of nations.

Seeking only diversion, with the usual leaven of business exigency, Sam found Destiny as well, in the person of a hollow-cheeked, eager-eyed Mexican, fed on disappointments but living on hope. He was an agent the revolutionist leader Juárez had sent to America. Financial ambassador of a great Indian empire with an overlay of western civilization, this unfortunate man was peddling, with little more success or dignity than an ordinary book agent, the bonds of Mexico's *de jure* government which former President Benito Juárez hoped to restore.

Washington had protested against French invasion of North America and the puppet monarchy of "Emperor" Maximilian, whose *de facto* rule satisfied no one but Napoleon III. However, Maximilian was still in power, supported by a great and friendly European country, and the financing of a revolt against him was not a good investment. Juárez' agent trying desperately to sell his bonds at 12½ cents on the dollar, was dismissed with fair words but no cash by the New York bankers. One of them, half in jest, said to the man, "Why don't you see Sam Brannan, the California millionaire? He'll buy *anything*, they tell me."

Benito Juárez' agent sought Sam out at once. He was at the end of his tether, his clothes threadbare, his body overworked and undernourished, his morale almost broken. No more pitiful pleader for an almost hopeless cause could well have been imagined. Yet he found a ready listener in Samuel Brannan.

He was ever responsive to a hard-luck story; the plight of the Mexican people, in bondage to a foreign power, would alone have appealed to his heart. But there were other and stronger considerations. Sam had hoped to capture California for the Mormons but had been too late; he had planned, in mind at least, a filibuster that might annex Hawaii to the United States. In this he had been, as it proved, premature. In the restoration of Mexico to popular rule, he saw a third and greater opportunity. Last of all there was the fact that Senator Benton, his old enemy, favored Maximilian, planned to colonize Mexico with Americans under special territorial concessions. . . . Two could play that game—in different ways—thought Brannan.

He bought Juárez' revolutionist bonds. He invested recklessly and prodigally every dollar he could raise by short sales and other sacrifices of valuable property. Badlam disapproved with all his might. It was the worst type of collateral security, for not one in a hundred believed that the revolution would succeed. But Sam was determined. He bought Juárez' bonds to the tune of $1,500,000 par value.

When Sam returned to San Francisco the town was full of discharged Union soldiers looking for work. The goldfields were no longer a bonanza, and times were both hard and uncertain.

Sam perceived an opportunity to answer the many appeals made to him for employment by organizing a fighting unit to support Juárez' revolt. He had placed his bonds in a safe-deposit box, but he had not shelved his hopes. The revolution, with Sam's cash behind it, was in full swing. Sam followed its progress eagerly. Lately it had met reverses. Time to raise the bet, thought Sam, who was an ardent poker-player.

He sent out a secret call for volunteers. The response was so large that it would have daunted anyone but him. He refused the service of none. With the aid of Juárez' agents he smuggled his men across the border in small groups that excited no suspicion.

Straggling into Mexico, their arms shipped under false labels, Sam's filibusters were assembled and equipped below the border into a formidable fighting unit. Many had been officers in the Civil War; some were skilled artillerists; most of them were adventurers who loved fighting. They were inconsiderable in number compared to Juárez' peon army but they meant much to that disorderly, untrained and badly accoutered organization.

Their appearance gave rise to a rumor that the United States was sending troops to support Juárez, and this immeasurably strengthened the flagging morale of the revolutionists. A new spirit and vigor entered the campaign against Maximilian, and though it is absurd to claim that Sam's fighters brought about his overthrow, there is little doubt they hastened that event with its pitiably tragic dénouement.

Sam reaped no immediate reward from Juárez' restoration beyond, perhaps, the moral satisfaction of it and the bafflement of Benton. He might have sold his bonds at a profit, but he had greater hopes. Other and more personal events engrossed him at the time. One of these was the return of his family from Europe.

He had sold the Mission Street house. The neighborhood was almost solidly commercial now, and the old plank toll road had long given way to a wide business street. He had auctioned the furniture, retaining only a few keepsakes against the chance of Lisa's return. Sam had learned to treat the periodical announcements of his wife's homecoming without undue seriousness. But now, after two years of promising or threatening—he could never quite determine which from her letters of variable mood—she had actually left Geneva. She had written to him from Dresden on her way to a German port. He realized with a startled glance of corroboration at the postmark on her letter that she might arrive within a fortnight.

It was thirteen years since Lisa Brannan and her brood had left a very different San Francisco from that which existed today. She would not recognize this growing, established commonwealth as the raw, gold-mad town of unstable architecture, lawlessness, stench and unpaved streets she had so joyously deserted.

She might fancy the new city—tolerate it, at least. Perhaps they might pull together after all these years apart. Sam hoped so, ardently. He loved his family. The domestic tradition was strong in him despite its continued frustration. If he might have his family around him, a home where he could bring his friends —and Lisa just a bit more patient with his admitted imperfections—life would form itself into a new and pleasant pattern.

Would she be as pretty as ever? he wondered. And what would the children be like? Sammy was twenty-two; he could scarcely realize it. A grown man! Addie was old enough to marry and Fanny not far from it. Even Alicia—whom he had always called Lizzie, to his wife's disgust; he must remember not to do that again—would be a big girl now.

He drove frantically about town, seeking a new home for them; over the hills and into the western addition, through the Mission District, to South Park and up on Rincon Hill. He thought, with his investor's instinct, that the hills north of Market Street overlooking the Bay were most likely to increase in price—a thing to be considered in the ever-shifting progress of San Francisco's realty values. Rincon Hill was already decadent, though some of the best families still clung to it. If they cut Second Street through as they talked of doing, it would ruin them. And South Park was becoming shabby. The trend was north of Market Street. Only steep hills hindered its development. Real-estate dealers talked of "marine views" to compensate for the pitch of streets whose grades were dangerous in wet weather.

"Would they like a marine view, do you think, Alex?" Sam asked his manager. "It might remind them of Switzerland." Badlam thought they would. Sam decided finally to take a big rococo house on Clay Street hill. It was modern and pretentious, with a sweeping prospect of the bay and its tangle of shipping. It included spacious grounds with trees and gardens, an ornate iron fence, a carriage block and a hitching post. There was a stable and carriage house, a weathervane topping the former, a rather splendid porte-cochère.

Entering, one came from the vestibule into an elaborate reception hall from which an imposing stairway ascended. Sam pictured Lisa coming down to join her guests at a *soirée*, looking queenly in an evening gown and jewels. It was this thought perhaps more than anything else which sold him the Clay Street house. He stood so long gazing at the stairway that Alex nudged him, wondering if his uncle had seen a ghost. Sam started at the touch. "I guess we'll take it, Alex, boy," he said.

They went over the place again before closing the deal. Sam wished to be certain there was plenty of room for servants. He knew, instinctively, that Lisa, setting up a home again, would want to "splurge."

He hesitated about furnishings and concluded wisely to let Lisa take charge of that. He would be certain to get things wrong.

At the Russ House, now the leading hotel, he engaged a suite of rooms: a parlor and drawing room, a bedroom for Lisa and himself, one for each of the children. It gave him a queer feeling to realize they were grown-up, so short a while ago it seemed since they were climbing over him, into his lap, playing with his watch and begging for sweets, which he invariably brought home from the office. No more of that. He thought of little Don, who had lived only two years. It was after his death that Lisa had gone away. Don would be nearly fifteen now if he were alive, mused Sam.

He bought himself new clothes. Johnny the barber went over him painstakingly. His boots shone from Leon the bootblack's ministration; even his nails were manicured. His family must be proud of him—or at least not ashamed. It was almost too much to expect that Lisa, after her years in Europe, would be proud of her western, money-grubbing husband.

Sam had to warn a certain lady that discretion would be in order. She did not accept the warning graciously. The opera season was on and she liked to attend performances leaning on the arm of a millionaire. *She* was proud of him, at any rate, mused Sam, a trifle grimly, and she would be jealous of Lisa. But she consented to take up her abode in Calistoga for a time. Sam had given her a cottage there and he could run up for week ends. . . . Her husband was too busy to care what she did —too busy even to suspect.

So all was in order when Lisa's ship docked at Long Wharf. She stood, surrounded by her children, staring at the town. It had improved incredibly. She hadn't believed all Sam wrote about it, but perhaps he had told her the truth after all.

The equipage with a liveried coachman was quite present-able, and so, she noted, with a sigh of relief, was her husband. One never could tell about Sam. She kissed him, noting with satisfaction that his breath smelled only faintly of liquor—tinc-tured with cloves.

Young Sam greeted his father shyly. He looked like his mother, a bit of a fop and perhaps a prig, his father decided after a searching glance. That would be only natural after the training he'd had and Lisa's coddling. But he was straight and well set up, with a good head and fine, rather dreamy eyes.

The girls were pretty and well groomed, thought Sam, though they had too much manner—for California, at least. Foreign schools gave them that overlay of specious refinement, smeared them with self-conscious affectations—pretty enough but unnatural.

They were, after all, his girls. They would outgrow and shed these veneers. Fanny was going to be a beauty, anyone could see that. And the other two, though plainer, were not going to be old maids, he decided approvingly. He kissed them all and handed them into the carriage, lifting his hat with pride to acquaintances as they drove to the hotel. It was altogether a propitious reunion, he thought. He must find Sammy a job. What the boy needed was to be on his own, to recognize and meet responsibilities. If he had learned anything of practical value in that fancy Freiburg school there ought to be plenty of chance. Above all, Sam thought a bit harassedly, he must watch his own step. Many things would have to be different from now on.

Rather to his surprise, Lisa approved of the house on Clay Street. She exclaimed about the view and went eagerly over the premises, deciding the disposition of rooms and spaces. She bought carpets, furniture, pictures, a new piano. Delivery vans toiled in a procession up the steep grade to her door; gardeners worked on the lawns and flowerbeds. A fountain was installed.

Lisa hired a retinue of "help": a cook, a chambermaid, a sort of upper housemaid and a butler to superintend them. The footman and coachman had quarters over the carriage house. Sam's horses and carriage were transferred from a downtown livery stable to his home. A riding horse was bought for Sam Junior and a pony for Alicia. The gardener came three days a week to water, prune and plant. The conservatory was bright with fresh flowers.

When Sam totaled his bills the first month after Lisa's return, he whistled. But he made no protest. "I guess I can stand it," he told Alex.

The butler was an imposing man with an odd combination of Oxford and Cockney accents. He wore knee breeches and a coat that reminded Sam of the ringmaster in Rowe's Circus. Under his air of honeyed politeness Sam sensed a secret contempt. But the fellow was efficient; he ran the household like a clock.

There were other elements in his new home life which disturbed Sam. He didn't like Lisa's guests. She entertained earnestly and, according to the papers, "lavishly." Most of the friends who remembered her after the long absence were of the old Southern crowd. They were not as important as before "the War of the Secession." They had become a social undercurrent. "Sponges," some people called them. But they still had grand manners and a certain prestige. To Lisa's rococo drawing room they brought a sprinkling of European aristocrats: frayed Royalists from France, impoverished Spanish grandees, titled English remittance men and Germans evading military service. Between them Lisa achieved something like a *salon*. They drank Sam's wines and disparaged American customs. Sam couldn't stand them. After an honest and unsuccessful effort he no longer tried. There was little social interchange between the two Brannan families. Sophie had visited her cousins and been snubbed. But Sam came often to his brother's widow's house. Brannan also found it more congenial than his own home. He had hoped to bring his friends home informally, but Lisa and the butler made them ill at ease. All was right when he dined governors, senators, distinguished visitors from the Atlantic States or abroad. Lisa then was graciousness itself; the butler punctilio personified. His children performed on the piano. The great ones were charmed. With Sam's cronies it was another affair. "They're common," Lisa flared at him when he upbraided her for lack of cordiality. When he answered, "So am I," she shrugged.

There was no open rupture between them; it was just as it used to be except that the children were grown. The girls came to him secretly for spending money. Fanny was keeping company with a young fellow named Schuyler, "a fine old Southern family," Lisa informed her husband proudly. That didn't mean much to Sam, but he liked Schuyler. He did not object.

Sam Junior had found no work. His father had sent him to a dozen men but without satisfactory result. Some of the jobs didn't interest him. He was rather proud of his Freiburg certificate. He talked big. "We need practical men," Sam's friends told him apologetically when they turned him down. Still, Sam had faith in the boy; he gave him money now and then to augment Lisa's somewhat meager allowance. Sammy must sow his wild oats. He'd turn out all right in the end.

Sam spent increasingly more time in Calistoga. He reopened his suite in the Express Building. When he came home late from the springs or elsewhere he stayed there overnight, or when he had tarried too long over wine. Old Tom Davidson, the janitor, was devoted to Sam, saw that he got to bed if need be and kept his mouth closed. There were other events and circumstances about which Tom was discreet. Sam was grateful for his loyalty. He made it worth Tom's while.

Sometimes Alex grew a little troublesome about expenses. Lisa's bills increased; and there were others annotated "See my father" by young Sam, bills from haberdashers, wine merchants, livery-stable keepers, gamblers—sometimes jewelers and furriers. Alex complained of them. He could no longer balance outgo with income.

"It's only a matter of time, Uncle Sam, till you——" he hesitated.

"Till I what?"

"Go broke," said Alex ominously.

Sam had another talk with Lisa. She was adamant. "We can't live cheaper. Sell some of your property. . . . You're land-poor, Sam; that's the trouble."

"It isn't a good time to sell," he answered, but she wouldn't listen to argument.

"You're a rich man, Sam. You needn't stint your family."

. *14* .

Bullets and Judgments

Sam took the stage for Calistoga after a night out. A policeman had taken him home. Old Tom had put him to bed and brought him an eye-opener in the morning. He was glad to get out of town. There was no longer any peace in San Francisco, he decided—between Lisa and Alex.

There wasn't too much peace in Calistoga either, he reflected broodingly as the stage jolted along through the April afternoon. Sam was in a surly mood unusual for him, nursing his wrongs, rebuffing the advances of fellow passengers.

"I must get the mill back," he said to himself over and over. . . . Damned if he'd tolerate any more nonsense from Warner Buck or his brother-in-law, Andy Snyder.

Two years before he had leased a parcel of land to Buck. It was near the stage road to the geysers—just inside the gates of Sam's Calistoga domain. On it were the steam sawmill and pumping plant. Sam had turned them over to Buck for operation. He didn't want to be bothered with them any longer.

But Buck hadn't paid his rent. He had evaded payments on one excuse after another until Sam, at Alex's advice, had brought suit to terminate the lease and reclaim the property. While the matter was in litigation Buck went into bankruptcy. Sam had an order from the sheriff of Napa County to recover his property. But Andy Snyder got himself appointed assignee of the estate. That was a smart trick—and a dirty one, Sam thought. Snyder had placed armed men in possession.

"We'll see about that," thought Sam angrily. The worst of it was that young Theo Larbig, a German boy he had befriended, was one of Snyder's gang. Sam had found Theo wandering, homeless, on the streets of San Francisco several years before. He'd given him food, a bed and new clothes. Later he'd taken the boy—he was only sixteen—to Mary Brannan and asked her to look after him. By and by he found work for Theo in Calistoga.

But Larbig, sensitive, high-strung kid that he was, got to drinking. "I can't lecture him for that," mused Sam. "But he might have known better than go against me. You can't trust anybody," Sam morosely told himself. "Nobody but Alex and old Tom."

It was dusk when he reached Calistoga—dinnertime. But Sam didn't feel like eating. He entered the bar and ordered champagne.

Milton McDowell was there—one of Snyder's friends.

"See here, Milt," said Sam. "I've come to take back my mill. Do you know that? That's what I'm here for."

"All right," said McDowell staring at him.

"To hell with your friend, Andy Snyder! Have a drink."

McDowell made no answer. Quietly he left the room.

Two of Sam's friends, Swift and Garrett, came closer. "You shouldn't have said that," Swift protested. "He's gone to warn Snyder."

"To hell with them both. . . . Have a drink."

They tried to quiet him; but Brannan was not to be soothed. "I'm starting for the mill," he shouted, flinging a gold piece on the counter. "Who's my friend? Who's goin' with me?"

Swift and Garrett made another effort to dissuade him. "Wait till tomorrow," Garrett urged. "Those men have guns."

"To hell with their guns! Stay here if you're scared."

They went with him. He was roaring, fighting drunk, and anything might happen. As they approached the mill voices called to them threateningly. "Stand back, you fellows. We'll shoot. We mean business."

Whether Sam heard them is a question. He continued to advance, swaying a little but undaunted. When he was about sixty feet off the voices once more warned. "Stand still, Sam Brannan, or we'll let you have it." That was Snyder's voice.

Sam shouted furiously, "I want my mill."

"Well, you can't have it," returned the voice. "I've got possession and I'm going to keep it."

Someone called to Swift, "Stand clear of him," and Sam, realizing, perhaps, that his friends were in danger, gave up his reckless design. "I'll come back tomorrow by daylight," he said. "I'll get the mill, damn you!"

He called to his companions, "Come on, boys." His back was to the mill now. Some one fired.

Smith cried, "Oh! I'm hit." Sam sprang toward him.

A voice within the mill yelled, "Give it to the sons of bitches." Several rifles cracked.

Brannan staggered a few steps forward and fell. His companions bent and raised him. "My God! He's all bloody," said Garrett. They picked him up, calling for help. Men came running from the hotel and adjacent buildings.

"It's Mr. Brannan. He's been killed," the cry went up. He was carried to his room in the hotel. Dr. Stillwagon came in haste and worked over Sam, removing his blood-soaked garments. He was still unconscious though he breathed.

"Is he going to die?" asked Swift. His own wound was superficial. He had forgotten it in his anxiety for Sam.

"I can't tell yet," answered the physician. "He's got a ball in the neck between the trachea and esophagus. That was a narrow squeak—just missed the jugular vein. . . . And he's got wounds in his arms and legs. Better telegraph Alexander Badlam. . . ."

Sam was conscious now. He was feeling for something. "Ouch!" he cried.

"What is it, Mr. Brannan?"

"My watch," said Sam, his voice barely audible. "Look in my clothes. I guess I lost it when I fell. Send someone to find it. I——" He lapsed into delirious mutterings.

Dr. Stillwagon gave him an injection of morphine. "Have to stop that sort of thing," he said grimly.

Alex and Dr. Rowell came up from the city next morning. Sam was conscious and wanted to talk, but Dr. Rowell quieted him firmly. "You've had a narrow escape," he said. "You've got to keep very quiet, Sam."

"I want a drink——"

"You can't have it," returned Dr. Rowell. Sam didn't press the point. He was too weak to argue. Later in the day he asked Alex if he had told Lisa. The latter nodded.

"I don't want her to come here," whispered Sam.

"She won't," Alex told him.

Sam stared at him an instant; then he closed his eyes. Dr. Rowell took Alex by the arm. They left the room.

"That was a funny look he gave me," Alex thought. He accompanied the physician to the dining room. The latter ordered wine. He made a good meal, but Alex wasn't hungry. "Damn it!" he thought. "She knows. And he knows she does."

He had informed Sam's wife of the shooting as soon as the telegram came. He had gone at once to her house and waited in the parlor till she came down. He said, "Uncle Sam's been shot. He's hurt badly."

And she had replied, with a flutter of hands like a bird that is frightened, "Will he die?"

"I don't think so, ma'am," Alex told her.

Suddenly, in order to cover her excitement, her alarm, or whatever it was, she spoke with a kind of forced anger. "Another saloon brawl? Or was it——" She had not finished the sentence. She cut it off sharply in the middle, flushing deeply and turning away.

Alex explained what he knew of the shooting; he had spoken reproachfully, rebukingly even. But she didn't let him finish. "It wouldn't have happened unless he'd been drunk," she said passionately. Alex made no answer to that; he knew it was true.

But it didn't justify her words, her attitude. She was his wife. . . .
"We're taking the first stage in the morning—Dr. Rowell
and I. Do you wish to go with us?"

"No," she said. "Sam doesn't need me. . . . I won't do him
any good."

"Good night, then," Alex answered and went out. Her last
words worried him. What had she meant? Sam would have to be
careful.

Sam's assailants gave themselves up to a friendly justice of
the peace and were released on their own recognizance. Snyder,
though a violent-tempered man, was not an evil one. He had
friends in Calistoga. But the local and San Francisco papers
raised a hue and cry.

> It is currently believed [declared the *Alta*] that this at-
> tempt at murder was the result of a long-prepared plan
> rather than an outburst of passion.
>
> The same spirit of envious hostility against intelli-
> gent enterprise murdered the late Osborn at Oak Knoll
> and in its lawless malignity destroyed 1,000 head of
> French and Spanish merino sheep which were driven in
> the night over a high precipice at the upper end of
> Napa Valley because they roiled the source of a stream
> which afforded water to parties below.
>
> Feeling in Napa Valley against such high-handed
> outrages is outspoken and decided and the outcome of
> the trial is awaited with great interest.

Sam, of all concerned, was the least excited by the shooting.
He had little to say of his assailants. They were rearrested and
held in default of $5,000 bail until the trial took place in St.
Helena on April 25. By that time Sam was able to attend. He
proved anything but a vindictive witness. He admitted that he
was drunk and had been warned to keep off the property held
by Snyder. He made so lamentable a witness for the prosecution
that the county attorney was disgusted. The case was dismissed.

"You might have sent them to prison," scolded Alex. "They
shot you in the back. They tried to kill you. *What's the matter
with you, Uncle Sam?*"

"The matter was Theo Larbig," Brannan answered. "I couldn't send that kid to jail."

He remained for a time in Calistoga. His wounds healed quickly. But some of his daring and his high good humor were gone. He was often depressed and allowed himself to be solaced too openly for Badlam's comfort.

"For God's sake, Uncle Sam, be careful. Watch yourself. . . . I think she knows."

Sam always promised, but he didn't keep his word. The rumor of his liaison became a byword. More of his friends grew cool in their manner toward him. Lisa's friends ignored him openly.

"To hell with them!" he said. He said that of many things and many people nowadays. He drank more, became more aloof. He had quarrels with Lisa. She demanded more and more money and Sam had less and less. He had to cut her allowance. The first time she said nothing. But the second time she accused him of adultery.

"If I divorce you I can get my rights," she lashed at him. "I'll make this town too hot to hold you and your——"

Sam took her by the shoulders, shook her into momentary silence. "Hush! For God's sake, Lisa!"

"Hush?" she cried hysterically. "For what? The children know it. And the servants. Everybody knows it."

"It's not true. . . . You can't prove anything."

"Oh, can't I? You just wait. . . . Tom Madison, the janitor——" She paused, a little frightened by his look.

"Tom's tcld you nothing."

"Well, I'll drag him into court. I'll *make* him tell——"

Sam raised his hand. He was upon the point of striking her. But he took a long breath instead. "Listen to me," he said. "You can have your divorce. You can get it on grounds of intemperance. I'll give you half my property. . . . But if you bring a woman's name into it—so help me God, I'll kill you!"

He gave her no chance to reply. He strode out of the room. Never again did he enter her house.

It was not many days after that—less than a week—when Alex handed him a folded paper. On the cover was written

"Ann Lisa Brannan *vs.* Samuel Brannan. Divorce." He opened
it and read with frantic haste:

> WHEREAS, The said defendant, Samuel Brannan, is ad-
> dicted to open and notorious intemperance and has be-
> come, by reason of this, unstable, unreliable and unfit to
> perform the duties of . . .

Sam tossed the summons back to Alex with a gusty laugh
of relief.

"To hell with her!"

He stalked out of the office. But a moment later he returned.
"Alex," he said, "see the papers tonight. Give each of them a big
advertisement for Calistoga."

San Francisco newspapers printed guarded stories of the
divorce action. None of them wished to offend Sam Brannan. He
was still a power and a heavy advertiser. Even the *Morning Call,*
which dealt in sensational news, contented itself with the comment that Mr. and Mrs. Brannan had spent little time together
in recent years. There would be no contest. It was rumored that
a property division had been arranged out of court.

Sam found sanctuary at the springs. Tom Davidson, as usual,
helped him pack. Sam disliked personal servants; he had never
employed a valet. But he liked old Tom, who had many a time
undressed him at night and brought in his breakfast next morning. Tom knew most of his employer's secrets and often spoke
his mind. That day, as he was leaving, Sam pressed a hundred-
dollar note into his hand.

"Thank ye, sir," said Tom. "Ye don't have to give me money."

"That's for what you didn't take—from others, Tom."

The old man winked at him. "God bless ye, Mr. Brannan,
sir. *Be careful.*"

"I will," said Tom. "To hell with women."

He had had a narrow escape. He kept his promise for a
while.

Lisa's lawyers called on him when he returned to San Francisco. They wanted to know about property settlements. Sam
had been prepared to act generously but he was astonished by
their demands.

"They're crazy," protested Alex. "It would cripple you, Uncle Sam."

There were many conferences. At last Sam and Lisa met in her lawyers' office to attempt a compromise. Sam pleaded with her. "Give me time," he said, "I'll treat you right. It's a critical period, Lisa. If my credit's impaired there'll be trouble——"

She would not listen. "You've brought it on yourself, Sam Brannan. . . . I've my children to look after."

"Suppose I refuse?" he asked.

She looked hard at him. "You know what happens then."

He took a step toward her. "It's blackmail," he said furiously.

"Don't dare to lay a hand on me. . . . I'll scream. . . . I— you'll be sorry."

He turned his back on her.

"Give her what she asks," he said to Badlam. "I can get more money."

Even so, it required much wrangling. Judge Morrison of the fourth district court in San Francisco granted Lisa a divorce November 11, 1870. He appointed Andrew J. Bryant and O. P. Sutton referees in the division of property. Their hopeless disagreement necessitated the appointment of a third referee: Abraham Seligman.

Not until the following year was a final order for the distribution of property filed. It exempted, after some dispute, 45,000 gallons of Calistoga brandy stored in New York, valued at $2.50 per gallon, or a total of $112,500. According to rumor Lisa's fear that money from such a source would not be "respectable" influenced her consent to the exemption. Sam grinned when he heard it. "Something to be said for sin, at any rate," he chuckled.

The property awarded Lisa Brannan included Armory Hall at the northeastern corner of Montgomery and Sacramento Streets, eight city blocks in the tract known as Horner's Addition, not far from Mission Dolores, fifteen lots in another section of this subdivision, two hundred shares of the original stock of the Central Pacific Railroad, 315 shares of stock in the Masonic Hall Association, 1,310 shares of stock in the Pacific Bank of San Francisco. Nor did the court order overlook such minute

items as Sam's half interest in a promissory note for $5,000 made
five years earlier on which Richard Chenery was still paying
interest at the rate of one and one half per cent a month.

In the township of Hot Springs, Napa County, Lisa was
awarded several large tracts the boundaries of which were
described in part as follows:

> Beginning at a corner on the right bank of Napa River,
> which corner is an oak, six inches in diameter from
> which an ash ten inches in diameter bears S. 38 E. 37
> links distant, thence S. 34½ West 18 chains 71 links to
> a stake G. 3 from which an oak 18 inches in diameter
> bears S. 62½ E. 8 links distant, thence South 55½ E. 12
> chains, 25 links to a stake in the middle of ditch, thence
> along the middle of ditch aforesaid N. 34½ E. 15 chains,
> 71 links to Napa River, thence continuing the same
> course to the fence near the mountains, thence along
> said fence N. 35¼ W. to the corner of the field, thence
> S. 45 W. 4 chains, 83 links to an oak 12 inches in diam-
> eter, marked with two notches on each side, thence
> S. 72 West 6 chains 28 links, thence N. 64 W. 3 chains
> 75 links to a stake from which an oak 15 inches in
> diameter bears North 69¼ E. 12½ links distant thence
> South 34½ W. 13 chains to the place of beginning.

Some of the property was encumbered. In the case of Armory Hall, Lisa was ordered by the court to release Sam from
the mortgage. On other property the obligation remained his.
But it was a fine haul for Lisa Brannan. She and her friends
said it served Sam right. Alex was furious.

"You've given her about half a million," he accused. "That
Pacific Bank stock alone was worth a hundred and fifty thousand dollars."

"To hell with it," said Sam.

. *15* .

Declining Fortunes

Alex had warned his uncle that unconditional financial surrender
to Lisa would cripple him. It was a warning to which Sam paid
little heed at the time. But in the months following his divorce
he realized, reluctantly, its truth. He was free of the drain of
his wife's heavy household expenses. But his securities were
sadly diminished—a fact his creditors were not slow to learn.
They pressed him ruthlessly, forcing sacrificial sales or fresh
loans at high interest. Much of the Calistoga property was
deeply involved.

Sam had seldom counted the cost. He had always said, "I
can get more money," and made good his boast. But he was not
the old Sam Brannan any more. Unbridled habits, Andy Snyder's
bullets and the practiced greeds of Lisa had combined to lower
his morale—his luck, he called it.

In San Francisco people said that the drink had got Sam
Brannan. He was fifty-odd and looked older, though he still
walked erect as ever and the old flash of indomitable purpose
was in his eyes. He had loyal retainers in Calistoga, and there
he stayed most of the time. Calistoga was his town. He had made
it and he loved it as he once had loved San Francisco. But in

the city people were forgetting Sam Brannan—all that he stood for, all he had wrought. Younger folk were at the helm. And Sam was no longer a millionaire. There were many others now richer and more important than he.

Lisa still lived in the big house on Clay Street hill. There was a cable railroad now that carried passengers over horsecar-defying grades. But Lisa was trying to sell, so Sam heard. He saw her sometimes during his visits to town—out driving in her carriage with the girls. Fanny had married young Schuyler. They were mentioned now and then in the social columns of the San Francisco papers.

Sam never saw the girls, but Sam Junior sometimes came to Calistoga—usually in quest of a "loan." Sam's affection for his son was tinged with a mild contempt. He feared that Sammy, as he still called him to the young fellow's embarrassment, had inherited the worst qualities of both parties. He dressed meticulously—"as if he'd just stepped out of a bandbox," Sam phrased it—and he had fine manners. People liked him but not many trusted him. "He's not good enough for a saint nor bad enough for a devil," Sam complained.

Sam stayed at the hotel. Of a morning he was usually sober. He attended to business. About mid-afternoon he started to drink. People who watched him walking down Calistoga's main street with its half dozen saloons smiled at each other. Some of them shook their heads. They knew he would go from one drinking place to another. He would order champagne and take off his hat when he drank it. That was one of his rites; what it signified nobody knew, and no one dared ask him, for Sam was quarrelsome about personal affairs. He would keep on drinking till his speech was thick and his legs unsteady. Then, usually, he would go to his room and to bed. Occasionally he had to be taken there. He grew careless of his attire; he was sometimes an unpleasant sight.

But always, wherever he went, Sam made himself felt. He did unexpected things. There were all sorts of tales about him. When "Doc" Lilley, veteran foreman of his ranch, died Sam ordered all hands to wash up and attend the funeral. He marched them, like an officer at the head of his company, to the church, where they stood silent and attentive through the service. Among them, his head bowed, his "plug" hat against his chest, stood Sam. Later he assembled them once more in military formation. They marched ahead of the hearse through the main street of Calistoga and over a bridge on the outskirts of town. There Sam barked an order and the men separated, allowing the hearse to pass between them. Bareheaded they watched it round a bend and pass from sight.

Sam marched his workers back to town and bought them each a drink. "Get back to work, boys," he said laconically.

Jeff Thatcher, the lad who had found and restored Sam's watch the night of the shooting, thought Sam had forgotten the service. He hadn't even thanked young Jeff. But a month or more after his recovery Sam sent for the boy. He looked Jeff over carefully. "Your clothes are pretty shabby, Jeff," he said.

The boy reddened. "They're all I've got, Mr. Brannan."

"Well, I'm going to buy you a new outfit," Sam told him, "from the skin out." He led the astonished Jeff to the town's leading clothier. "What size undershirt do you wear?"

"I—don't know," the boy stammered.

"Why don't you?" asked Sam looking stern.

"I don't wear any undershirt, sir."

Sam laughed and laughed. "It's not too late to learn." He bought Jeff three suits of underwear, a dozen pairs of socks, six shirts. "The best in the house," he kept saying. He bought Jeff a new suit of clothes, a hat, three neckties and a pair of shoes.

"Now you can go out and spark the girls."

He brushed aside Jeff's inarticulate but fervent thanks with a gruff "That's all right." He pulled from his pocket the watch Jeff had brought back to him covered with blood and dirt. It was bright and clean now. Sam gazed at it fondly. "I wouldn't have lost it for a thousand dollars," he mused. "You thought I'd forgot what you did for me, didn't you, lad?"

"N-no, sir," answered Jeff politely.

"You're a liar. Now get out of here. . . . And remember: Sam Brannan never forgets a favor."

On New Year's Eve he strode into the church, where a watch meeting was being held, close to midnight. He was drunk. He could scarcely walk. The preacher paused apprehensively in the midst of a prayer. Everybody turned and stared. They didn't know what Sam might do. He was like a potential bull in a china shop.

Sam paused a moment as if trying to collect his wits. Then he took off his hat and sat down. The prayer was resumed; the services continued. Sam sat very still—somnolently or reverently, they could not tell. But with the ringing of bells and other sounds which announced the old year's passing, Sam got to his feet and went about shaking hands. His breath smelled of liquor but his legs were steadier now, his manner affably decorous. He beckoned two boys to his side and asked if they could find a big market basket. "Y-yes, sir," they answered half fearfully.

"Take this, then," he gave them a gold piece. "Buy all the oranges and candy in town and bring 'em here."

When they returned, staggering under their load, Sam distributed the purchases. When the final orange, the last piece of candy, had been handed out, he bade them good-by.

"God bless you all! A happy new year!" he called from the doorway.

He devoted many hours to planning the hotel gardens. From the world's far places came rare flowers, plants, exotic shrubs. He planted many of them himself. He was happy and morose by turns.

The hotel no longer paid. Sam turned it over to Joe Tichenor, who made a roadhouse out of it. Parties came from San Francisco and other places to hold high carnival. Sometimes Sam joined them; he was always welcome because he bought champagne for everybody. But more often he went to bed. Sometimes he complained that they kept him awake.

His first act in the morning was to read the San Francisco papers. They were a day old when they reached him, but it didn't matter. Propped up in bed he scanned the real-estate news and the movements of stocks. The "homesteading movement" goaded him, sometimes to a kind of grim fury. Every available foot of San Francisco was being laid out in allotments. The buying fervor was tremendous and the prices paid for small parcels of land—such as the Horner's Addition lots he had deeded to Lisa—was unprecedented.

It was just as he had expected. That was why he had pleaded for time with Lisa, tried to hold his residential property for the coming rise. He hoped, charitably enough, that Lisa would take advantage of the boom. It mightn't last long. Rumors came to him of her speculations in Nevada Mining stock. Sam distrusted that—as an investment. The big bugs had made their pile and the mines were petering out. Sam hoped, for the children's sake, that Lisa wouldn't lose, senselessly, all he had worked for and given her at so grave a sacrifice.

Sam was interested in the Citizens' Independent Party. He attended some of their meetings, made speeches for them. They were progressives and reformers, and the time was once more ripe for reform, Sam thought. But he was genuinely surprised when he received the new party's nomination for senator. A special committee notified him. Fortunately he was sober. They took Sam with them to the old district-court room where the convention was being held. The delegates rose and cheered as Sam entered. There were only half a hundred of them, but they made quite a noise. Sam had beaten William Piper on the second ballot. "Speech! Speech!" they yelled.

It warmed Sam's heart more than liquor, that reception. It was like old times. He made them a speech that rang—through the town and the state. Let the city own its gas works and waterworks, said Sam. The people were paying too much to monopolies. Socialist! the other parties shouted.

Sam raised another issue: Keep out the Chinese. Coolie labor! Robbing American workmen! The masses cocked up their ears at that. . . . If the Chinese were not kept out by ballots the people would have to use bayonets soon, Sam stormed to cheering crowds. Dennis Kearny, a teamster who had been a sailor and wanted to be a labor-leader, appropriated Sam's slogan and rose to fame on its wings.

San Francisco wasn't ready for reform. Sam worked hard for

his party and Alex gave him support. Alex, now a member of the board of supervisors, was running for office himself. He promised, if elected, to make the big corporations pay thousands in taxes instead of the hundreds they paid now. He won his election, but Sam lost. He was on the wrong ticket, people said regretfully.

C. H. Swift, who was wounded with Sam in the siege of Snyder's mill, bought some of the latter's land near the springs. O. P. Coleman bought another piece. Sam was glad to get the money. When the Calistoga Real Estate Company made him an offer for 2,282 acres he accepted it with a kind of grim resignation. He made many small sales to newcomers for whatever he could get. Judge Palmer drew three hundred deeds for Sam within a year and received three dollars each for them. It amounted to more than his salary.

Bit by bit Sam's properties dwindled away. He still had a few rents from his San Francisco buildings; a few stocks paid him irregular dividends. What remained of his property in Napa County was heavily encumbered.

Alex was deep in politics. Sam's affairs no longer required much of his time. He attended to them in his leisure hours.

Sam seldom went to San Francisco any more. People no longer recognized him. He looked like a tramp, his friends said. Sometimes he felt like one. One day he sought out Johnny the barber. Johnny shook his head. "The way you let yourself go, Mr. Brannan! It's too bad!"

"Fix me up, Johnny," Sam pleaded. "Make me look like I used to."

Johnny worked on him for hours. He had Sam's clothes cleaned and pressed. He shaved and trimmed and shampooed and polished till the transformation was complete. Sam looked in a mirror. He laughed his old laugh. "By God! It's a miracle, Johnny. I look different. I feel different. I'm going up to Odd Fellows' Hall."

He gave the barber a gold piece he could ill afford and went forth to meet the boys. "Why, Sam!" they exclaimed and shook his hand. "You look *fine*."

"I feel fine. . . . Let's have a little drink."

"How long has it been since you came to San Francisco, Sam?" asked one of his older friends.

"It'll be thirty years the end of July."

When Sam had gone there was talk about him. "He looks like himself again. Perhaps he's behaving——"

"Too late now . . . He'll never reform," said another.

"Thirty years since he brought the old *Brooklyn* into Yerba Buena! Let's make an anniversary of it. He's done more for this town than anyone else. . . . Let's give him a banquet."

So they gave Sam a banquet. The Musical Fund Society and the California Pioneers arranged it. Professor Spadini composed a special march for the occasion: "The Sam Brannan March." San Francisco's best orchestra played it. The old guard, to a man, turned out to do him honor. The mayor and others told of Sam's accomplishments, the fervor of their praises growing with each round of drinks. Sam Brannan had brought law and progress to the city. There was scarcely an important development for the public good that Sam hadn't boosted or started. At one time in San Francisco's history it was only necessary to call on him to assure support of any worthy enterprise.

"Here's to good ol' Sam! Hip! Hip! Hooray!"

Sam listened proudly and a trifle grimly. He wished he had some of the money he'd scattered so lavishly in olden days. He thought of his Mexican bonds in a safe deposit box. They had a par value of a million and a half—and he was on the verge of bankruptcy.

They gave him three cheers and a tiger as he rose smiling, bowing. What? They wanted him to make a speech. All right. By God, he'd do it!

Thirty years ago he'd sailed into the harbor. What did it look like then? Like the devil, beggin' their pardon. He remembered it well: a long beach pimpled with sand dunes; scrub oaks here and there; hides drying in the sun and cattle bones between them; donkeys with loads of wood as big as themselves strapped to their backs staggering along; a dozen rickety shanties that looked as though the wind would blow them over, and

Indians sprawled close to the water, the waves lapping their feet. "That's what I found," said Sam, "when I brought almost three hundred men and women from the States. I drilled them to fight with Mexico, but they beat their swords into plowshares." He was proud of 'em by God! said Sam. And proud of San Francisco. . . . "Here's to the good ol' town!"

He hoped all would "die in good health and live to a green old age."

The following day he lunched with Alex. He looked somewhat disheveled. "I had a grand time, Alex, boy. Did I make a big fool of myself?"

"No, no, Uncle Sam. You were all right. Your speech was elegant."

Sam grimaced. "Alex, I'm goin' to turn what's left of Calistoga over to the Sacramento Savings Bank. I want you to sell all my property here. How much'll that leave me—when I've paid my pressing debts?"

"About a thousand dollars," Badlam said regretfully.

"That was what I figured. Well, let's clean her up. I'm goin' to Mexico."

"Mexico, Uncle Sam! What for?"

"To market my bonds. I'm goin' to make a new start, Alex."

In the spring of 1877 Sam said farewell to Calistoga. The townsfolk saw him standing on top of Mount Lincoln early in the morning.

Below and all around spread the acres he had developed from wilderness into growing, productive farms. The slopes that reached toward Mount St. Helena were green with orderly vineyards grown from cuttings he had searched out oversea and brought there from a dozen countries. The landscape was dotted with houses he had built or financed and in which hundreds of families were now cooking their morning meals. He could see the smoke from their chimneys rise straight and dark in the windless welkin, forming a pattern turbulent and fantastic— like the pattern of his life. At the foot of Mount Lincoln the geysers spouted their white plumes. And the ornate gardens of the rambling, ivy-covered hotel gave their fragrance to the spring atmosphere.

Sam loved it all. But he was saying good-by. He had turned over what was left of his lands to the Sacramento Savings Bank. He had cleaned his slate so far as he was able.

He stood for a long time on his hill, staring down at the tomb wherein lay the bodies of his aged, drunken father and his innocent infant son. So much of him and his had come to Calistoga! So little of it had flowered. He had lost a great deal of money and almost his life. The dream was finished.

A new dream filled his heart now: Mexico! If he could exchange his bonds for land he might colonize that vast, fertile country. Its uncharted, fallow stretches, watered by great rivers, might be made into a paradise for American homesteaders. *There* was a prospect to live for. A gateway to redemption and fresh fortune.

Sam descended from his height and paused at a kiosk supported by pillars of petrified wood. It was there the "Soup Spring" flowed. He noted, disapprovingly, that there were no crackers beside the bubbling bowl. He must speak to Tichenor about that.

He took a long drink of the water and made a face after it. Then he returned to the hotel.

"Put my bags on the train when it comes," he said to the porter and gave him a silver dollar. That was a comedown for Sam, but he couldn't afford to tip gold pieces any more.

Presently the train rolled in and Sam climbed aboard. He shook hands with a few bystanders. The train started. Sam kept his eyes ahead, suppressing a desire to turn for a last look at his vanishing empire—his no longer. He stared at the countryside. Eight years ago he had owned most of the green meadows on both sides of the track. Eight years ago he had been a king. Now he was a refugee.

But there were other things ahead. Mexico—the biggest dream of all! Forward, Samuel Brannan! Life's not finished yet.

. 16 .

The Mexican Bubble

Sam Brannan did not go direct to Mexico. He made an intermediate trip to Monterey, California's first capital, where life was little changed from the old days of Spanish rule, where men and customs were much as they used to be before the gringos came.

In Monterey dwelt Manuel Castro, aging but still shrewd and active. He had engineered the overthrow of Governor Micheltorena in 1844 and defied the American invaders under Captain Burrows with a troop of Californian *caballeros* two years later. He had driven Fremont from Gavilan Peak and in the late '50's had aided Peter Sherraback in his abortive claim to a large portion of San Francisco.

Sam knew his history well. In California Castro was little better than the relic of a past regime, but he had connections in Mexico City, where Sam needed an ambassador. So Samuel Brannan and Manuel Castro, impoverished soldiers of fortune, drank together in the *cantinas* and discussed the future. Castro wrote to relatives and friends in Mexico. Presently he followed his letters.

Sam went to New York. There, in a safe deposit box, were

the bonds bought of Juárez' agent thirteen years before. Juárez was dead now, but his government carried on. Sam took his bonds to the Mexican consulate. . . . He met Don Manuel Piniche, late senator from Yucatán in the Mexican Congress. They, too, drank and counseled together.

Alex had not sold his uncle out completely. He realized more clearly than Sam how long and arduous a task the awakening of a government's memory of past favors might be. What remained of Sam's income, carefully nursed by Alex, was sufficient to pay Sam's hotel bills and nominal expenses. No more champagne drinking; not even much whisky—but enough to keep up a front while the claim was being pressed.

Poor Uncle Sam! He'd had a lot of tough luck lately. Alex was not a moralist; he didn't hold with Lisa that it served Sam right. He thought his uncle was a grand old party. Even if he got nowhere with the Mexican scheme it wouldn't do to let him starve. He sent Sam a check each month with a statement of rents collected which was kinder than the truth. Sam's letters were enthusiastic. Castro was pulling wires. He had friends in President Gonzales' cabinet. Pressure was being exerted. Results were certain in the end.

The grant would have to be made through Castro with the understanding that he turn it over to Sam. Alex didn't like that, for he had no confidence in Castro; but he had learned enough of Latin ways to understand the exigencies of political indirection. Sam was in Mexico now. He would look out for himself.

Now and then Tom Davidson, Johnny the barber, or some other old retainer asked Alex about "the boss." "God bless him!" they'd say. "He's a prince. I hope he comes back with a million."

Otherwise the town had pretty well forgotten Sam. On November 4, 1879, the Sacramento *Union* printed a story about him which the San Francisco papers ignored:

Sam Brannan is in New York negotiating with the Mexican Government through their minister for $1,500,000 worth of land in Sonora. Because this land is supposed to include rich mines the grant has been delayed but all is reported going favorably, and when the deal is completed. Brannan will return to San Francisco and place himself at the head of an enterprise for the development of the huge land project.

More than a year went by before further news of Brannan reached the public. Again it was the Sacramento paper that printed it. The story, dated Mexico City, January 18, 1881, read as follows:

General Manuel Castro who commanded the native Californians against the "Gringos" in 1846 is with Sam Brannan in Mexico City negotiating for lands in Sonora. Brannan declares that his claims are allowed and that former reports of their refusal are false. He is waiting for a grant that will be made to Castro with a proviso that he turn it over to Brannan in redemption of the latter's aid against Maximilian when Juárez's agent came to peddle worthless, deflated Mexican bonds and get arms and financial backing in the war against France. Everyone except Brannan laughed at him. But Brannan bought many bonds, paid and arranged for arms shipments and equipped a company of frontiersmen to fight against Maximilian at a cost of $30,000.

In the same newspaper, though the significance was noted by few, was an item reporting an Indian rebellion. Men and women had been killed, it was admitted, and federal troops had been unsuccessful in forays against the Yaquis.

Alex was one of those who noticed the second item and put two and two together. He wondered whether his uncle was being used as a cat's-paw. If the Mexicans gave him lands which the Indians controlled, might they not hope for American aid in subduing aborigines who had defied them? And might not Sam lose his scalp to bring it about?

The next news came from San Diego, where George Ripley, a broker, received a telegram from Sam, February 16, 1882. It read:

MY GRANT FOR COLONIZATION IS CONFIRMED FOR 1,000
FAMILIES. IT CONSISTS OF 1,500 LEAGUES IN SONORA, IN-
DEPENDENT OF MY OTHER CLAIMS.

The San Diego *Union* which printed Sam's telegram, added the
following item:

Manuel Castro, late of California, has been appointed
to a position in the Mexican Army. He will command
in Sonora where he and Brannan's agent, J. B. Methies,
will proceed.

So they were going to provide military protection for Sam's enterprise, mused Alex. Well, it was at least a gesture.

In April the papers were full of Sam Brannan and his plans.
Ripley had gone to New York to meet Sam after his return from
Mexico. The Sonora colony had tendered him a banquet. Sam
and his Mexican advocate, Don Piniche, had received an ovation.
Eastern financiers were interested in the scheme to colonize
Sonora.

Sam was in his glory. He heard himself eulogized as "the
friend of Mexico and the pioneer of colonization." He had helped
the oppressed people of Mexico in their darkest hour, and that
country had honorably recognized the debt by a valuable
concession.

Fervently Sam responded. The greatest dream of his ambitious life showed in his eyes, his words, his gestures. He would
create a new world in Sonora—a world of small farms, happy
homes, in a vast, fertile valley watered by great streams. The
Indians were friendly. If Americans would follow he would lead
them to a poor man's paradise, a "promised land."

He sat down amid loud applause. Don Piniche followed.
Mexico, he said, esteemed the Señor Brannan. Mexico did not
forget her friends. She wished to cultivate, in spite of past mis-
understandings, the friendship and co-operation of Americanos.

The Honorable Dwight Townsend, portly and swaying,
proposed a toast to the United States, "whose friendly arms will
clasp her sister in their close embrace and lead her on to
Fortune."

"That's the stuff!" cried Sam. He was having champagne tonight. He was extraordinarily happy.

Issues grew slightly confused toward the close of the banquet. E. C. Kemble, now agent of the Associated Press, rose unsteadily to a toast: "The electric telegraph which makes all nations neighbors." He paid little attention to his subject. He had sailed with Sam in 1846 on the *Brooklyn* and had helped to edit the *California Star*. He had known Sam for thirty-five years as a pioneer of peaceful settlement and civilization. There would be no filibustering in Sonora. Sam's energy and will would bring success. . . . He talked on and on. A snore at last interrupted him rudely. The guest of honor was asleep.

By the end of May, Sam was back in San Francisco. He was more like the blustery, self-confident protagonist of great affairs than he had been since the '60's, thought Alex. But, studying his uncle more closely, he noted that drink and the defeats of recent years had taken their inevitable toll. There were pouches under Sam's eyes, an almost imperceptible tremor in his dramatically gesturing hands, an occasional quaver in his still-ringing, ever-persuasive voice. And he dealt in too many superlatives—as if he were afraid you wouldn't believe him.

But he talked to newspapermen boldly. They flocked to his hotel. A newspaper had referred to him as "Colonel" Brannan. Whence came the title? they asked, half tauntingly. These young men were not the ones who used to hang on Sam's words. They were of a new generation whose members had no respect for tradition or vanished glories.

Nevertheless, they departed impressed. Sam still had a way with men. He laughed about the title. That was Mexican courtesy. South of the Rio Grande you were either a peon or a personage. So they'd dubbed him "coronel," which was Spanish for *colonel*. It didn't mean a thing in San Francisco. Here, among the boys, he was *Sam*. And he wanted a drink. Would they join him? He could talk better over a glass.

"Well, then, here it is, boys," he said. "The Mexicans are a fine people. They never forget——"

"Like the elephant, eh, Sam?" asked one of the newsmen.

"Like the Indian," corrected Sam. "It's a great Indian empire, is Mexico. . . . And in 1866 it was likely to become a French colony——"

"But you and Juárez stopped all that," the newsman once more interrupted.

"Shut up!" the others shouted.

Sam went on: "I gave 'em a little help, as my young friend has stated. And what did they do? Forget me when they had their country back again? When I was broke and needed help myself? *Not the Mexican government!*" He set down his glass and waved both hands in a sweeping gesture. "Eighty square acres of land they gave me; the great plateau watered by the Yaqui and Mayo rivers. . . . The finest land on God's green footstool, boys; fertile, tillable soil with no mountains between it and the coast. . . ."

"What about the Yaqui Indians?" asked a reporter.

"The most cordial relations have been established with the Yaquis and Mayos. They're good workers. We'll get them to work on our farms. All we have to do is make arrangements with the chiefs."

"When will you open this big tract?" they asked him.

"As soon as it can be surveyed and subdivided. I've sent surveyors out from Tucson and Mexico City; but I need fifteen or twenty more. . . . We'll lay out a central city with small farms around it. I don't want rich men on my project. I want men and women from the Pacific Coast—Washington, Oregon and California—that'll work their own land. Every alternate lot or farm will go free to a settler who'll pay his share of surveying costs. And everything that's left at the end of a year will be sold for the benefit of the community. Every dollar of the proceeds goes into the treasury of Sonora City. How's that for a plan, boys?"

"Wonderful!" said one.

Another snickered. "How will people get there?" asked a third.

"For the present they'll have to stage it from Tucson.

There'll be one trip a week to begin, and more later. But that's nothing. We're goin' to build a railroad, boys, as soon as things get started . . . and that won't be long."

They had another drink. The reporters departed. Sam visited Johnny the barber. "Fix me up fine, Johnny," he said. "I'm goin' to a banquet at the Palace Hotel tonight."

Johnny looked his patron over critically and went to work. "What Mr. Brannan needs," he confided to Alex later, "is a good woman to look after him."

Sam looked quite presentable when he took his seat at the big horseshoe-shaped table in the Palace banquet hall. He had even a flower in his buttonhole. Johnny had put a little dye on his graying hair, slicked his sideburns and goatee with brilliantine.

Once more the old guard turned out to honor Sam Brannan. Once the guests around his table would have spelled the flower and power of San Francisco; now they were the pioneers and ghosts of yesteryear, but not without distinction. Frank Pixley, editor of the *Argonaut,* was there; Frank Soule the writer, Judge Freelon, State Senator Winans, Captain Patten, General Castro, Don Tinocs and the Honorable James G. Eastland. By no means an assemblage to be ignored. Once again Sam heard himself praised as the pioneer of civilization and friend of Mexico. Once again he responded, a bit unsteadily, outlining his hopes and plans.

A few days later he made a talk in Pioneer Hall. It had been widely advertised: SAM BRANNAN'S PARADISE. THE NEW LAND OF OPPORTUNITY. Newspapers had given the project good send-offs. But there was not a big crowd as Sam had expected and as Alex—despite his better judgment—had hoped. Too many people had forgotten Samuel Brannan, California's first millionaire. There was plenty of land for colonization in California. Mexico was a faraway region.

Sam talked forcefully and well. Alex in a rear seat, trying to feel out the popular reaction, had to admit that. But he could no longer rouse a crowd as he used to in the days when they cheered him and milled round him, eager to climb aboard any ship of enterprise that Sam Brannan sailed. Tom Davidson was there with his savings bankbook in his pocket, willing to risk all he had on "the boss's" scheme, and a few others like him. But the majority had little confidence. To most Sam was only a man with a plausible scheme to coax dollars out of their pockets.

"Ain't them Yaquis hostile Injuns?" someone shouted.

"I've seen worse on Market Street," Sam countered. There was a laugh. That heartened him. "The Yaquis are quite friendly," he declared. "They'll help us till the land—the richest land on God's green footstool. . . . And Sam Brannan wouldn't tell you that unless 'twas true."

He had their interest now. They asked more questions, and Sam answered them glibly. But that was as far as it went. The crowd had little money. Times were hard.

"If any of you are engineers," said Sam at last, "I'll give you land to do surveying."

Several men came forward. Sam referred them to Alex. He'd make contracts with them. They could start at once.

Sam was undaunted by the failure of his colonization rally. "They want time to investigate," he told Alex. "I'll advertise all over the country. I'll put the deal through."

"That'll take a lot of money, Uncle Sam."

"Yes, I know, lad." Brannan's voice was tired. "But I'll get it somehow."

He left soon after that. He borrowed the fare to Mexico from Alex. He had friends there, Sam said, who would outfit him. He must get into the field and superintend operations. Perhaps it was too soon to start colonizing. Things hadn't progressed far enough.

Alex did not hear from him directly. But he watched the papers. On July 21, the *Alta* printed news of Sam's recent movements:

A Guaymas dispatch reads: "Sam Brannan was paid $10,000 by the Mexican Customs House and is returning by the steamer *Newburn,* the federal judge having allotted him permission to survey his lands. Owing to a rebellion among the Indians the land is not the same as that originally allotted."

Alex showed it to his friends. That disposed of the Indian problem, he said. Now the work would progress without further interruption. But a later dispatch dashed his hopes:

> A Mexican federal court has refused permission for the survey of a land grant made to Samuel Brannan because of Brannan's failure to comply with the conditions imposed. Brannan and Castro with their engineers have returned to Mexico City to await developments. The grant was made to Manuel Castro by the Governor of Sonora without adequate authority, it seems. But even if the grant were allowed, Brannan's failure to meet the conditions imposed would cause it to revert to the Government. According to *El Fronteriza* at Tucson, the *Constitution* says article 30 of the contract provides that a survey shall at least be begun within three months. Article 22 explains how terms will be suspended in case of unexpected accidents except in measurement of land which may not be delayed beyond the period provided. It is now, since February 22, more than three months past the signing of the contract and nothing has been done on the rivers in regard to surveying the lands and everything is as it was, so the contract is voided. Article 20 voids for failure to commence marking and measuring the limits and bounds of vacant lands within three months.
>
> The governor of the state has notified the Central Government that the Colonizing Company has not commenced marking or bounding the limits of the Yaqui and Mayo rivers and asks authority to void the contract.

Still no letter from Sam. Alex pictured him going from his lodgings to the various bureaus in Mexico City with Castro or Piniche to interpret for him. Sam's Spanish was not good enough to carry on such negotiations. It disturbed Alex. He knew how

aging men, especially foreigners, were shunted from one office
to another, month after month—sometimes year after year, as
poor old Sutter with his claim for stolen lands had been evaded
and ignored in Washington until his death.

Finally a letter came from Sam. It was a hopeful letter.
Negotiations were in progress. There had been some misunderstanding but pretty soon everything would be smoothed out.
Could Alex let him have a small loan? It required money to get
things started. But after that there'd be plenty for all. Alex sent
him a money order.

On August 10 the *Alta* printed another story:

> Sam Brannan's Mexican grant is now dead without hope
> of resurrection. It never had any chance of being opera-
> tive. It covered the valuable land that since time im-
> memorial has been held by the Yaquis and other indus-
> trious but warlike Indians. The Mexicans have wished
> to deprive the Indians of this land and were willing to
> let Americans do the necessary fighting.
>
> Brannan made no effort to survey or subdivide the
> land, which would have required a small army. The
> grant lapsed. The Governor of Sonora reported the fact
> to the Central Government and now President Gon-
> zales has formally abrogated the contract which was
> made with Castro, a Mexican, it being understood that
> he would transfer it to Brannan. It is not probable that
> Brannan will secure another grant in lieu of the lapsed
> one.

So that was the end of it, mused Alex. He had hoped that
Sam would, somehow, triumph over his adversaries. Well, he
could take care of his uncle. Alex was well-to-do. In a year or
two he would quit politics and manage his own investments as
for ten or twelve years he had managed Sam's.

Alex seldom saw his Aunt Lisa or his cousins. Sam Junior
had gone to Arizona. He was interested in copper mines and had
made some money. Lisa Brannan had speculated in Nevada
silver stocks and lost nearly all of hers. They lived in shabby

genteel fashion with much of their old dignity. Lisa had "paying guests." One of the girls, already a widow, lived with her. She made "souvenirs" and sold them to tourists on the beaches Sunday afternoons.

John Ricketson dropped in to see Alex toward the end of autumn. He had a letter from Sam. It was mailed from Comoripa on the Yaqui River and made no mention of the cancellation of his grant. Perhaps Sam hadn't learned of it—in the field where he was, remote from sources of communication. Perhaps he had decided to ignore it. Ricketson didn't know. He had been in Mexico with Sam and was going back again. The damned thing might still go through he said. But Alex shook his head. He read the letter, dated September 28:

> Arrived here from Eglisia and Mullatus. I was in the saddle one month and twenty days. Will go to Guaymas sixth Proximo.
>
> This letter is sent to you by one of our men to the railroad station. I have traveled with only two men and a guide and no weapon on my person. There are worse Indians in San Francisco than in Sonora. I wish you had been with me as a companion. The citizens of Guaymas thought we would never return. I shall forward full details of our exploration from Guaymas.

A few weeks later Alex received a letter from Sam dated Guaymas. He wanted a bottle of perfume and a book about General Sheridan. Alex wondered a little about these requests. His uncle was neither a fop nor a reader. But he had always admired Sheridan. And after two months in the saddle it might be pleasant to read. He sent both.

Ricketson came in again. "I hear they're living above a little *pulqueria*—a candy store—in Guaymas."

"They? Who?" asked Alex.

"Why, Sam and his woman . . . Haven't you heard?"

"His *woman?*"

"Yes, Carmelita Carmen. She's the daughter of a refugee."

"Refugee from what?"

"The Maximilian overthrow—at least her father was. Sam picked her up somewhere. . . . She's about half his age. Good-looking—and devoted."

"You say they're not married?" asked Alex.

"The *parroco*—the priest—in Guaymas won't marry 'em because Sam's a Protestant. But they're going to Tucson one of these days for a wedding, Sam says. He's all right. He'll make an honest woman of her; don't you worry."

Alex laughed. "I wasn't worrying. Where did you learn all this?"

Ricketson, it seems, had learned it from one of Sam's engineers recently returned.

"I'm glad," said Alex after Ricketson had gone. He said it aloud and was surprised by the sound of his own voice.

Poor Uncle Sam! He needed someone to look after him, as Johnny the barber had said. "He's never had a woman in his life worth shooting," thought Alex angrily.

It was not long till he received direct news from Sam. He had married Carmelita Carmen in Tucson. They were keeping house in Guaymas. "She is a good girl," he wrote. "She loves me and takes good care of me. We are poor but happy. . . . I am going back to Mexico City to get more land. Address me in Guaymas as Don Samuel del Brannan."

A second letter followed. Sam was leaving for the "Yakee" River. He would visit the chief in company with the second chief. "I'll be gone six days if I don't lose my scalp," he wrote. "My wife doesn't want me to go because her father was killed by order of an old chief when he visited the Indians to make a treaty. She was a young girl then."

Sam was interested in a thirty-ton sloop "to carry brick from the Yakee River to Guaymas" and in the agency for Wrigley's portable houses, "Numbers 1, 2 and 3 with single and double walls."

"I want a lot of circulars," he wrote. "Also an agency for canned meat, fish and fruit. I shall establish a town on the upper Yakee in December and there will be a large demand for these

things." Another thing Sam desired was "a buggy made in
Benecia with fresh-water tanks under the seats to hold fifteen or
thirty gallons for desert travel."

He was full of business and ambitions. "I'm glad you're
going to quit politics, lad," he wrote. "There's nothing in it
unless you steal."

Alex smiled at that. Who should know it better than an honest man? he thought a shade ruefully.

Sam sent him another letter before leaving Guaymas, dated
August 19, 1882:

Our vessel did not get off yesterday, which gives me an
opportunity of writing a few more lines. I want a first-
class artesian-well borer. There is one here but he is on
the railroad and cannot leave before the road is finished.

I have three ranches of 5, 4 and 3 leagues each.
The R.R. runs through two of them. The five-league
ranch is thirty miles from here. If I can strike water on
it, it is a fortune in itself. Level land, good soil, well
timbered and I can have a station made there if I can
strike water on both sides of the road. There is the best
clay in the state there for making brick.

I want a first-class man and him to have a half
interest in the business and pay his half of the expenses.
Let me know what the tools can be had for and the
cost of pipe.

Ricketson is out of town and very busy. I have to
do my own writing with my lame arm. I shall remove
Vassault from the agency. If you don't want it get me
another man. Ask Vassault to let you have my map of
Guaymas. You take a copy of it. I shall send it to New
York when I return from the River. Send me a copy and
I will make some corrections before it goes.

Send me two weekly *Cronicles* [*sic*] for one year
and send the bill to George Vincent. Tell the *Cronicle*
to make John Ricketson their agent and they will have

no more trouble: the *Bulletin* and *Post* the same.
(Weekly.)

Yours truly,

UNCLE

The letter contained Alex's first intimation of a number of facts. He was unaware that Ricketson had returned to Sam's service. He wondered about the lame arm. Sam's writing was scrawly as if his control of nerves and muscles was impaired. But what astonished Alex most was the apparent fact that Sam had obtained another land grant in Mexico. Truly, he mused, the man was dauntless; nothing could balk him. A short time ago he had been a pauper. Now he had a young wife to love and care for him in his declining years. He owned three great ranches apparently free from Indian claims. He was in new enterprises up to his neck. There was something deathless and inconquerable about Sam Brannan.

More demands were forthcoming: "Send the old letter press (By Wells Fargo); the large picture at the house, in my room (By Wells Fargo)." He was going in for family portraits, Alex thought, smiling. Perhaps that oil painting of himself was for Carmelita. Then he wrote:

Send the following by George Vincent on the steamer:

One ice pitcher (not packed. George will use it coming down) for Mrs. B., the following engraving on the same:

CARMELITA B. DEL BRANNAN,
GUAYMAS, MEX.

Two China silk handkerchiefs.
Three pairs of thick cotton socks for a foot 8½.
Three pairs of   *do.*   *do.*   for Mrs. B., white, thick for Winter. The size of leg the length of string enclosed; the size of foot from knot to the longest end.

Two China umbrellas.

One pair China slippers for Mrs. B., same size.

                                        ($1.00 or $1.50)

One   *do.*   for my foot (8½)

Six shirt Bussums [Alex decided that *bosoms* were indi-
    cated]; two with stand-up collars; two tan down;
    two with no collars.

Ask Mary to send me a pair of red shirt-and-
drawers.

If Hooper has not sent my album, give it to George
Vincent. I can bring them all ashore without permit
from the Custom House. Wrap all the articles separate
and mark contents on the same. Make out bill and price
of the different articles and add fifteen percent premium
for gold. Give it to Vincent and I will pay the money
here when it comes down.

                                        SAMUEL BRANNAN

P.S. Send me three pairs of eye glasses, No. 14 that
cost $1.00 each. A small pocket barometer. Find them
at the pawn shop.

Alex dispatched the articles promptly. He "forgot" to enclose a
bill.

. *17* .

The Final Years

Sam wrote frequently though briefly to Alex during the year
that followed. Ricketson brought at times more definite news.
Sam was aging. His arm gave him trouble. His tongue was thick
—not from drink, though he still imbibed freely—but from a
kind of paralysis which affected one side of his face. He couldn't
ride horseback any more but was trying to direct the development of his lands from Guaymas—without much success.

"He's done everything a man could," said Ricketson sorrow-
fully. "He's *still* doing it, for that matter: offering engineers big
blocks of land if they'll only survey his property. He's willing
practically to *give* the land away to homesteaders . . . and it's
good land too. But he can't get the cursed thing started. It's all
there—the image of a great colony—in the back of his mind.
And his mind's as active as ever . . . but his body's old and sick.
Poor Sam!"

"Do you think we ought to put him in a home of some
kind?" asked Alex.

"Good Heavens, *no!*" cried Ricketson. "You'd murder him.
. . . He'd never go. Besides, he's *got* a home. His wife looks
after him."

"I only want to do what's right," said Alex.

"Let him play his dream out, then. He won't live so many more years."

"John," said Alex disturbedly, "I wonder if this whole Mexican bubble hasn't been a cruel joke on my uncle. Don't you suppose they've used him as a buffer in their war against the Indians? Haven't they handed him gifts on a string and then jerked them away? And laughed up their confounded sleeves?"

"The Mexican government?" asked Ricketson. "No, I think they've tried to play fair with Sam. They hate gringos, but they like him. He's one of their own kind—full of fancies and hopes. . . . Sam started too late, that's all. He drank too much and too hard. Now he's paying the piper." He shook his head. "I'm going to the Odd Fellows. They ought to help Sam. He gave them a block of land for their cemetery and it's worth forty thousand dollars today."

"He did things like that for hundreds," said Alex. "Not many remember it now."

"Well, the Odd Fellows are rich . . . and they're pretty good at remembering. They've got five thousand members now, and lots of them are Sam's old friends. . . . If one of them would bring it up before the lodge, they might do something. . . ."

Adam Willard, United States consul at Guaymas, sat in the patio of his official *casa* one morning in midsummer, sipping a drink and trying to concentrate on a report when a Mexican servant entered.

"The Señor del Brannan," he announced, "desires to speak with your excellence."

"Who in hell is the Señor del Brannan?"

"He is the old *Americano* who resides above the *pulqueria* with a Mexican woman."

"What does he want?"

The peon shrugged his shoulders and spread his hands. "*Quien sabe,* Excellence."

"Send him in."

He finished his glass with a sigh, dismissed the report from his mind and observed presently a strange, shambling figure. The man walked with difficulty and one side of his face seemed distorted. But his eyes were very bright. "Are you the consul?"

"Yes," said Willard.

"I'm Sam Brannan and I'd like to talk with you, sir."

"Sit down, Mr. Brannan. Have a drink?"

Sam eased himself into a chair with difficulty. "No thanks," he said. "It was drink brought me to this." He indicated his affliction with a sidewise glance. "I'm through with it." He spoke with difficulty. He looked shabby and old. But there was a certain dignity about him which impressed the consul.

"What can I do for you?" he asked.

"I'd like you to record a will—my last will and testament."

"You wish me to make it out for you?"

"No, thank you. I've done it myself." He fished in his pocket with its torn lining and presented a folded paper. Willard read the document.

"Hm!" he remarked. "It's a trifle irregular, but I suppose it'll do."

"What's irregular about it?"

"Well, the form for one thing," said the consul with a shade of irritation.

"It tells what I want done with my property, doesn't it?"

"Yes, it does that," Willard admitted.

"Then—you'll sign it and make it official?"

"Yes, I'll sign it and affix the seal," said Willard. "Wait. We'll have to get a couple of witnesses." He called the servant and gave him instructions. After a time he returned with two men. "Do you know Mr. Brannan?" asked Willard.

"Sure, we know old Sam," they chorused.

"Then put your John Hancocks on this will," said Brannan. They did so.

"Have a drink?" asked the consul. They did not decline.

Sam restored the paper to his pocket and departed. He had had great difficulty in writing it with his afflicted hand. He had regained more use of it recently—since he quit drinking. It almost killed him at first, but now he was better for his abstinence. Slowly he mounted the narrow flight of stairs which led to his quarters above a Mexican sweetshop. A woman rose from an old-fashioned rocker and came toward him. She was young, though her blue-black heavy tresses already had touches of gray. She had rather fine eyes, and her figure, though full, was attractive. She led Sam to the rocker, pulled off his boots and brought slippers. Sam's glance lingered on her fondly. "Here is the paper," he gave her the will. "Keep it in a safe place, Carmelita. You'll need it after I'm gone."

"Do not speak of that," she protested. "Already you are much better. You will live to be an old man."

"I am an old man now," he said sadly.

"It is only because you are ill. My father was much older than you. And he was a strong man and active—till they killed him." Her eyes darkened.

Sam put his lame arm awkwardly about her waist and kissed her.

Alex received a copy of the will a month later. Sam asked him to keep it in his safe-deposit box. It was a queer document even for a holographic will:

In the name of God, Amen, I declare all former wills null and void this day.

1.—I bequeath and give to my son, Samuel Brannan, Jr., one dollar and to my eldest daughter, Adelaide, one dollar; and to my third and youngest daughter, Lizzie Brannan, one dollar.

The reason I bequeath so small a sum is that I gave their mother at the time of my divorce from her a large fortune of over half a million dollars and she took charge of the children and alienated them from me and I have learned that she has squandered it away in gambling on mining stocks, which I am sorry to hear.

2.—And I give and bequeath to John Ricketson now residing in New Guaymas, Mexico, one half of all my property in New Guaymas or Point Arena, Mexico, Block 9.

My nephew, the oldest son of my sister, Mary Ann Badlam, now residing in San Francisco, to share and share alike in one half of each of my ten Mexican claims of land and railroad franchises or moneys, Ricketson paying one half of the land cost to me in New Guaymas, Eight hundred ($800) dollars.

They, Ricketson and Badlam, paying all my honest debts and my funeral expenses to be levied on my property in Block 1, New Guaymas, Mexico; they to prosecute all those claims against Mexico not paid.

SAM'L BRANNAN

Witnessed by   *Attested by* A. WILLARD, *U. S. Consul*
JOHN WILSON   *at Guaymas, to whom the signer*
JOHN YOUNG   *personally appeared and was known.*

In the same mail which brought this copy of his uncle's will, Alex received a marked copy of the San Diego *Union*, dated July 4, 1883—less than a week after the filing date of the will. It read:

The Mexican Government has made over to Samuel Brannan 200,000 acres on the Tagin River between the towns of Comeripa and Superaipa on that stream, the lands being principally agricultural.

Alex sighed. It was a Chinese puzzle. He cut out the news article and filed it away with Sam's will.

"Let him play his dreams out. He won't live many more years," Ricketson had said. Yes, that was the best thing to do. He wondered what John had done about getting the Odd Fellows to make Sam an allowance. Nothing, apparently, had happened.

In 1884 Alex had a letter from Sam, the first in many months. It was dated Nogales. Sam had evidently abandoned his plan for colonizing the small concessions near Guaymas to which his

great Mexican grants had dwindled. The 200,000 acres on the
Tagin River had reverted to the government because Sam had
had no means to survey them. But he was still enthusiastic about
Mexico. He wrote that Mexico was a great country. Valuable
land could be bought for a dollar an acre. He declared:

> The best route is by water from San Francisco to Guay-
> mas; thence twenty-three hours by rail. The Mexican
> Government will establish within sixty days a customs-
> free zone which will create a good market for Ameri-
> cans. Rough labor is cheap; only $1.00 or $2.00 a day.
> The Indians are friendly and property or life is as safe
> here as anywhere in the United States.

"Wherever he goes, he smells out opportunities like a
pointer pup," said Ricketson when Alex showed him the letter.
"But he's too old to flush 'em any longer. He's seen a dozen of
his big schemes fail—and yet he's just as eager for the next one."
He shook his head. "I'm going to stir up the Odd Fellows again."
Another brief note came for Alex:

> My hand trembles too much to write. I have ten letters
> to answer. I shall have to go out and get someone in
> the morning to write for me. I will send you a list of
> my property when I return tomorrow night. Must write
> it myself.

Again he requested naïvely:

> Please send me a pair of pants so that I will have a
> change. The Indians have stolen so many of my things
> including surveying instruments which I cannot replace
> and other articles.

It was his only complaint against the Indians.

Now and again fragmentary notes reached Alex from Guaymas. Sam was still dreaming of colonization, planning to settle
his land. There were almost unreadable pencil jottings captioned
"Points of Will." One of the items read:

> My youngest daughter Ann Lizia, one hundred acres
> of land in Sonora, Mexico, of land to be derived from
> Federal Government, to be selected by Alexander Bad-
> lam, Jr.
> All the residue of my property, what or wherever,
> real or personal, to my nephew Alexander Badlam, Jr.,
> now residing in San Francisco; he to loan his sister
> $3,000 without interest from my effects after paying my
> debts and funeral expenses.

Another note, less clear, apparently indicating some bestowal
on his wife, was as follows:

> Five hundred acres of land to be derived from Mexican
> Government in Sonora to be selected by Alexander
> Badlam, Jr., and the $200 due me for reducing the
> mortgage on her house. Her name is Carmelita Carmen
> del Brannan.

It didn't make sense, but Alex thought he understood. Sam
wished his wife to be provided for. Alex grimaced as he read
the note again. He didn't believe the "land to be derived from
the government" was worth a plugged nickel. But he would see
that Carmelita didn't suffer. He wrote to Sam that he would
take care of everything, including other items:

> My body to be buried in Sonora City any time after
> the lapse of one year and my father and son, Don B.,
> now buried in Calistoga in a tomb on Mary Carpenter's
> lot. And tomb to be her private property after their
> removal.

Poor Uncle Sam! thought Alex. The dream was almost played
out.
Venerable figures of the old days who frequented the Bank
Exchange and Yellowstone bars talked of Sam Brannan as a
tradition. He'd been a great fellow. A prince. God rest his soul!

But Sam wasn't dead. Far from it, Ricketson reported after a trip to Guaymas. He was writing a history of California—a few lines at a time because he couldn't always control his hand. He was planning with a lawyer named Doud to present a claim for cash settlement against the Mexican government. He had quit drinking, Ricketson reported. He looked better and his mind was ambitious as ever.

"He's going to southern California—San Diego, I believe."

"Why *southern* California?"

"Sam has an idea there's money in fruit ranching. He's going to raise figs . . . and he thinks there's money in land. He's going to speculate."

"*Speculate!* What with?" asked Alex in amazement.

"God knows. . . . That never bothered Sam," said Ricketson.

Apparently it was true. Sam wrote to Alex. Could he borrow a little money?—a few hundred would be enough. He had a chance to buy a hundred acres in Escondido, near San Diego. He thought he'd feel better there. He was sick of Mexico.

Alex sent him the money. Soon afterward he received a letter on neatly printed stationery:

Office of

SAM BRANNAN

Dealer in Real Estate

He'd decided to begin all over again, Sam wrote, in San Diego, whose harbor was second only to that of San Francisco. He felt certain he could recover health and fortune there. Alex heard from him at lengthening intervals. Finally curiosity got the better of the younger man and he journeyed to southern California. Sam was no longer in north San Diego, where his previous letters were postmarked. He had gone inland to Escondido, where his ranch was located. Sam was promoting the "back country," Alex was told.

Alex hired a horse and rode the thirty-odd miles over rolling hills to a little inland hamlet known as Escondido—Spanish for *hidden*, Alex mused. And well named. Along the winding road, in some places little better than a trail, he observed, at intervals signs which read:

SEE SAM BRANNAN
Homes for Health and Husbandry
Escondido, California

Before the door of a white cubicle, conspicuously emblazoned with a similar announcement, Alex found his uncle. All around, as far as human vision reached, lay the hillocks of San Diego's "hinterland," wooded and virgin. Sam was smoking a pipe.

"Hello, Uncle Sam!" shouted Alex, dismounting.

The man in the chair rose to his feet with an odd, unbalanced alacrity. It was plain that a part of his body was less articulate than the rest. He seemed to Alex at once very old and surprisingly nimble. One of his arms hung limp as if useless; one side of his face was perceptibly drawn. His smile was a trifle distorted, but none the less hearty; his eyes held their old, imperishable gleam.

"By God Almighty!" he exclaimed. It was the same voice, thought Alex; the voice that used to ring over the town and sway thousands. "By God Almighty! It's *Alex.*"

The grip of his good arm was strong Alex noticed. "Yes, it's I—come to see you, uncle."

"Well, you young —— —— ——," cried Sam with profane affection. "So you've quit politics and gone into business! Well, so have I. Sit down."

They chatted for an hour eagerly. Sam did most of the questioning. He called the roster of his old friends. Were they still in San Francisco? Did they ever speak of him? What were they doing? He laughed and slapped his knee or sighed and shook his head according to the nature of the answers. "Not many of the old crowd left," he said.

"What about yourself? What are *you* doing, Uncle Sam?"

Sam waved an arm toward the hillocks. "All this is new country, Alex, fresh and fertile, good for man or beast. And it'll

grow anything—anything in the world." He laid a hand per-
suasively on his nephew's arm. "Better come down here and
join me, Alex. We'll sell thousands of acres. . . . We'll dot these
hills with farms, like Calistoga."

The old dream! thought Alex compassionately. "And how
are you feeling, uncle?"

"Wonderful," said Sam. "This climate makes you young
again. . . . You should have seen me at Guaymas. I could
scarcely move. It was terrible, Alex. But now I can walk. I can
even use this arm." He raised the dragging member with an
effort. "I can hold a fork with it. I've quit drinking . . . and I eat
good food. The woman at my boarding house is a fine cook. . . .
When I have a misery in the guts she makes me broth and
gruel. . . ."

"But—your wife, Uncle Sam?"

"Carmelita left me down in Guaymas, Alex." Sam spoke with
an effort.

"Oh, I'm sorry."

"Yes; she doesn't like the gringos. She was homesick for her
people in Chihuahua and——"

"Yes, Uncle Sam?"

"She lost patience with me, Alex, when I didn't make the
money I talked so much about."

Sam consulted his watch. "Dinnertime," he said. "You must
be hungry, lad, after the long ride. Did you leave your horse
at the stable?"

"Yes, the livery stable, Uncle Sam."

"We'll walk to my room and wash up; then we'll eat." Once
more he half sprang and half twisted his body out of the chair.
At Alex's side he hobbled along surprisingly fast. Sam pointed
out a green patch on a hillside. "That's my ranch," he said. "A
hundred acres of figs—all young trees and growing like weeds.
I'll sell 'em for a fortune some day."

They traversed the rambling main street for several blocks
and paused before a two-story wooden building. The ground
floor had plants in its show windows and curtains back of them.
"That's the dining room," said Sam. He led Alex up a short stair-

way to his room. It contained a bed, a bureau and a commode with a white porcelain pitcher and bowl. There was little else in the room, few belongings, Alex noted as he washed his hands and face. They went down together and entered the cool, wide dining room with its two long tables set with heavy china, clockwork fly fans and big pewter castors. An ample, maternal-looking woman, dark-skinned and comely, brought them food. It was good food, as Sam had declared. The woman smiled at them and Sam introduced his nephew.

"I guess he was worried about me," Sam told her with a grin. "He came all the way from San Francisco to see how I was."

The woman patted Sam on the shoulder. "Don't worry about your uncle. We'll take care of him," she said.

Alex felt better about Sam when he returned to San Francisco. "He's in good hands," he told John Ricketson. "He seems to be happy. Did you hear about his wife?"

"Yes. I guess all women are alike——"

"Tut! Tut!" protested Alex, who was happily married.

"Well, *Sam's* women, anyhow. I'm going to see the Odd Fellows again. They ought to do something."

At last the Odd Fellows did. The tract of land Sam had given them a quarter of a century ago to bury their dead had become gilt-edge property. The cemetery was a dividend-payer. Out of its income a fund was set aside for Sam. A letter brought him the news. It was delicately worded with no sting of charity about it; it was signed by old friends who wished his age, like theirs, to be secure.

Sam wiped his eyes in secret when he read it. Bread upon the waters! he thought. From all the largess of his castings this was the first to return. But it was, for that very reason, doubly precious. He wrote to Alex not to send him any more money. He had an income now. Doud, the lawyer, was pressing his claim against Mexico for a cash settlement, and Castro was helping. It seemed a long time, but they wrote the chances were good. Of course, he would have to divide with them.

Alex smiled as he read the letter. What would Sam do with a large sum of money if, by some fantasy of fate, he should receive it? Alex had heard of Doud, an "international lawyer" whose reputation was not the best. He dismissed the matter from his mind.

And then, one day, the impossible happened. Word reached him that Sam had been awarded $49,000 in lieu of his land claims. Doud, by some hook or crook—mostly crook, Alex decided—had met with success. Sam wrote, "Alex, get out my books. Find all to whom I owe money. Put it down in black and white. I want to pay my debts, Alex. There'll be plenty for that."

Alex did as he was told. When Sam appeared, dragging one leg a little, his face still screwed up, but marvelously like his old self in fashionable clothing and a shiny top hat, Alex gave him the list to look over: rather a formidable list of debts, large and small. Many of the older ones had, no doubt, been written off or forgotten; but there they were. Sam studied the list carefully, inserting a name and amount here and there in a shaky pencil scrawl as he remembered some informal, unrecorded loan. He added the amounts half a dozen times, correcting errors, before he handed the list back to Alex.

"Pay 'em out of that," he said, tossing a bulging wallet on his nephew's desk. The latter, after counting the contents glanced up disturbedly. "It'll take nearly all you've got, Uncle Sam."

"Doud and Castro got the rest," said Sam. "But never mind. Sam Brannan pays his debts."

He had been drinking a little, Alex noticed, but he was sober enough to know his own mind. Alex did not argue with his uncle. He had tried that often enough—to no purpose. Old and sick as he was, Sam would brook no interference with this plan. He was as immovably determined as ever, as true to form. He would cancel his obligations. And with what was left he would have a final fling. He would be the old Sam once more—an hour, a day or a week—till the rest of the money was gone, flinging gold pieces about, emptying his pockets for anyone who made a demand upon him.

After all, why not? thought Alex tolerantly. He had it coming, poor old man, at the end of his disillusions, his pains and privations.

"All right," he said, "I'll pay your debts for you, if that's what you wish. Tomorrow you won't owe a dollar."

And the day after tomorrow he wouldn't *have* a dollar, thought Alex harassedly. He recounted the bills and checked Sam's addition.

"Here's five hundred dollars—all that's left."

"I want it in gold," said Sam. "I hate greenbacks." Alex got him the gold from his safe. As soon as Sam was gone he began sending notes to people on the list; others he reached by means of the new telephone recently installed in his office. Within a few hours a queue formed in front of his door.

Sam was behaving better than Alex had expected. He met his uncle on the street a number of times, chatting with old acquaintances or stalking about lonesomely, looking lost amid scenes once so familiar to him to which he had become a stranger. Johnny the barber was dead and old Tom Davidson had gone east to visit relatives. Even at the Pioneers' Society and the Odd Fellows Lodge there were few to hail him as a friend.

Only at the Bank Exchange was he happy. Little had changed there. The same bartenders as in the days of his prosperity mixed the same old drinks. They were whitehaired now but dexterous and affable as ever. Most of the patrons remembered Sam and slapped him on the back with ribald endearments. They discussed old friends, lamented old days.

So-and-so was dead and What's-his-name had gone back to England to claim an estate. Blank, the town drunkard, had reformed. He was in Congress now—if you could believe it. Bill G——, the unluckiest man in San Francisco, had grubstaked a prospector in the Paniment Range with his last hundred dollars and was a rich man now. Who would have thought——

"Fill 'em up again, bartender."

At the end of the week Alex received a phone call from the Pioneers' Society.

"Better look after Sam Brannan," the secretary told him. "He's ill at the Occidental Hotel."

Alex found his uncle prostrate but cheerful. "It's the old gut trouble," Sam explained. "When I have it I can't eat solid food. It's a nuisance. But you can't expect everything."

"Have you had a doctor, Uncle Sam?"

"Sure. Old Doc Cruse was in to see me. He cussed me out for drinkin'. He gave me some medicine. It stops the pain."

"Hadn't you better go to a hospital?"

"No, I want to go home. A boat leaves tomorrow." He made an impatient gesture. "I've had enough of this town. . . . All the good people are dead or gone—except you, Alex."

"But—do you think you can travel?"

"Of *course* I can travel." He reached in the pocket of his trousers hanging on the bed post and fished out a couple of gold pieces. "Here. Buy me a ticket and pay my hotel bill, Alex. . . . And you can give Doc five dollars for his visit and medicine. He looked as if he could use it." Sam chuckled.

Alex dropped in to see Dr. Cruse. He put the five dollars in his pocket and looked at Alex gravely. "Get him home as quick as you can. The medicine will quiet his pain. But he won't last long. The next attack——"

"Would a hospital do any good?"

The physician shook his head. "It's too late."

Sam stood in the stern of the coastwise steamer. His arms were full of packages to which, for some reason, he clung. They held a silk dress, a pair of gloves and a bottle of perfume for the boarding-house woman.

The next attack came soon after Sam's return. The boarding-house woman and her son put him to bed. She made him soup and gruel as usual, but this time it didn't work. Sam was "out of his head." He talked sometimes in English and again in Spanish. They sent for a doctor, but apparently nothing could be done. The old man was dying.

After she had washed her supper dishes, the boarding-house woman went upstairs and sat beside Sam's bed.

"Listen, my dove," he said. He reached for her hand and she let him hold it. "Listen to me. I am Samuel del Brannan. I am rich. I have millions in gold. Give me my pants."

She brought him his trousers. Weakly his hand explored the

pockets and emerged grasping a twenty-dollar gold piece. He held it up to her triumphantly.

"Parley Pratt, the Mormon elder, said I'd die without a dime. I fooled him. I've got gold in my hand *and my good wife beside me.*" He laughed aloud.

"I'm a great man, Carmelita. Once I was the richest man in California. . . . I drove the hooligans and shoulder-strikers out of San Francisco and put up the first stone buildings. . . . Calistoga . . . Bullets in my back . . . And Lisa. She took my children away . . . all gone . . . Everything. I don't care. I've got you, Carmelita. Hold me. . . . The pain——"

The boarding-house woman bent down, held his agony-contorted face against her breast, crooning.

"It's better," he said in a whisper. "Ahh!"

For a time she held his limp body tightly, almost unconsciously against her own. At last she released it gently and pulled the blanket over his face.

Appendix

In Lieu of Bibliography

Despite the varied and prominent roles he had enacted on the stage of California's history, I found adequate historical research for a biography of Samuel Brannan a difficult task. The reference libraries of San Francisco, including those of the Historical Society and the Society of California Pioneers, contained meager records of his extraordinary career. When I began my work only a thin booklet, reprinted from a magazine article by the late James A. B. Scherer, had dealt with Brannan's multifarious activities under the title "The First Forty-Niner"—which was inaccurate, for Brannan came to San Francisco in 1846. It proved a fragile and sometimes misleading skeleton for the work I planned to build, but I was grateful for it none the less.

After my biography was completed but before it appeared in print, two biographies of Brannan appeared, one under the aegis of the Mormon Church and another written by the granddaughter of a member of the Original Quorum of Twelve Apostles. Both, having access to Mormon records which were denied to me, contained certain facts which I had been unable to discover. But as I do not consider my work seriously incomplete without them, I have made no attempt to "crib" them. One, for instance, dealt with the date when Brannan ceased sleeping with his wife, from whom in his later years he was estranged, then divorced. I found the latter volume useful however, as a check to my own researches and discovered little conflict—none, in fact, of importance.

A small but historically rich record entitled *Minutes of the Proceedings of the Legislative Assembly of the District of San Francisco, March 12, 1849, to June 4, 1849, and the Record of*

Proceedings of the Ayuntamiento or Town Council of San Francisco, August 8, 1849, to May 3, 1850, yielded much authentic, detailed information. Brannan's connection with and activities in these bodies was character-revealing.

Histories of Napa County by Slocum and Menefee provided data concerning Brannan's life in Calistoga. Oscar T. Shuck in *Representative and Leading Men of the Pacific Coast* shed light on the shooting which almost cost Brannan his life.

I was fortunate enough to contact several of his relatives, the first being Miss Sophie Brannan of New York, then visiting San Francisco. She is Brannan's grandniece, daughter of his nephew, Thomas Brannan, in turn the son of Sam's elder brother John. Miss Brannan showed me transcripts of the Brannan family genealogy, several well-preserved letters in her granduncle's handwriting and numerous newspaper clippings bearing on his life.

Mrs. Maud Pettus, daughter of Sam's nephew and one-time business agent Alexander Badlam, permitted me to copy Sam's holographic will, together with notes concerning it and other matters found among her father's papers. She gave me much information about Brannan's long and intimate association with her father.

Mrs. Sophie Haight, daughter of Sam's elder brother John, proved my most valuable source of news. She was eighty-six but in full enjoyment of her faculties and possessed of a remarkable memory. From the anecdotes she related, her comments on his relatives and friends, her witty, character-revealing stories of his personal and general reactions, I received a picture of Sam Brannan that seemed clear and true, as well as extraordinarily dramatic. She had a knack for painting mental pictures. Through her eyes I saw Sam's first wife Hattie Hatch, his daughter Almira, who was for a time an inmate of Mrs. Haight's household, Ann Lisa, the "highfalutin, nosey" social climber with her spoiled and snobbish children.

From Mrs. Waldemar Young, daughter of Mrs. Haight, I learned that Sam sought his first wife on the eve of second marriage but could not locate her. According to one story she fled and hid herself when she learned that Sam was about to take another wife. Mrs. Haight, however, told me that Hattie divorced her husband when he ran after women. The reader may take his choice.

From Saco, Maine, I obtained a transcript of the birth, death and marriage records of the Brannan family from 1775, the date of Sam's father's arrival from Ireland, to 1889, the time of Sam's death.

The New York public records contain no vital statistics prior to 1853. Therefore it is impossible to learn the exact date of Brannan's marriage to Ann Lisa Corwin or the birth of their son, Samuel Brannan, Jr.

A "broadside," or printed announcement publicly displayed, accusing Brannan and two companions of stealing and destroying mail on the steamer *Gamecock* en route to Honolulu represents an ill-supported and fantastic bit of evidence, for, though the issue was pursued somewhat farther in the press, Brannan seems to have escaped subsequent publicity. A Mr. Hanna brought libel proceedings against James H. Tanner, author of the broadside, but the case was dismissed by a Hawaiian court. A man named Petrovits is said to have admitted destroying three letters addressed to Prince Alexander of Hawaii, one to the Catholic bishop and one to the British consul in Honolulu. Apparently he was not punished, though the Code of the Kingdom provided a penalty of imprisonment for one to five years. Doubtless the Polynesian court decided that it had no jurisdiction in case of a crime committed on the high seas. I am indebted to Andrew Farrell of the Honolulu *Advertiser* for his painstaking investigation of island archives in my behalf.

In the California State Library at Sacramento, with the assistance of Librarian Mabel Gillis and of Miss Wenzel of the California Room, I found a rich and varied source of information: complete files of California newspapers dating back to the first copy of Brannan's *California Star, The Friend,* a Honolulu weekly, recording the passenger list of Brannan's ship *Brooklyn* with a list of births and deaths aboard that vessel, and also photostats of many Brannan letters. From this voluminous, though in some respects incomplete, data I was forced to make some personal interpretations. One historian claims Brannan met Commodore Stockton of the sloop-of-war *Congress* at Honolulu. I regard this as inaccurate. On the same page of *The Friend* reporting the *Brooklyn's* arrival is printed a letter from the *Congress's* chaplain dated "At Sea." It is prefaced by the following statement:

> Only six months have elapsed since the date of the following communication [December 6, 1845]. It was cut from a late overland paper and, thanks to the individual who forwarded it, found publication in our columns.

It is my conclusion that a six-months-old letter from anyone aboard the *Congress* would not have appeared in *The Friend* July 2 (a day before the departure of the *Brooklyn*) if the *Congress* itself had been in Honolulu waters.

With the statement of another historian—that Brannan personally financed the entire *Brooklyn* venture for transporting a large colony of Mormons halfway around the world—I must again disagree. It is written that he invested $16,500 of his own money in the ship and then sought capital to buy equipment. I do not think it jibes with probability. How could a young man like Samuel Brannan, owner of the tiny print shop at 7 Spruce Street, accumulate so considerable a sum within a few years?

What probably occurred is that he collected that sum in advance fares from his 238 passengers at seventy-five dollars per head, the forty children being carried at half price. Brannan doubtless expended all of it for remodeling the *Brooklyn*, provisioning her for six months and paying the owners $1,200 a month for her use. Captain Richardson, who piloted her around the Horn to San Francisco, did not receive his $1,000 stipulated salary until a number of the Mormon colonists had chopped enough wood and sold it to accumulate that amount.

Between Honolulu and San Francisco the social storm which had been brewing earlier in the voyage broke in all its fury. Charges were filed, a trial was held aboard ship and certain passengers were convicted of "licentious and wicked conduct." Brannan wrote the Brethren at Nauvoo after his arrival in California: "A council was called, the matter investigated and a list of evidences given of the most disgusting character." From this I deem it fair to conclude the Seventh Commandment had been violated. Subsequent to the colony's discharge in San Francisco, Isaac Addison and others were excommunicated as a result of charges brought by Brannan.

By process of elimination, I deduced that Mary Addison was the girl who caused Henry Harris to join the Mormon ship at Honolulu. In histories Harris' inamorata is referred to merely as a pretty girl among the *Brooklyn*'s passengers. Only two unmarried females on the ship were listed as "daughter," indicating that they were minors of perhaps marriageable years: Miss Addison and Miss Aldrich; the others, one would infer, were old enough to travel alone and therefore doubtless were spinsters—much less likely to attract the emotional attention of a youth. Miss Lizzie Winner, listed among George Winner's "six children," married Basil Hall soon after landing.

The Addisons arrayed themselves against Brannan during the latter part of the voyage, and Harris, soon after the arrival in San Francisco, preferred serious charges against him. It seems a reasonable supposition that the Addisons might succeed in turning the young man's sympathies away from Brannan through emotional appeal if he were infatuated with Isaac Addison's daughter; there would be the motive of reprisal, whereas Prudence Aldrich, widowed during the sea journey, would have no such incentive, assuming her daughter to have been Harris' beloved.

In the reconstruction of the ship trials and the romance of Henry Harris, I took certain liberties, there being no way to determine the exact truth concerning minutiae.

From Sacramento I turned to Calistoga, where, I had been told, the hotel built by Brannan still stood. This was incorrect, as the old Calistoga Inn had been destroyed by fire many years ago. But I was so lucky as to meet and enlist the good offices of Charles E. Butler, who had been a half-grown boy in Brannan's time and whose brother was the great man's employee.

"Charlie" Butler proved a mine of information and helpfulness in an otherwise unproductive field. He told me many anecdotes of Sam Brannan either from first-hand memory or from recollection of his brother's tales. He recalled the building of the tomb wherein reposed the bodies of Sam's father and infant son. Butler, in fact, had dynamited and razed the tomb not many years before my visit to Calistoga when the property on which it stood was sold. He refuted a rumor that a geyser had spouted under the tomb, boiling the corpses it contained and causing a stench which almost depopulated the neighborhood. There were no bodies in it when he took it down, said Butler, only a small iron box containing papers, then of no value.

Butler related to me the anecdotes of Barnum and the boiled fish spouting from a pipe, of the "Soup Spring" and details of divers episodes in Brannan's life at the springs. He showed me an old ledger in which were entered the realty transactions of Brannan up to the time of his final departure in 1877. He had discovered in the home of a pioneer the discolored and worn but still photographable panorama of Calistoga in the '60's. And he set me on the track of a court order for the division of property between Samuel and Ann Lisa Brannan subsequent to their divorce—a handwritten record in one of the old files of Napa County. It included property in San Francisco as well as Napa County and was a find, because all San Francisco records prior to 1906 were destroyed in the great fire of that year.

W. Aird Macdonald, one-time newspaperman, an elder of the Mormon Church in Piedmont, California, supplied me with a picture of Brannan's tomb at Calistoga—the one destroyed by Butler—and with details of Sam's conversion to Mormonism. He told me how "the hand of fellowship" had been withdrawn because of charges made presumably by Wilfred Woodruff, of Brannan's hasty trip to Nauvoo to combat them and of his triumphant return. From Macdonald I received copies of the notorious Benson-Kendall contract with the Saints and Brannan's letters to Brigham Young concerning it. These letters and the related contract I later re-encountered in a book called *The Mormon Battalion.*

From Leon O. Whitsell, railroad commissioner of San Francisco, I obtained accurate data concerning Brannan's relations with the Masonic Fraternity. And through Mr. Whitsell I gained the privilege of reading a thesis written by Florence Dunlap on Samuel Brannan in 1928. From this I gleaned a number of minor but interesting details which had hitherto escaped me.

There are some accepted episodes in Brannan's life which I have not included in this biography. There is such a paucity of detail concerning them, important as they sound, that I decided against them.

The first is Sam's reputed participation in the Nevada silver-mining boom. It is unlikely that he would overlook such an opportunity. He is credited with buying agricultural and timber land in Steptoe Valley, building a sawmill, constructing toll roads and establishing a smelter near Mineral City. It is possible—even probable—he did all these things. They were doubtless among the incredibly varied investments he made and abandoned during the feverish, reckless years of his domestic difficulties.

In 1868 Brannan is said to have bought 170,000 acres of land from Abel Stearns in "the cow counties," as southern California was then dubbed. He is believed to have divided the huge Stearns estate into small farms and sold it to incoming settlers. I cannot believe the latter portion of this story—not because it wouldn't be a project dear to Sam's heart but because it would have required all his time and energies during a period when his every thought was centered on the problem of making Calistoga pay—a problem complex enough to engross the undivided attention of any man, even Samuel Brannan.

So, I believe, if he bought this immense grant in Los Angeles County, he turned it over to the first bidder, unloaded and forgot it, as he did with so many schemes. Because I frankly do not know the truth about it—and don't wish to guess too blindly—I omitted the Stearns transaction from my story.

In 1863 Sam Brannan, with Peter H. Burnett, once governor of California, and Joseph W. Winans, who married Sam's niece, started the Pacific Accumulation Loan Society, later called the Pacific Bank. It is said to have been the first chartered commercial bank in California and was probably of moment in financial history.

But Sam Brannan's interest in this institution was largely financial. He had no intimate concern with it aside from lending his name to the directorate and his cash to its development. It proved a good investment, but it was no brainchild of Sam's. Its establishment neither added to nor took away from his character. Therefore I discarded it, with other nonessentials, as story material.

A number of reports from varying sources indicated that Brannan died in the arms of his young Mexican wife Carmelita. It made rather an effective climax of which I might have availed myself with all the gusto of a sometime fictioneer. But it was not to be. In Escondido I discovered John Dart, physically feeble but mentally as young as myself. He was eighty-five and had been a friend not only of Sam Brannan but of his son. He was for a time an inmate of the Brannan home. He knew Lisa Brannan and her daughters and supplied me with photographs of them taken in Dresden just before their return to America.

Said Dart, "Sam never had a woman with him here in Escondido. The people with whom he boarded took care of him during his last illness. I never saw the Mexican wife. She must have left Sam in Guaymas—if she ever existed."

There is no doubt as to her existence. Brannan mentioned her in several letters as his wife.

Little more may be told of Sam Brannan. His body was removed after his death, May 5, 1889, to a vault in San Diego by order of the Escondido lodge of Masons. It was embalmed by Breese & Company, San Diego undertakers, but whether any service was held over it one can only conjecture. Brannan's body lay in the vault for sixteen months—the reason for which appears to be another mystery. At the end of that time Alexander Badlam, Jr., received a letter from the law and collection agency of Collier, Hammond & Mulford demanding payment of ninety-five dollars for embalming and other expenses. Badlam settled this account and had his uncle's body interred in Mount Hope Cemetery. His daughter showed me the following receipt:

May 14—To entrance fee for the remains of
the late Samuel Brannan in vault $5.00
To 16 months' rent at $1.00 per month 16.00
(June 1, 1889, to October 1, 1890)
To dig grave October 1 5.00
To removal from vault to grave in
cemetery 5.00

$31.00

Received Payment October 1, 1890.
S. WHITMORE,
Superintendent, Mount Hope Cemetery

Sam's fig ranch apparently reverted to the former owner. The following is an inventory of his property:

Right of redemption of mortgage of $1,000 and interest on 20-acre tract 5 blocks 182 in town of Escondido.
Lots 5, 6, 7, 8, 9, 10 and 11 in Block 34 town of Escondido upon which $200 was paid September 30, 1888. Balance due to get title $600 and interest.
Lots 6, 7, 8, 9, 10, 11, 12 and 13 in Block 33 Escondido. $50 paid. Sold 21 of September 1888. Balance due $650 and interest at 10%.
164 Certificates of stock (2,900 shares) Sonora City and Improvement Company.
One cloth house [probably a tent] in town of Escondido.
Two trunks containing articles of no value.
One silver watch.
Garden tools.

Sam Brannan's fig trees were uprooted and the land replanted to citrus fruit. The frame building on Grand Avenue, where for a time he lived and where he died, has been supplanted by a more modern structure.

Sam Brannan's body lay for thirty years under a neglected mound of earth, at the head of which a narrow slab of redwood dimly announced his name. Later J. Harvey McCarthy, whose father was Brannan's friend, replaced the wooden stick with an adequate headstone.

Lisa Brannan died in San Francisco many years ago, aged ninety-three. She had long been impoverished. Sam Brannan, Jr., lived eighty-six years. He had made some money and lost it. For years preceding his death in San Diego he lived on an allowance made him by the Pioneers' Society. One of his sisters was the inmate of a home for aged persons during her declining years, maintained there by the charity of members of her church. Brannan's eldest daughter by his first wife, Hattie, died in want.

These facts I learned from papers in the possession of Mrs. Pettus, through long talks with Mrs. Haight, records of the Pioneers' Society and newspaper clippings.

Some of my data came from historical sketches in old San Francisco directories.

I am sincerely grateful to the Historical Society, to Mrs. Helen Van Sicklen, former secretary of the Society of California Pioneers, and to all those other good people mentioned or, perchance, inadvertently forgotten who have helped me construct this book.

Index

California history books by
James Stevenson Publisher:

Memoirs of the Vallejos
ISBN 1-885852-02-9

William B. Ide, President of California
ISBN 1-885852-01-0

Sam Brannan, Builder of California
ISBN 1-885852-05-3

Historical and Descriptive Sketchbook of Napa, Sonoma,
Lake, and Mendocino, 1873
ISBN 1-885852-00-2

The Capital That Couldn't Stay Put,
The Complete Book of California's Capitols
ISBN 1-885852-04-5

History of Solano County, 1879
ISBN 1-885852-03-7

To order, request price list by phone, fax, mail or e-mail.
To phone: (707) 434-0210
To fax: (707) 434-0760
To write: James Stevenson Publisher- address on title page.
To e-mail: stevensn@community.net

World Wide Web page may be found by searching for
"California history" using search engine in Netscape or other
browser.